Commercial Integration between the European Union and Mexico

Gerhard Niedrist (ed.)

Commercial Integration between the European Union and Mexico

Multidisciplinary Studies

PL ACADEMIC RESEARCH

Bibliographic Information published by the Deutsche Nationalbibliothek
The Deutsche Nationalbibliothek lists this publication in the Deutsche Nationalbibliografie; detailed bibliographic data is available in the internet at http://dnb.d-nb.de.

EGADE. Business School TECNOLÓGICO DE MONTERREY | Cátedra de Estudios Europeos sobre Desarrollo y Competitividad | EGAP. Gobierno y Política Pública TECNOLÓGICO DE MONTERREY

Library of Congress Cataloging-in-Publication Data

Commercial integration between the European Union and Mexico : multidisciplinary studies / Niedrist, Gerhard (ed.).
pages cm
ISBN 978-3-631-64831-5—ISBN 978-3-653-03734-0 (ebook)
1. European Union countries—Foreign economic relations—Mexico.
2. Mexico—Foreign economic relations—European Union countries.
3. Free trade—European Union countries.
4. Free trade—Mexico. 5. European Union—Mexico. I. Gerhard, Niedrist, 1977–
HF1531.Z4M53 2013
382'.9142—dc23
2013034248

ISBN 978-3-631-64831-5 (Print)
E-ISBN 978-3-653-03734-0 (E-Book)
DOI 10.3726/978-3-653-03734-0

PL Academic Research is an Imprint of Peter Lang GmbH.

Peter Lang – Frankfurt am Main · Bern · Bruxelles · New York · Oxford · Warszawa · Wien

www.peterlang.com

Table of Contents

Foreword 11

The Impact of the EU-Mexican Trade Agreement on Revealed Comparative Advantage
Bonnie J. Palifka & José de Jesús Salazar Cantú 15
1. Introduction 15
2. Review of Literature 18
3. Methodology and Data 22
4. Results 23
5. Conclusions 33
References 35

The EU-Mexico Agreement: What Has Happened to Trade and Capital Flows since 2000?
René Cabral & Daniel Villarreal Cabello 39
1. Introduction 39
2. Trade in goods 41
   2.1 The EU total trade 42
   2.2 Mexico's total trade 45
   2.3 EU-Mexico trade 48
3. Foreign Direct Investment Flows 49
   3.1 The EU's FDI 50
   3.2 Mexico's FDI inflows 52
   3.3 Mexico's reception of FDI by sector 53
   3.4 FDI flows from the EU 55
4. Trade and FDI determinants 56
5. Conclusions 59
References 60

Mexican-European Union Free Trade Agreement: Liberalization Process and Mexican Export Performance
Sergio Ortiz Valdés ... 61
1. Introduction ... 61
2. General Characteristics of the Mexican – European Union Free Trade Agreement ... 62
3. Mexican-EU FTA Tariff Elimination Scheme for Mexican Products ... 67
4. MEX-EU FTA Commercial Liberation for Mexican Food Products ... 69
5. Mexican Exports to European Union before and after the Mexican-EU-FTA ... 73
6. Agro-Food Mexican Exports to the European Union ... 80
7. Mexican exports of processed food to the European Union (Section IV of the HS) before and after the Mexican-EU-FTA. ... 83
8. Conclusions ... 89
References ... 91

Mexican Firms' Entry Strategies to the European Union Market
Laura Zapata Cantú, Mariela Quiroga & Ana Luisa Cabrera ... 95
1. Introduction ... 95
2. The European Union and Mexico Free Trade Agreement ... 95
3. Mexican Imports from the European Union ... 97
4. Mexican Exports to the European Union ... 97
5. Chapter objectives ... 99
6. Literature Review: International Strategies ... 100
7. Traditional Motivators in International Trade ... 101
8. New Motivators ... 102
9. The Meaning of Internationalization: Prerequisites and Processes ... 103
10. The evolution of a mentality: from an international strategy to a transnational strategy ... 106
11. The mode of entry strategies into the European Union by Mexican firms ... 109
12. Conclusions ... 115
References ... 116

The EU-Mexican FTA and Art. XXIV GATT
Gerhard Niedrist ... 119
1. Introduction ... 119
2. Trade creation vs. trade diversion ... 120
3. Art. XXIV GATT ... 122
4. The external criteria: Art. XXIV:5b GATT ... 123

5. The internal criteria: Art. XXIV:8b GATT 124
6. The EU-Mexican FTA in the light of Art. XXIV GATT 126
6.1 The CRTA 126
6.2 Trade Data 127
7. Conclusions 129
References 130

Investment Protection Standards in the Mexico –
European Union Bilateral Investment Treaties:
Fair and Equitable Treatment and Full Protection and Security
Gabriel Cavazos Villanueva & Magda Carolina Sánchez Navarro 133
1. Introduction 133
2. The new EU investment policy 136
2.1 General Framework of the new policy 136
2.2 Evolution of investment regulation in the EU 138
2.3 BITs Concluded by EU Member States prior to the entry into force of the Treaty of Lisbon 140
2.4 BIT Arbitration under the proposed regulation 140
2.5 Substantive investment protections under the new investment policy 141
3. Fair and Equitable Treatment in the context of the Mexico-EU BITs. 142
3.1 General notion of FET 142
4.3.1 The interpretation of FET in accordance to international law principles 143
3.1.2 The interpretation of FET as a standard linked to customary international law 145
3.1.3 The interpretation of FET as a self-contained standard 147
3.1.4 Tecmed 149
3.2 The relationship between FET and other standards of investment protection. 155
4. Full Protection and Security 157
4.1 FPS linked to Customary International Law 159
4.2 FPS as a self-contained standard 159
5. Conclusions 160
References 162
Cases 164
Treaties 165

Reputations and Supportive Behavior of Spanish and U.S. Firms in Mexico
William Newburry, M Abrahim Soleimani & Armando Borda 167
1. Introduction 167
2. Hypotheses 168
   2.1 Foreign Headquarters 169
   2.2 Degree of Internationalization 173
   2.3 Individual-Level Demographic Influences 173
   2.4 Supportive Behavior 176
3. Methodology 178
   3.1 Sample 178
   3.2 Dependent Variables 178
   3.3 Independent Variables 179
   3.4 Control Variables 180
   3.5 Analysis 180
4. Results 180
   4.1 Corporate reputation 183
5. Supportive behavior 184
6. Discussion 184
7. Conclusions 187
References 188

Regulatory Changes of the Financial Industry in the E.U.
Roberto Joaquín Santillán Salgado 195
1. Introduction 195
2. The origins of the 2007-2009 financial crisis in the United States 197
3. The European Union's Financial Regulation Framework: Some Antecedents 200
4. The First Bank Directive 201
5. The Second Bank Directive 202
6. The Investment Services Directive 203
7. The Capital Adequacy Directive 204
8. Financial Services Action Plan 204
9. The Commission of Wise Men and the Lamfalussy Report 205
10. Why did the existing regulations fail in 2007-2009? 206
11. The integration of the financial markets in Europe, national regulations and the convergence efforts 208
12. The Larosière and Turner Reports 209
13. Lord Turner's Report 213
14. Concluding Remarks 216
References 217

An Approach to the CSR of European Companies Operating in Mexico
Florina Guadalupe Arredondo Trapero, Verónica del Carmen Maldonado de Lozada & Alfonso Benito Fraile 219
1. Introduction 219
2. European and Mexican Conceptions of CSR 219
3. The Millenium Development Goals (MDG) as Reference for CSR in Mexico 222
4. The Stakeholders' Role in Defining CSR Objectives 224
Spanish Companies in Mexico and their CSR 225
5. BBVA 227
6. Santander 227
7. Gas Natural Unión FENOSA 228
8. Gas Natural Mexico 229
9. Telefónica 230
10. Sol Melia 231
11. CSR of Spanish Companies in Mexico in the EUMFTA framework 232
12. Conclusion 239
References 240

Foreword

International Agreements have been part of our economic and political landscape in recent decades. This is why, after thirteen years of operation of the Free Trade Agreement between the EU and Mexico (EUMFTA), we believe this to be a good moment to explore how far we have come. It is noticeable that although the North America Free Trade Agreement (NAFTA) has been the subject of plenty of academic analysis, this has not been the case for EUMFTA. This adds interest and value to the present book, which incorporates the study of the evolution of such agreement from different perspectives.

Trade, investment, business strategies, regulations and trend analyses constitute the subject matters of the series of essays presented in this work by a group of academics. Every essay explores the challenges and opportunities of the agreement from specific standpoints, incorporating the data, correlations, and other statistical analysis that provide the evidence for the relationships and hypotheses under study.

Although the EU - Mexico treaty is a truly comprehensive one (sometimes called Global Agreement or the Economic Association, Political Dialogue and Cooperation Agreement), with its three identified pillars: political dialogue, trade and cooperation; not one single essay refers to the agreement as a whole; rather, each one deeply exploresa specific topic, but most of them centered on the economic association part of the agreement. Regarding trade in goods between Mexico and the European Union, the first essay takes a look at the evolution of the comparative advantage in Mexico and in Europe resulting from the FTA launched in 2000. The study renders very interesting results, concluding that Mexico has acquired a clear comparative advantage on certain industries, such as iron and steel and optical apparatus, for example; whereas the EU has on aircraft, mineral fuels and paper articles, among others.

Another essay shows that trade has increased significantly between Mexico and the European Union. It compares the EUMFTA and the NAFTA performance in trade, during the first nine years of both agreements, and concludes that the dynamism of the one with Europe was greater. Furthermore, the analysis also concludes that EUMFTA brings trade creation and not trade diversion.In the realm of capital flows, the rise in Foreign Direct Investment (FDI) is also noteworthy, becoming a complement to the one coming from the US and Canada. However, the authors also note that despite the agreement, the level of FDI from Europe is still very small compared to the one going from Europe to Central America and Brazil. An essay which focuses on specific manufacturing and agricultural exports of Mexico to the EU, concludes that there has been a very limited response of the latter to the liberalization, but also acknowledges that the agreement was much more restrictive in terms of liberalizing agricultural products. Some authors, however, state that the distance between the Mexican producers and the European market has not been reduced because of the FTA.

Whereas some essays suggest that the objectives of Mexico and the EU with respect to economic diversification and to the strengthening of EU´s presence in Latin America have been so far fulfilled, others argue that Mexican operations in the European Union did not stem from the agreement but rather go back yearsprior to it. This is the case of a group of Mexican firms that have entered the European Markets. Given the still wide array of opportunities for Mexican firms in the European markets under the EUMFTA, it is interesting to observe the distinct strategies that Mexican companies (some manufacturing, some service firms) who have established in Europe have followed to become global within that region.

The geographically strategic position of Mexico that places this country as a "bridge" between Europe and Latin America is identified as one of its main assets in regards to the FTA; however, there are also two relevant aspects that place Mexico at an advantageous position: the cheaper cost of labor and the availability of lower cost of capital. Does this circumstance pose a question of inequality for one partner over the other?

This Free Trade Agreementon the one hand, grants the European Union preferential access to the NAFTA region and is therefore very important to it; on the other hand, the FTA is one of the first cases of a cross-regional preferential agreement which gives Mexico an advantage over other countries. Is this a case of regionalism or multilateralism?

An examination of the legal aspects of the FTAconcludes that it is foreseeable to expect a more harmonized conception of the relevant standards, but maybe not in the short run, not at least on the EU side.As for the analyzedfinancial regulatory framework,advice is given towards a greater cooperation among national authorities in the European Union which would promote more efficiency in the provision of financial services.

The challenge of foreign companies gaining legitimacy in Mexico is also explored. This essay studies the role of corporate reputation on its stakeholders, looking at whether or not Mexican citizens will be inclined to purchase European goods over local ones, because of the reputation of the firms.Finally, on the field of corporate social responsibility, the question arises about practices being directed to resolve genuine social needs,over only makingcompanies look good before society.

The appraisal of outcomes and challenges offered by these essays presents us with the opportunity to reflect upon the impact of the Global Agreement between Mexico and the European Union over each partner-country, as well as to assess if the opportunities that opened are being used or should be looked upon for further action. The essays also point towards the need to explore comparative advantage in different products and sectors, the opportunities to attract more Foreign Direct Investment, the promotion ofbilateral investment treaties which provide conditions for greater capital flows, and the need to design the appropriate strategies for Mexican firms that want to enter the European markets.

From all the above considerations, it seems that the EU-Mexico Free Trade Agreement has rendered a positive balance for both sides, but that such balance could become even greater. There are much more opportunities out there for businesses to undertake, and I would argue that authorities should design the appropriate public policies to induce such undertaking.

Dra. Ma. de Lourdes Dieck Assad
President of EGADE Business School, Tecnológico de Monterrey
Mexican Ambassador to the European Union from 2004 to 2007

The Impact of the EU-Mexican Trade Agreement on Revealed Comparative Advantage

*Bonnie J. Palifka** *& José de Jesús Salazar Cantú*†

1. Introduction

The EU-Mexico Free Trade Agreement took effect in July of 2000, eliminating import tariffs on Mexican manufactured goods to the European Union by 2003 and on European manufactured goods to Mexico by 2007. Unlike the North American Free Trade Agreement, this agreement has received almost no academic attention. Mexico had signed agreements with the European Union in 1975 and 1991, but these were limited in nature and had little impact. In 1997, the two parties signed the EU-Mexico Economic Partnership, Political Coordination and Cooperation Agreement, which entered into force on July 1, 2000. According to the European Commission (2009a), this treaty

> "... has considerably strengthened bilateral relations between the EU and Mexico. It governs all relations between them, including a regular high-level political dialogue. It is based on shared values, such as democracy and human rights, and reflects Mexico's relevance on the international scene".

Figure 1. European (EU-15)-Mexican Trade, 1995-2008

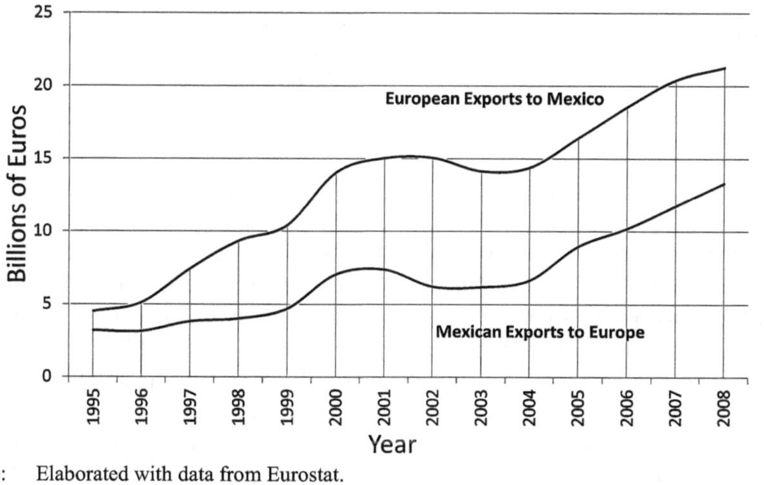

Source: Elaborated with data from Eurostat.

---

*, † Department of Economics, Tecnológico de Monterrey.

The Agreement has established a Free Trade Area (FTA) between the EU and Mexico that has enshrined their bilateral trade relations in a preferential framework and has helped to enhance their bilateral economic ties. The FTA has allowed significant growth in bilateral trade and has acted as a catalyst for investment flows. (European Commission, 2009a)

Figure 1 shows the evolution of trade flows between Mexico and the EU-15. Bilateral trade has, indeed, increased dramatically since the agreement took effect. Between 2000 and 2008, European exports to Mexico increased 51%; Mexican exports to the EU-15 increased 89%.

According to the European Commission (2009b), Mexico now occupies the 26th place among Europe's trading partners, ranking 16th in European exports; Europe is second only to the United States as an export market for Mexico. As Figure 2 illustrates, Europe and Mexico engage in a considerable amount of intra-industrial trade: three of the four main commodities traded coincide, representing 66.4% of Mexico's exports to Europe and 54.8% of Europe's exports to Mexico.

Figure 2. Principle commodities in European-Mexican Trade, 2007

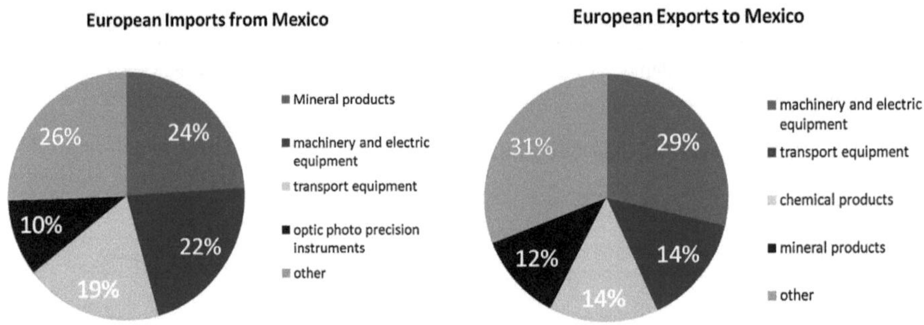

Source: elaborated with data from the European Trade Commission (2009)

Because the European tariffs were already quite low relative to Mexican tariffs in 2000, Europe stood to gain the most in trade from this agreement, while Mexico might have expected to benefit in other areas, such as investment. Figure 3 illustrates the increase in net foreign direct investment, favoring Mexico. Indeed, as of 2006, Mexican investment in Europe was only one-tenth the level of European (EU-27) investment in Mexico (European Commission, 2009).

This agreement, however, was not signed in a vacuum. In 2001, China joined the World Trade Organization, representing a major competitor for many Mexican products. After September of the same year, the world entered into a recession triggered by the terrorist attacks in the United States. Furthermore, in the years since 2000, Mexico and Europe have signed dozens of free trade agreements with other partners, while the European Union has increased from fifteen to twenty-seven members. All of these events complicate the task of identifying the benefits of this agreement for either side using simple graphs such as Figures 1, 2, and 3.

Ten years have passed since this agreement went into force, with almost no academic analysis of its effects. The purpose of this chapter is to examine the evolution of comparative advantage on both sides of the EU-Mexico Free Trade Agreement, in order to determine whether the agreement has benefited either or both sides. Although the treaty is comprehensive, covering trade in goods and services, investment, intellectual property, and cooperation in areas of mutual interest such as technology, agriculture, public administration, culture, and the fight against drug trafficking, this study is limited to trade in goods. We calculate the revealed comparative advantage for each two-digit industry for each partner in the other market in order to identify those industries with the strongest comparative advantage in the partner market, both before and after the agreement went into effect. This is purely a descriptive exercise: we leave the estimation of factors determining comparative advantage for future studies.

Figure 3. Net FDI, EU-15 in Mexico, 1995-2007

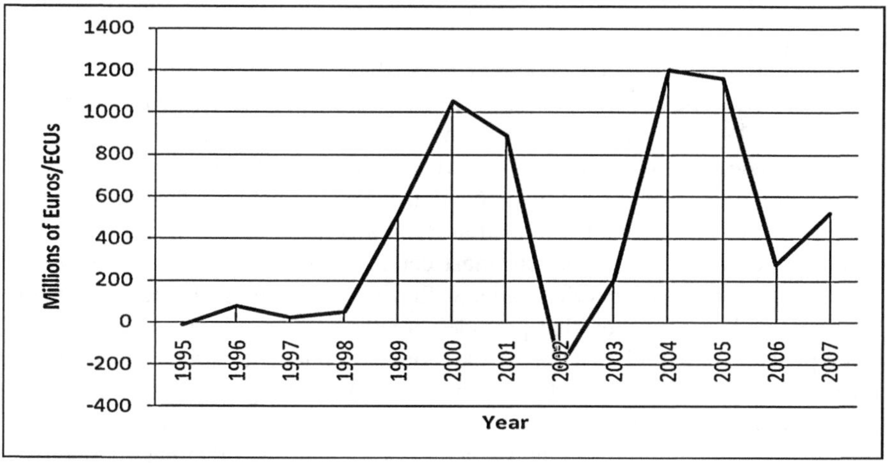

Source: elaborated with data from Eurostat

We find that the agreement led to an initial increase in the number of industries enjoying comparative advantage, but that this advantage began to dissipate as early as 2003. Certain industries, however, have flourished under the treaty on each side. For Mexico, the three industries with the greatest revealed comparative advantage in the European market are Vegetable plaiting materials, Zinc and articles thereof, and Optical and similar apparatus. For Europe, the top three industries are Cork and articles of cork, Works of art, and Pharmaceutical products.

The chapter proceeds as follows: section 2 reviews the relevant literature; the model and data are described in section 3; results are in section 4; and section 5 concludes.

2. Review of Literature

The Classical and Neoclassical models of international trade theory argue that trade liberalization leads to more efficient resource allocation, an increase in production, and an increase in national consumption. The gains from trade theorem formally demonstrates this, establishing that, given the relative prices in free trade, the consumption bundle in general equilibrium is of greater value than the consumption bundle under self-sufficiency with the same prices. Figure 4 shows this. Beginning at equilibrium A (self-sufficiency), opening up to foreign trade exposes the country to new relative prices (represented by the slope of the tangent pp^*) and leads to a new equilibrium in production, A', and in consumption, A''. A'' is unattainable under self-sufficiency; the higher indifference curve attained through trade reflects the increase in national wellbeing.

A variety of conditions in economic policy have led countries to adopt barriers to foreign trade. The empirical evidence (e.g., Wacziarg and Horn, 2003; Rodriguez and Rodrik, 1999; Hoeller, Girouard, and Colecchia, 1998; Edwards, 1997; and Sachs and Warner, 1995) tends to show that trade liberalization is correlated with higher economic growth, although Corden (1993) concludes that the benefits from trade are lesser when liberalization is unilateral.

Free trade is an ideal situation: most countries still use tariffs and non-tariff barriers to promote or restrict trade, with various motives. Trade agreements have emerged as an option that provides greater trade freedom and certainty to participants. Whalley (1996) shows that countries pursue a variety of objectives when entering into a free trade agreement (FTA), among them: an increase in consumption, to secure access to markets, to provide a better framework for other macroeconomic reforms, and as a means to enter into other negotiations.

In theory FTAs allow each country to specialize in the production of those goods and services in which it enjoys a comparative advantage, exporting those goods and services to the other market, while accepting the import of goods and services in which the partner has a comparative advantage.

Figure 4. Gains from trade

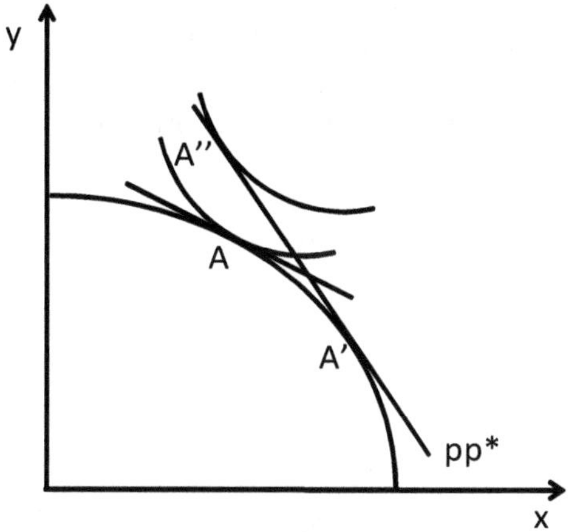

While FTAs may be a step toward increased trade and, therefore, an increase in productive efficiency, production, and income, they also pose a threat to sectors at a disadvantage. Although provisions are usually made to help these sectors adjust, it is also commonplace for countries to try to make post-treaty unilateral corrections to protect particular sectors that suffer more than expected. These actions tend to be protectionist and often violate the treaties signed. Sherer (1994) uses game theory to show that the dominant strategy in trade agreements is non-fulfillment, resulting in a sub-optimal equilibrium.

Trade theory also considers the effects of treaties on non-member countries. Viner (1950) initiated the analysis of the effects of trade agreements and introduced the terms *trade creation* and *trade diversion*. Trade creation occurs when lower-cost imports from a member nation replace higher-cost production in the home country and result in an improvement in wellbeing for consumers derived from the lower-priced imports. Trade diversion occurs when higher-cost imports from a member country replace lower-cost imports from a non-member country, due to differentiated barriers; the result is less efficient international production. Figure 5 illustrates these effects on the partial equilibrium of good *X*.

Three countries interact: the home country, a small country which before the treaty and given its import tariffs on *X* applied to the rest of the world, has a price of Px_d; the partner country whose price is Px_p; and a third country, from which the home country imported *X* before the treaty at a price Px_w and applied a tariff equal to $(Px_d - Px_w)$. The elimination of tariffs between home and the partner will lead home residents to import *X* from the partner country, since Px_p is lower than Px_d, and therefore consumer surplus will increase by areas *a*, *b*, *c*, and *d*. The elimination of tariffs will cost the home government areas *c* and *e*, while home producers lose area *a* of their surplus. The total economic effect on the home surplus will therefore be equal to $b + d - e$, of which *b* and *d* correspond to what Viner calls benefits from trade creation, where home imports increase from Qx_2-Qx_1 to Qx_3-Qx_0, while $-e$ represents trade diversion, the loss in terms of trade derived from importing goods at a higher price than that which would prevail in universal free trade.

Figure 5. Trade creation vs. trade diversion

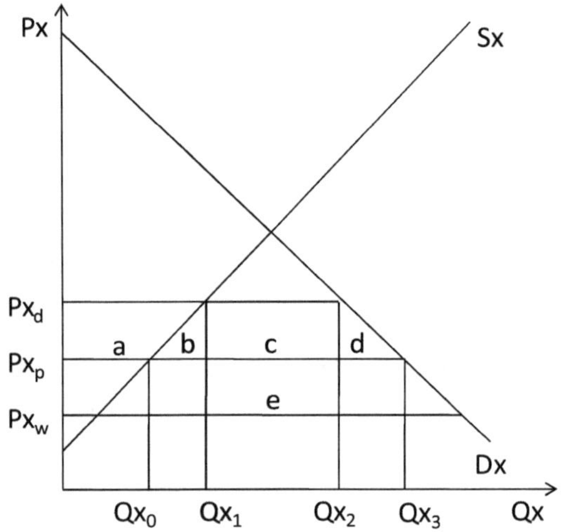

Since the more efficient supplier is displaced by a less efficient supplier, there is a loss of efficiency in world production. If $b+d$ is less than the absolute value of *e*, then the agreement diverts more trade than it creates and wellbeing is reduced both in the home country and in the world. In the opposite case, home wellbeing is improved, but world production is still less efficient, since the wellbeing in the displaced country may be affected adversely and world resources are used less efficiently. This situation has led the World Trade Organization (WTO) to recommend that FTAs be signed between countries that already enjoy close trade relations, which reduces the gap between Px_p and Px_w, increasing areas *a* and *b* and reducing area *e*.

From Viner's (1950) result we can infer that there is no unique outcome from trade agreements and that FTAs do not necessarily imply benefits for the member countries, nor for the world as a whole. Kemp and Wan (1976), and Krishna and Panagariya (2002) explore the conditions under which a treaty will benefit its members without causing damage to any non-member country.

Whalley and Xin (2007) show that the proliferation of regional trade agreements has led to greater trade among the members of the large trade blocs, which has resulted in greater regionalization than internationalization of foreign trade. This result does not preclude the possibility that net diversion of trade may be occurring and that, therefore, the state of trade relations is sub-optimal; it may cause greater benefits for members and losses for non-members. A similar result is described by Winters (1997) in an analysis of the effects of European integration, concluding that such losses exist but are small. The increase in trade and reduction of adverse effects for non-member countries would imply, as Baldwin (2006) indicates, a multilateralization of regionalism and reduce the free rider problem identified by Bhagwati (1990); to achieve this, Baldwin suggests, requires a less passive role for the WTO. Winters argues that estimating these effects is not simple, as it requires the creation of the counter-factual scenario of no trade agreement in order to contrast it with the observed conditions. At the same time, it is often difficult to obtain information on prices, production, and trade at a sufficiently disaggregated level. These measurement problems reinforce the validity of descriptive studies of changes in trade patterns and comparative advantages, such as this chapter undertakes.

Balassa (1965) studies the possible effects of trade liberation on the relocation of productive resources to different industries in each country, in light of the Kennedy Round of GATT negotiations. The lack of information for similar years of production, prices, trade flows and factors of production employed in the various countries led Balassa to propose a method requiring little information. The method proposed and applied by Balassa detects *ex post* comparative advantage, in contrast with neoclassical theory, in which comparative advantage is determined *ex ante* by the relative productivity of labor (David Ricardo's theory) or by the relative abundance of factors (the Heckscher-Ohlin-Samuelson theory). The term employed by Balassa and later by other authors (e.g., Garanina, 2009; Yen-Chum and Chia-Wen, 2008; Cinquetti, 2008; Hisanaga, 2008; Geda and Meskel, 2008; Abidin and Wai, 2008; Faber, 2007; Rae and Sollie, 2007) is *revealed comparative advantage* (RCA). Almost half a century after Balassa's seminal paper, the empirical proof of the changes effected by trade liberalization on patterns of comparative advantages continues to face important problems related to the availability of information: while countries now have abundant databases of information on the productive environment and trade, the methodologies and data-collection timing differ from one country to another. At the same time, the classifications used for trade data are not always the same as those used for data on the primary, industrial, and service sectors.

Using indices of revealed comparative advantage (RCA), Chiquiar, Fragoso, and Ramos-Francia (2007) find that the trade pattern of Mexico is closely related to the performance of Mexican exports to the United States; they also find that the RCA indices have fallen for the majority of Mexican exports since 2001, especially in industries which compete with developing countries.

Trade agreements with other countries, and in particular with those of the European Union, in theory would provide Mexico with an opportunity to participate more intensely in markets in developed countries, where comparative advantages would be expected to differ from those of Mexico. This, however, is not necessarily so. Hoeller et al. (1998) found that the patterns of European specialization in trade with both the United States and Japan, are biased toward labor-intensive industries, with low-qualified labor and low wages, which suggests a bleak outlook for potential trade growth between Mexico and the European Union, since Mexico would be expected to derive competitive advantage through specialization in goods intensive in low-qualified labor. Amoroso, Chiquiar, Quella, and Ramos-Francia (2008) find that Mexico is, indeed, abundant in this resource; in addition, they find that the countries of the European Union are not major competitors to Mexico, which leaves open a window of opportunity for success in the agreement. Their study is focused on the manufacturing sector and considers mainly the countries with comparative advantages similar to those of Mexico. In contrast, the analysis in this chapter considers the entire spectrum of external trade and refers specifically to trade flows between Mexico and the European Union.

3. Methodology and Data

We apply the Balassa methodology as used in Chiquiar, et al. (2007)[1] to determine whether Mexico's Revealed Comparative Advantage (RCA) in the European market (and vice versa) improved after the FTA went into effect. For example, the RCA of Mexico in the European market for each two-digit industry is calculated as in Equation (1):

$$RCA_i^{Mexico} = \left(\frac{X_i^{Mexico} \Big/ \sum_{i=1}^{n} X_i^{Mexico}}{X_i^{World} \Big/ \sum_{i=1}^{n} X_i^{World}} \right) \quad (1)$$

Where

RCA = Revealed Comparative Advantage

X = exports to Europe

i = two-digit industry

1 This application of the index differs from Balassa's in that the original Balassa index measures the revealed comparative advantage of a country in the entire world market for a given industry, while this one is limited to a particular market: in the case of Chiquiar, *et al.* (2007), the US market; in our study, the Mexican or European market, respectively.

If $RCA_i > 1$, then Mexico is revealed to hold a comparative advantage in that industry. This means that the products in industry *i* represent a greater proportion of Mexican exports to Europe than do the same products in the total of exports to Europe by all nations.

We used the Commodity Trade Statistics Database (COMTRADE) published by the United Nations to carry out the analysis using two-digit Harmonized System industries in order to match categories to the tariff elimination schedules. In order to circumvent the difficult reality that countries joined the European Union after the Mexican-EU Free Trade Agreement became effective, we have limited our sample to the fifteen member countries in 2000 (EU-15). We calculated the RCA for each two-digit industry for each year from 1990 to 2008; due to space limitations, we report only selected years.

4. Results

In this section, we report the top ten and bottom ten industries, ranked by RCA, for Mexico and for Europe, for the years 1990, 1999, and 2008. We also report the ten industries that enjoyed the greatest increase in RCA and that suffered the greatest decline in RCA for Mexico and for Europe, in the ten-year period 1998-2008.

Tables 1 and 2 contain, respectively, the ten highest and ten lowest RCAs for Mexico and for the EU-15 in 1990. Mexico had a revealed comparative advantage (RCA>1) in only three industries, all of them in the primary sector. Not surprisingly, petroleum dominated Mexican exports to Europe. Europe, by contrast, had a revealed comparative advantage in the Mexican market in 42 industries from all three sectors.

By 1999 (Tables 3 and 4), the 2000 treaty was under negotiation and Mexico had developed a comparative advantage in 19 industries. Although the primary sector continued to be predominant, certain manufacturing industries began to appear in the top ten. In Table 3, we can further observe that Petroleum (Chapter 27) had been displaced by two other chapters in terms of RCA. Note also that Lead (Chapter 28), which was among the top ten in 1990, had moved to the bottom ten by 1999. Europe had a comparative advantage in 33 chapters in 1999; Table 4 shows the top ten and the bottom ten industries. Beverages, spirits, and vinegar (chapter 22) continues to be the only industry that is in the top ten for both parties, indicating intra-industry trade. Vegetable plaiting materials (Chapter 14) is the most advantageous Mexican industry, but among the lowest for Europe.

Table1. Highest and lowest RCA, Mexico 1990[2]

Chapter		RCA
27	Mineral fuels, oils, distillation products, etc.	22.07346
14	Vegetable plaiting materials, vegetable products nes	3.247819
7	Edible vegetables and certain roots and tubers	1.090957
78	Lead and articles thereof	0.765398
26	Ores, slag and ash	0.711206
22	Beverages, spirits and vinegar	0.517572
74	Copper and articles thereof	0.497707
65	Headgear and parts thereof	0.455539
8	Edible fruit, nuts, peel of citrus fruit, melons	0.415677
9	Coffee, tea, mate and spices	0.395211
	…	
48	Paper & paperboard, articles of pulp, paper and board	0.002703
67	Bird skin, feathers, artificial flowers, human hair	0.002572
36	Explosives, pyrotechnics, matches, pyrophorics, etc.	0.002298
30	Pharmaceutical products	0.002065
35	Albuminoids, modified starches, glues, enzymes	0.001863
89	Ships, boats and other floating structures	0.001665
76	Aluminum and articles thereof	0.000501
80	Tin and articles thereof	0.000464
10	Cereals	0.000149
15	Animal, vegetable fats and oils, cleavage products, etc.	0.000008

Tables 5 and 6 respectively show the top and bottom RCAs for Mexico and the EU-15 in 2008. Mexico had a comparative advantage in 16 industries; Europe in 30. Note that Chapter 14 continues to occupy the first place for Mexico, although its RCA has fallen from 12.9 to 6.3. (This may be a result of trade diversification.) Six of the top ten (chapters 79, 90, 87, 85, 25, and 96) were not among the top ten industries for Mexico in 1999; three of these (79, 90, and 96) had a comparative *disadvantage* (RCA<1) in 1999. Zinc (79) was in categories A and B, with

2 Only chapters in which Mexico exported to Europe are presented. Mexico had no exports to Europe in 16 chapters in 1990. These were: 2 Meat and edible offal; 11 milling products, malt, starches, inulin, wheat gluten; 17 Sugars and sugar confectionery; 18 Cocoa and cocoa preparations; 19 Cereal, flour, starch, milk preparations and products; 31 Fertilizers; 43 Furskins and artificial fur, manufactures thereof; 45 Cork and articles of cork; 50 Silk; 51 Wool, animal hair, horsehair yarn and fabric thereof; 53 Vegetable textile fibres nes. paper yarn, woven fabric; 75 Nickel and articles thereof; 79 Zinc and articles thereof; 86 Railway, tramway locomotives, rolling stock, equipment; 88 Aircraft, spacecraft, and parts thereof; 91 Clocks and watches and parts thereof. In ten of these, Mexico began exporting to Europe the following year.

base rates between 0 and 2.5%.[3] The industries in Chapter 90 were also in categories A and B, with base rates between 0 and 4.2%; Figure 2 in the Introduction shows that this industry is one of the strongest Mexican exporters to Europe. Those in Chapter 96 were almost entirely tax-free at the time the treaty entered into force. The comparative advantage developed in these industries may, therefore, be due to factors other than the reduction in trade barriers.

Table 2. Highest and lowest RCA, Europe 1990[4]

Chapter		RCA
80	Tin and articles thereof	8.949238
49	Printed books, newspapers, pictures, etc.	8.686705
22	Beverages, spirits and vinegar	7.851523
20	Vegetable, fruit, nut, etc. food preparations	7.843625
45	Cork and articles of cork	7.590942
11	Milling products, malt, starches, inulin, wheat gluten	7.552255
16	Meat, fish and seafood food preparations nes	7.294346
19	Cereal, flour, starch, milk preparations and products	7.106933
6	Live trees, plants, bulbs, roots, cut flowers, etc.	6.508665
3	Fish, crustaceans, molluscs, aquatic invertebrates	6.506305
	...	
25	Salt, sulphur, earth, stone, plaster, lime and cement	0.037579
91	Clocks and watches and parts thereof	0.03232
65	Headgear and parts thereof	0.031146
81	Other base metals, cermets, articles thereof	0.022932
86	Railway, tramway locomotives, rolling stock, equipment	0.021083
23	Residues, wastes of food industry, animal fodder	0.018811
26	Ores, slag and ash	0.010119
88	Aircraft, spacecraft, and parts thereof	0.008639
47	Pulp of wood, fibrous cellulosic material, waste, etc.	0.002786
92	Musical instruments, parts and accessories	0.000108

Interestingly, the industries in which Mexico had the greatest comparative advantage in the European market do not coincide with those identified by Chiquiar *et al.* (2007, 10) as most advantageous in the world market in the period 1996-

3 See the Appendix for a summary of tariff elimination schedule categories.

4 Note: Only chapters in which Europe exported to Mexico are presented. Europe had no exports to Mexico in four chapters in 1990: 14 Vegetable plaiting materials, vegetable products nes; 78 Lead and articles thereof; 36 Explosives, pyrotechnics, matches, pyrophorics, etc.; 75 Nickel and articles thereof.

2005, with the exceptions of chapters 87, 22, and 85.[5] Chapter 87 – Vehicles – is the fourth largest export category from Mexico to Europe, as shown in Figure 2.

Table 3. Highest and lowest RCA, Mexico 1999

Chapter		RCA
14	Vegetable plaiting materials, vegetable products nes	12.92428
9	Coffee, tea, mate and spices	3.846705
27	Mineral fuels, oils, distillation products, etc.	3.316553
32	Tanning, dyeing extracts, tannins, derivs. Pigments, etc.	2.553129
26	Ores, slag and ash	2.279973
58	Special woven or tufted fabric, lace, tapestry	2.082302
7	Edible vegetables and certain roots and tubers	1.923688
8	Edible fruit, nuts, peel of citrus fruit, melons	1.894984
22	Beverages, spirits and vinegar	1.805609
92	Musical instruments, parts and accessories	1.805301
	...	
47	Pulp of wood, fibrous cellulosic material, waste, etc.	0.008645
66	Umbrellas, walking-sticks, seat-sticks, whips, etc.	0.006241
79	Zinc and articles thereof	0.005379
75	Nickel and articles thereof	0.004563
78	Lead and articles thereof	0.004148
10	Cereals	0.002116
89	Ships, boats and other floating structures	0.002032
88	Aircraft, spacecraft, and parts thereof	0.00188
50	Silk	0.000863
67	Bird skin, feathers, artificial flowers, human hair	0.000071

For Europe (Table 6), there are also six newcomers to the top ten: chapters 97, 6, 88, 50, 93, and 33; of these, one (88) had a comparative disadvantage in 1999. Chapter 88 was in Category A (immediate tariff elimination), with base rates between 0 and 20%. Cork (Chapter 45) continues in first place, as in 1999, but with a slight decrease in RCA.

Tables 7 and 8 reveal the industries in which the RCA grew and fell the most, for Mexico and Europe, respectively, in the ten year period from 1998 to 2008. For Mexico (Table 7), six of the top ten are in manufacturing industries. While some products in chapters 87 and 85 had relatively high base rates, most of the chapters with the greatest gains already had low base rates when the treaty went into effect; three of the top ten were duty-free before the treaty. Likewise, five of

5 Chiquiar *et al.* (2007) use SITC codes rather than Harmonized System categories.

the industries that lost the most either were duty-free or were subject to immediate tariff elimination when the treaty went into effect. Thus, it seems that factors other than tariff elimination are at play in determining which industries gained or lost the most in terms of competitive advantage.

Table 4. Highest and lowest RCA, Europe 1999

Chapter		RCA
45	Cork and articles of cork	5.85947
30	Pharmaceutical products	5.210492
50	Silk	4.628215
19	Cereal, flour, starch, milk preparations and products	4.444149
22	Beverages, spirits and vinegar	4.050936
69	Ceramic products	3.330715
49	Printed books, newspapers, pictures, etc.	2.766531
4	Dairy products, eggs, honey, edible animal product	2.449296
51	Wool, animal hair, horsehair yarn and fabric thereof	2.270618
13	Lac. Gums, resins, vegetable saps and extracts nes	2.246407
	…	
80	Tin and articles thereof	0.096498
14	Vegetable plaiting materials, vegetable products nes	0.088884
26	Ores, slag and ash	0.054644
2	Meat and edible meat offal	0.033504
7	Edible vegetables and certain roots and tubers	0.029823
8	Edible fruit, nuts, peel of citrus fruit, melons	0.028972
47	Pulp of wood, fibrous cellulosic material, waste, etc.	0.025481
67	Bird skin, feathers, artificial flowers, human hair	0.016507
46	Manufactures of plaiting material, basketwork, etc.	0.007798

It is noteworthy that Chapter 88 (Aircraft, spacecraft, and parts thereof) appears in the top ten list for each side, indicating, perhaps, an increase in intra-industrial trade. This chapter was among the bottom ten for Europe in 1990, but in the top ten by 2008; Mexico had no exports to Europe in this chapter in 1990 and in 2008 still suffered a disadvantage, but Mexican exports to Europe in this category were approximately 13% of European exports to Mexico in the same category.

Table 5. Highest and lowest RCA, Mexico 2008[6]

Chapter		RCA
14	Vegetable plaiting materials, vegetable products nes	6.272852
79	Zinc and articles thereof	5.239742
90	Optical, photo, technical, medical, etc. apparatus	4.012246
87	Vehicles other than railway, tramway	2.606863
9	Coffee, tea, mate and spices	2.300306
26	Ores, slag and ash	2.112527
22	Beverages, spirits and vinegar	2.048641
85	Electrical, electronic equipment	1.886927
25	Salt, sulphur, earth, stone, plaster, lime and cement	1.753669
96	Miscellaneous manufactures articles	1.489015
	...	
43	Furskins and artificial fur, manufactures thereof	0.009912
66	Umbrellas, walking-sticks, seat-sticks, whips, etc.	0.006493
19	Cereal, flour, starch, milk preparations and products	0.006206
46	Manufactures of plaiting material, basketwork, etc.	0.005519
31	Fertilizers	0.004419
67	Bird skin, feathers, artificial flowers, human hair	0.003918
86	Railway, tramway locomotives, rolling stock, equipment	0.00307
47	Pulp of wood, fibrous cellulosic material, waste, etc.	0.000421
50	Silk	0.000169
1	Live animals	0.000021

Table 6. Highest and lowest RCA, Europe 2008

Chapter		RCA
45	Cork and articles of cork	4.431031
97	Works of art, collectors pieces and antiques	3.438147
30	pharmaceutical products	3.364813
6	Live trees, plants, bulbs, roots, cut flowers, etc.	3.136746
88	Aircraft, spacecraft, and parts thereof	2.911997
50	Silk	2.805285
93	Arms and ammunition, parts and accessories thereof	2.580083
33	Essential oils, perfumes, cosmetics, toiletries	2.506225
19	Cereal, flour, starch, milk preparations and products	2.213142
51	Wool, animal hair, horsehair yarn and fabric thereof	2.191197
	...	

6 Note: Mexico had no exports of meat, fish and seafood food preparations (16) to Europe in 2008.

Chapter		RCA
36	Explosives, pyrotechnics, matches, pyrophorics, etc.	0.122908
16	Meat, fish and seafood food preparations nes	0.072483
12	Oil seed, oleagic fruits, grain, seed, fruit, etc.	0.068735
5	Products of animal origin, nes	0.054574
7	Edible vegetables and certain roots and tubers	0.046758
47	Pulp of wood, fibrous cellulosic material, waste, etc.	0.023691
26	Ores, slag and ash	0.018459
2	Meat and edible meat offal	0.006694
8	Edible fruit, nuts, peel of citrus fruit, melons	0.003042
10	Cereals	0.000495

Table 7. Industries with the greatest change in RCA, Mexico, 1998-2008

Chapter		Δ RCA	Base rates	Schedule Categories
79	Zinc and articles thereof	5.224666	0-2.5%	A & B
90	Optical, photo, technical, medical, etc. apparatus*	2.723543	0-4.2%	A & B
87	Vehicles other than railway, tramway	1.629497	0-15.4%	A & B
36	Explosives, pyrotechnics, matches, pyrophorics, etc.	1.430537	0%	A
10	Cereals**	1.244345	0-1.3%	1 & 5
78	Lead and articles thereof	1.003405	0-2.5%	A & B
96	Miscellaneous manufactures articles*	0.998184	0-2.5%	A & B
85	Electrical, electronic equipment	0.596948	0-9.8%	A & B
26	Ores, slag and ash	0.596041	0%	A
88	Aircraft, spacecraft, and parts thereof	0.582528	0%	A
	…			
17	Sugars and sugar confectionery	-1.57943	-	5, 6, & 7
37	Photographic or cinematographic goods	-1.58719	0%	A
3	Fish, crustaceans, molluscs, aquatic invertebrates	-2.02313	0-23%	1, 2, 3, 4a
92	Musical instruments, parts and accessories	-2.24249	0-3%	A & B
71	Pearls, precious stones, metals, coins, etc.*	-2.2468	0-1.7%	A
97	Works of art, collectors pieces and antiques	-3.15182	0%	A
9	Coffee, tea, mate and spices	-4.3697	0-9.5%	1, 2, 4
27	Mineral fuels, oils, distillation products, etc.	-4.41256	0%	A
58	Special woven or tufted fabric, lace, tapestry	-5.83972	4.2-9.7%	B
14	Vegetable plaiting materials, vegetable products nes*	-23.9407	0-30%	1

* Most categories had a 0% base rate.

** Most products had no base rate and are in category 5. Buckwheat and millet are in category 4, with per-weight tariffs rather than value-based tariffs (€44/ton and €66.3/ton, respectively). Maize was the only product subject to a tariff of 1.3%.

Sources: Authors' calculations based on COMTRADE data European Commission (2004)

Table 8. Industries with the greatest change in RCA, Europe, 1998-2008

Chapter		Δ RCA	Base rates	Schedule Categories
88	Aircraft, spacecraft, and parts thereof	2.07314	0-20%	A
97	Works of art, collectors pieces and antiques	1.811983	0%	A
93	Arms and ammunition, parts and accessories thereof	1.295188	0-20%	A
6	Live trees, plants, bulbs, roots, cut flowers, etc.	1.236903	0-20%	1
27	Mineral fuels, oils, distillation products, etc.	1.112423	0-10%	A, B+, C
43	Furskins and artificial fur, manufactures thereof	0.880395	10-20%	1, A
24	Tobacco and manufactured tobacco substitutes	0.851957	20-67%	1, 2, 5
1	Live animals	0.766135	0-45%	1, 3, 4, 5
57	Carpets and other textile floor coverings	0.592968	20%	A, B+, C
38	Miscellaneous chemical products	0.526971	0-15%	A, B, B+, C
	...			
86	Railway, tramway locomotives, rolling stock, equipment	-1.05497	0-20%	A, C
30	pharmaceutical products	-1.2662	0-20%	A, B, B+, C
19	Cereal, flour, starch, milk preparations and products	-1.37656	N/A, 10%	1, 2, 3, 5
50	Silk	-1.4602	10-15%	1, A
53	Vegetable textile fibres nes. Paper yarn, woven fabric	-1.56481	0-15%	1, 3, A, C
4	Dairy products, eggs, honey, edible animal product	-1.66703	N/A, 0-20%	1, 5
45	Cork and articles of cork	-2.02745	10-20%	A
69	Ceramic products	-2.28064	0-20%	A, C
49	Printed books, newspapers, pictures, etc.	-2.30428	0-20%	A, B+, C
22	Beverages, spirits and vinegar†	-3.31323	10-20%	1,2, 3, 4, 4a, 5

† Three products have a composite base rate of 10% or 20% plus $0.39586 pesos per liter.

Sources: Authors' calculations based on COMTRADE data; European Commission (2004b).

European exports to Mexico, in general, faced higher initial tariffs. As noted in the introduction, Europe thus stood to gain more in terms of market access through the free trade agreement. In Table 8, we observe that five of the top six industries that gained the most enjoyed immediate tariff elimination; only one was duty-free before the treaty. It is difficult, however, to detect a strong pattern in either the chapters that gained the most or those that lost the most, as the base tariff rates are in approximately the same range and all the tariff elimination schedule categories appear both in the top ten and in the bottom ten chapters. For

Europe, then, as for Mexico, there seem to be other reasons behind the comparative advantage gains and losses.

Table 9 reveals the number of industries in which each party to the agreement enjoyed a comparative advantage in the partner market, in each of the years from 1990 to 2008. We observe an increase after the signing of the 1991 agreement, followed by a decline in the latter half of the 1990s, and a renewed increase after the 2000 agreement, which peaked in the 2003-2006 period. For Mexico, the benefits of the Mexico-EU Free Trade Agreement, in terms of comparative advantage in the European market, are less than those derived from the combination of the 1991 Mexico-EU agreement and the North American Free Trade Agreement. The number of Mexican industries currently enjoying a comparative advantage in the European market, and vice versa, is comparable to the number during the early 1990s. Thus, the short-term gains in comparative advantage of the 2000 treaty seem to have dissipated over time, although total bilateral trade has increased. This result is similar to that reported by Chiquiar *et al.* (2007) for Mexico's participation in the U.S. market: that study found the decline to begin as early as 2001, with the entry of China in the WTO.

Tables 10 and 11 reveal those industries, which maintained a comparative advantage from 1999 to 2008, those which were at a disadvantage in 1999 and enjoyed a comparative advantage in 2008, and those which had a comparative advantage in 1999 but lost it by 2008. In the case of Mexico, there is an apparent shift from comparative advantage in primary-related industries to somewhat more advanced industries. It is especially surprising that Mexico lost its advantage in chapter 27 (mineral fuels, oils, distillation products, etc.) while Europe gained a comparative advantage in the same industry. The opposite movement occurred for chapter 79 (Zinc and articles thereof). Given that Europe is typically considered to have an advantage in capital-intensive industries, an impressive proportion of the European industries that either maintained or gained comparative advantage are related to the primary sector.

Table 9. Number of industries with a comparative advantage in the partner market

Year	Mexico	EU-15
1990	3	42
1991	7	32
1992	8	29
1993	16	27
1994	28	36
1995	35	40
1996	33	38

Year	Mexico	EU-15
1997	26	38
1998	31	37
1999	19	33
2000	18	35
2001	20	34
2002	18	38
2003	21	42
2004	21	42
2005	24	40
2006	23	42
2007	21	40
2008	16	30

Source: Authors' calculations based on COMTRADE data.

There are several possible reasons for the loss in comparative advantage of industries on both sides. First, as mentioned in the Introduction, China has become a major world competitor since joining the WTO. Second, each side has continued to sign treaties with other nations and regions. Third, twelve countries have joined the EU since 2000, representing competition both to Mexico and to the EU-15. Fourth, the very diversification of exports may dilute the comparative advantage index as calculated for each industry. Fifth, the countries analyzed in this chapter may not be doing enough to remain competitive in light of increasing globalization. This suggests that each side could benefit from policies designed to improve the competitiveness of its products in the partner market.

Table 10. Mexico: Industries that maintained, gained, or lost comparative advantage between 1999 and 2008

Industries that maintained an advantage	Industries that gained an advantage	Industries that lost comparative advantage
14 Vegetable plaiting materials, vegetable products nes	79 Zinc and articles thereof	41 Raw hides and skins (other than furskins) and leather
87 Vehicles other than railway, tramway	90 Optical, photo, technical, medical, etc. apparatus	32 Tanning, dyeing extracts, tannins, derivs. Pigments, etc.
09 Coffee, tea, mate and spices	96 Miscellaneous manufactures article	84 Nuclear reactors, boilers, machinery, etc.
26 Ores, slag and ash	36 Explosives, pyrotechnics, matches, pyrophoric, etc.	07 Edible vegetables and certain roots and tubers
22 Beverages, spirits and vinegar	10 Cereals	29 Organic chemicals
85 Electrical, electronic equipment	13 Lac. Gums, resins, vegetable saps and extracts nes	92 Musical instruments, parts and accessories
25 Salt, sulfur, earth, stone, plaster, lime and cement	72 Iron and steel	

Industries that maintained an advantage	Industries that gained an advantage	Industries that lost comparative advantage
08 Edible fruit, nuts, peel of citrus fruit, melons	78 Lead and articles thereof	71 Pearls, precious stones, metals, coins, etc. 27 Mineral fuels, oils, distillation products, etc. 03 Fish, crustaceans, mollusks, aquatic invertebrates 38 Special woven or tufted fabric, lace, tapestry 56 Wadding, felt, nonwovens, yarns, twine, cordage, etc.

5. Conclusions

This chapter represents a preliminary analysis of the evolution of comparative advantage in Mexico and in Europe resulting from the Free Trade Agreement that went into effect in 2000. Our results indicate that there was an initial overall trade benefit for each side, but that the comparative advantages have dissipated over time. Notwithstanding, the Revealed Comparative Advantage indices show that Mexico has matured in the European market, as evidenced by an increased comparative advantage for several manufacturing industries that were previously at a disadvantage, such as Optical and photo apparatus, and loss of comparative advantage in several primary-related industries, most notably Mineral fuels. Europe, meanwhile, continues to have more industries with a comparative advantage in the Mexican market than vice-versa.

Table 11: Europe: Industries that maintained, gained, or lost comparative advantage between 1999 and 2008

Industries that maintained an advantage	Industries that gained an advantage	Industries that lost comparative advantage
45 Cork and articles of cork 97 Works of art, collectors pieces and antiques 30 Pharmaceutical products 06 Live trees, plants, bulbs, roots, cut flowers, etc. 50 Silk 93 Arms and ammunition, parts and accessories thereof 33 Essential oils, perfumes, cosmetics, toiletries 19 Cereal, flour, starch, milk preparations and products	88 Aircraft, spacecraft, and parts thereof 27 Mineral fuels, oils, distillation products, etc. 96 Miscellaneous manufactures articles 01 Live animals	64 Footwear, gaiters and the like, parts thereof 87 Vehicles other than railway, tramway 83 Miscellaneous articles of base metal 70 Glass and glassware 59 Impregnated, coated or laminated textile fabric

Industries that maintained an advantage	Industries that gained an advantage	Industries that lost comparative advantage
51 Wool, animal hair, horsehair yarn and fabric thereof 22 Beverages, spirits and vinegar 53 Vegetable textile fibresnes. Paper yarn, woven fabric 35 Albuminoids, modified starches, glues, enzymes 38 Miscellaneous chemical products 72 Iron and steel 34 Soaps, lubricants, waxes, candles, modeling pastes 13 Lac. Gums, resins, vegetable saps and extracts nes 24 Tobacco and manufactured tobacco substitutes 68 Stone, plaster, cement, asbestos, mica, etc. articles 84 Nuclear reactors, boilers, machinery, etc. 29 Organic chemicals 90 Optical, photo, technical, medical, etc. apparatus 69 Ceramic products 32 Tanning, dyeing extracts, tannins, derivatives. Pigments, etc. 89 Ships, boats and other floating structures 82 Tools, implements, cutlery, etc. of base metal	48 Paper & paperboard, articles of pulp, paper and board	49 Printed books, newspapers, pictures, etc. 4 Dairy products, eggs, honey, edible animal product 79 Zinc and articles thereof

The next step in this analysis should be to examine why certain industries have a comparative advantage, based on factor costs, joint ventures, or other factors. Such detailed, industry-level analysis is beyond the scope of this chapter, but is necessary for those interested in exploring ways to promote Mexican products in Europe and vice-versa. In an ever more integrated world, in which trade barriers are no longer a viable tool of economic policy, it is increasingly important to develop other economic strategies to maintain or gain comparative advantages.

References

Abidin, M. & Wai, H. (2008). Revealed comparative advantage of Malaysian exports: The case for changing export composition. *Asian Economic Papers*, 7 (3), 130-147.

Amoroso, N., Chiquiar, D., Quella, N., y Ramos-Francia, M. (2008). Determinantes de la ventaja comparativa y del desempeño de las exportaciones manufactureras mexicanas en el período 1996-2005. *Banco de México*, documento de investigación 2008-01.

Balassa, B. (1965). Trade liberalisation and revealed comparative advantage. *The Manchester School of Economics and Social Science*, 33, 99-123.

Baldwin, R. (2006). Multilaterilising. regionalism: Spaghetti bowls as building blocs on the path to global trade. *National Bureau of Economic Research*, working paper 12545.

Bhagwati, J. (1990). Departures from multilateralism: regionalism and aggressive unilateralism. *The Economic Journal*, 100, 1304-1317.

Chiquiar, D., Fragoso, E. & Ramos-Francia, M. (2007). La ventaja comparativa y el desempeño de las exportaciones manufactureras mexicanas en el periodo 1996-2005. *Banco de México*, documento de investigación 12.

Cinquetti, C. (2008). Multinationals and exports in a large and protected developing country. *Review of International Economics*, 16 (8), 904-918.

Corden, M. (1987). Protection and liberalization: A review of analytical issues. *International Monetary Fund*, occasional paper 54.

Edwards, S. (1997). Openess, productivity and growth: What do we really? *National Bureau of Economic Research*, working paper 5978.

European Commission, External Relations. (2009a) The EU and Mexico (United Mexican States), http://ec.europa.eu/external_relations/mexico/index_en.htm, accessed February 23, 2010.

European Commission, Trade. (2009b) "Mexico" http://ec.europa.eu/trade/creating-opportunities/bilateral-relations/countries/mexico/index_en.htm, accessed February 24, 2010.

European Commission (2004a), Annex I: tariff elimination of the Community, http://trade.ec.europa.eu/doclib/docs/2004/october/tradoc_111724.pdf accessed February 23, 2010.

European Commission (2004b), Anexo II: Calendario de desgravación de México, http://trade.ec.europa.eu/doclib/docs/2004/october/tradoc_111768.pdf, accessed February 23, 2010.

European Commission, "Actos Legislativos y Otros Instrumentos; Eliminación arancelaria (relativa al artículo 3 de la Decisión), Anexo II Calendario de desgravación de México", http://trade.ec.europa.eu/doclib/docs/2004/october/tradoc_111768.pdf.

Faber, B. (2007). Towards the spatial patterns of sectoral adjustments to trade liberalisation: The case of NAFTA in Mexico. *Growth & Change*, 38 (4), 567-594.

Garanina, O. (2009). What beyond oil and gas? Russian trade specialisation in manufactures. *Post-Communist Economies*, 21 (1), 1-29.

Hisanaga, M. (2008). Revealed specialization: Evidence on U.S. international services. *International Trade Journal*, 22 (4), 378-414.

Geda, A. & Meskel, A. (2008). China and India's growth surge: Is it a curse of blessing for Africa? The case of manufactured exports. *African Development Review*, 20 (2), 247-272.

Hoeller, P., Girouard, N. & Colecchia, A. (1998). The European union's trade policies and their economic effects. *OECD Economics Department* Working Papers 194.

Kemp, M. & Wan, H. (1976). An elementary proposition concerning the formation of customs unions. In Murray Kemp, *Three topics in the theory of international trade: Distribution, welfare, and uncertainty*. Amsterdam, Netherlands: North Holland.

Krishna, P. & Panagariya, A. (2002). On necessarily welfare-enhancing free trade areas. *Journal of International Economics*, 57, 353-67.

Rae, D. & Sollie, M. (2007). Globalisation on the European Union: Which countries are best placed to cope? *OCDE, Economics Department* working paper 586.

Rodriguez, F. & Rodrik, D. (1999). Trade policy and economic growth: A skeptic's guide to cross-national evidence. *National Bureau of Economic Research*, working paper 7081.

Sachs, J. & Warner, A. (1995). Economic convergence and economic policies. *National Bureau of Economic Research*, working paper 5039.

Sherer, F. (1994). *Competition policies for an integrated world economy*. Washington, DC., EE.UU.: Brookings Institution.

United Nations (2009). Commodity Trade Statistics Database.

Viner, J. (1950). *The Customs Union Issue*. New York, EE.UU.: Carnegie Endowment for International Peace.

Wacziarg, R. & Horn, K. (2003). Trade liberalization and growth: New evidence. National Bureau of Economic growth: New evidence. *National Bureau of Economic Research*, working paper 10152.

Whalley, J. (1996). Why do countries seek regional trade agreements? *National Bureau of Economic Research*, working paper 5552.

Whalley, J. & Xin, X. (2007). Regionalization, changes in home bias, and the growth of world trade. *National Bureau of Economic Research*, working paper 13023.

Winters, A. (1997). Regionalism and the rest of the world: Theory and estimates of the effects of European integration. *Review of International Economics*, 5, 134-147.

Yen-Chum, J. & Chia-Wen, L. (2008). National port competitiveness: Implications for India. *Management Decision*, 46 (10), 1482-1507.

The EU-Mexico Agreement: What Has Happened to Trade and Capital Flows since 2000?

René Cabral[*] *& Daniel Villarreal Cabello*[†]

1. Introduction

It is well documented that Mexico embarked in an ambitious openness campaign in 1986 when it became a member of the World Trade Organization (WTO; previously, the General Agreement on Tariffs and Trade (GATT)). This campaign took a new dimension in 1994 when Mexico became a partner of the United States and Canada in the North American Free Trade Agreement (NAFTA). The aggregate positive effects of NAFTA were many, with not just trade rising considerably but also, with total foreign direct investment (FDI) inflows rising from figures below 4.3 billion in 1993 to nearly 30 billion by 2001. A number of studies have analyzed the direct and indirect economic effects of NAFTA from different perspective (for assessment of NAFTA's effects on trade and investment see, for instance, Ramirez (2006), Lederman (2005), Montenegro and Soloaga (2006) and Nica et al. (2006), among others).[1] Most of them find significant positive effects from the agreement for Mexico.

A few years later after the enactment of NAFTA, Mexico took another important and definitive step in its openness campaign by negotiating a broader cooperation agreement with the European Union (EU). The so called 'EU-Mexico Economic Partnership, Political Coordination and Cooperation Agreement' was signed in 1997 and entered into force in 2000.[2] The three pillars of this agreement are political dialogue, trade and cooperation. In our view, for Mexico and the EU, economic diversification and strengthening of its presence in Latin America are, respectively, the most important objectives of engaging in this broad cooperation agreement. This is specially the case for the economic dimension of the agreement, which focuses on trade and investment relations.

---

*, † EGAP Gobierno y Política Pública, Tecnológico de Monterrey.

1 For more specific indirect effects NAFTA on, for instance, the labor market, see Mollick and Cabral (2009). For the effects on the agreement on real wages, see Hanson (2004) and Cabral et al. (2010).

2 More precisely, commercial negotiations started in 1998, these concluded with the signing of a Free Trade Agreement which subsequently entered into force in July 2000 (goods) and March 2001 (services and investment).

After nearly 10 years since the bilateral accord entered into force, this chapter evaluates the effects of the agreement on trade and investment. We do this by setting the North America Free Trade Agreement (NAFTA) as the benchmark. First, we assess whether both parts have been able to accomplish their aforementioned diversification and growing presence objectives. Secondly, we observe whether the EU-Mexico agreement might have had a detrimental effect on the trade or capital flows of Mexico with other economic blocks. That is, we are interested in investigation whether trade diversion or creation resulted from the agreement. As for investment, we assess the particular impact of the agreement on the Mexican economy. Finally, we also examine the response of trade and investment to the developments of certain variables, such as the exchange rate and the rate of economic growth.

The main sources of data for the analysis in this chapter are Mexico's National Institute of Statistics (INEGI) and Ministry of Economy. For EU data, the main sources are the OECD and Eurostat. Other data on trade and FDI employed in the analysis comes from the International Monetary Fund. Since over the period under analysis the size of the EU has changed due to the addition of new member states, in this paper we refer to the EU considering the 25 sovereign states that comprise the EU before December 31, 2006.

Our statistical analysis shows that although Mexico's trade with the EU is significantly less than with its partners in North America, the United States (US) and Canada, it has increased significantly since the EU-Mexico agreement entered into force. We observe that for the first nine years of the agreement (2000-2008), the rate of growth of trade with the EU is higher than it was in the first nine years of NAFTA (1994-2002). On average, total trade grew by 12.7% in the first nine years of NAFTA (14.5% for exports and 10.9% for imports), relative to 13.4% after the Mexico-EU agreement was enacted (14.2% for exports and 13.2% for imports). Moreover, we find no evidence that this happened at the cost of lower trade with other regions, as Mexico's exchange of goods with Asia and Latin America over the same period grew by 21.3% and 17.7%, respectively. Overall, our agregate data suggest that the EU agrement, as well as other bilateral agrements signed by Mexico, have promoted trade creation rather than trade diversion from the NAFTA region.

As for investment, our examination of statistical data shows that over the last few years, FDI flows from the EU have also changed in size, behavior and structure. By 2000, the year in which the EU-Mexico trade agreement entered into force, FDI from the 25 EU members reached USD3,259 million, this compared with USD1,964 million observed in the year of 1994. Average annual FDI flows were only USD2,341 million for the period 1994-1999, compared with USD7,800 million between 2000 and 2007. Interestingly, we observe that the direction of EU's FDI flows have followed a very different pattern than those of the US in recent years. For the period 2000-2007, the correlation coefficient between US and EU FDI is -0.33, as compared to 0.91 for the period 1994-1999. This suggests not only an increasing contribution of the EU to Mexico's FDI total flows but also, a complementary role of those capital flows to the FDI that Mexico receives from the US and Canada. We argue that such complementarity benefits the Mexican economy by exerting a countercyclical force on FDI receipts from North America.

Despite the beneficial effects that the EU's FDI could have on counteracting business cycles, another interesting fact that emerges from the data analysis is the very small role that Mexico has on attracting FDI from the EU. According to our analysis, over the period 2005- 2007 Mexico captured less than 1% of the extra EU total FDI. We show this is very little compared with, for instance, the FDI received by Central America or Brazil. For the same period, these two economies captured, respectively, more than 10 and about three times the FDI attracted by Mexico from the 25 EU economies.

Finally, we empirically explore the effects of GDP growth and the nominal exchange rate on trade and capital flows of Mexico with the EU and the USA. We observe very different responses in general. We argue that these findings are, however, consistent with the unequal behavior of trade and capital flows described above.

The rest of this chapter continues as follows. Section 2 reviews the evolution of Mexico's total trade with the EU between 1993, the year before NAFTA was enacted, and 2008. Section 3 observes the origin of foreign direct investment received by Mexico between 1994 and 2007. It also looks at the reception of FDI by industry and pays particular attention to the flows of FDI that Mexico has received from the EU. Section 4 analyses the effect of the exchange rate and GDP growth on the trade and capital flows received by the US and the EU. Section 5 presents some conclusions of the assessment.

2. Trade in goods

Trade is perhaps the most important pillar of the Mexico-EU agreement signed in 2000. This section provides a picture of the importance of Mexico in the EU's trade and vice versa. We evaluate the evolution of trade before and after the agreement was enacted and we compare the performance of trade between Mexico and the EU with that of Mexico and the rest of the world. We do so while paying particular attention to the NAFTA region.

2.1 The EU total trade

The European Union, as a commercial union, dates back to the 1950s. Ever since then, it has evolved to become the world largest economic producer and consumer of goods and services. These days the EU represents roughly 20% of the world's total trade. According to OECD data, in 2007, the EU's total trade (exports plus imports) surpassed the outstanding figure of USD3 billion (USD1.6 billion for exports and USD1.4 billion for imports).[3] While most of its trade is with other EU members, the EU block represents an attractive market for world exporters, as well as a significant source of imports.

Figures 1 and 2 show the evolution, origin and destiny of the EU's exports and imports measured in constant 2005 US dollars. It is clear from these figures that, by and large, EU members trade mostly with other EU members. Between 1994 and 2007, more than two-thirds of their exports and imports were exchanged inside the union. NAFTA (16.3% of its exports and 16.2% of its imports) and Asia (9.4% of its exports and 8% of its imports) are the two regions that trade the most with the EU. The US plays a significant role on NAFTA's trade with the EU; it is the source of 14.8% and 14.9% of the total EU exports and imports, respectively. China plays the most important role in Asia; it is the destination of 7.2% of the EU's exports and the source of 8.6% of its imports.

Figure 1. EU's Total Trade Evolution 1994-2007

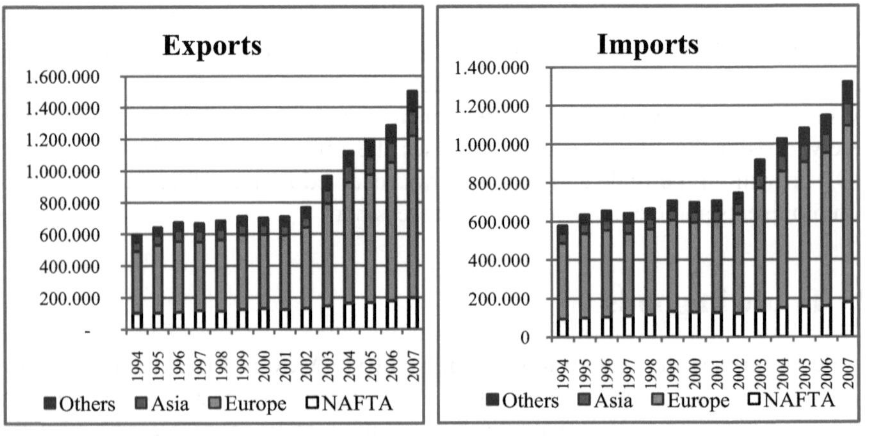

Source: Elaborated with data from the OECD.

3 We refer here to a billion of United States dollar as $1X10^{12}$ or $1,000,000,000,000 USD.

While trade with South and Central America has more than tripled in real terms over the 1994-2007 period, it still represents a small proportion of the EU's total exports. On average, only 2.6% of the EU's exports and 2.7% of its imports are allotted to this region. In the following section, we observe and discuss the origin and destination of the EU's trade to Latin America in more detail.

Figure 2. EU's Average Export and Import Shares 1994-2007

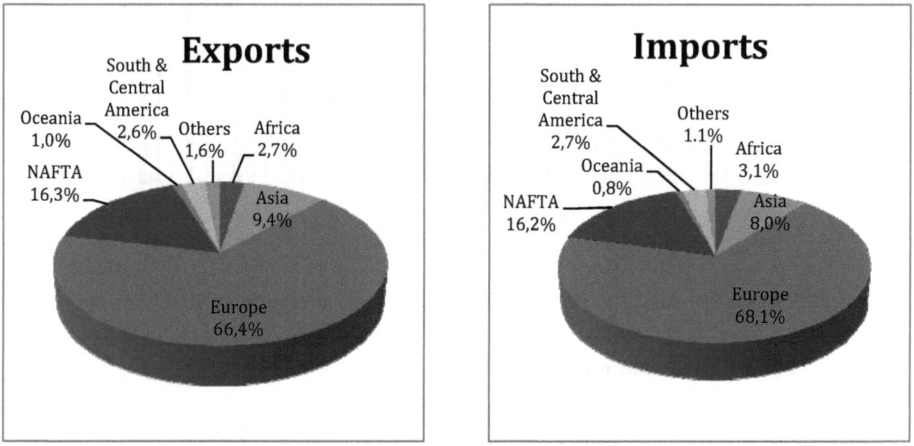

Source: Elaborated with data from the OECD.

EU trade with Latin America

Over the last 15 years, the EU has significantly increased its trade with Latin America.[4] Between 1994 and 2007, exports and imports with the region grew annually, on average, 8.1% and 10.3%, respectively. Figure 3 shows the evolution of the EU's trade with Latin America, its trade balance and the trend regression of the trade balance. Considering that several currencies are mixed in the composition of these trade flows, it is notable that there is not only a trend towards greater trade between the EU and Latin America but also a trend towards a more favorable trade balance for Latin America in the later years. Ever since 1998, the trade balance has evolved in favor of the region.

4 Latin America, as a region, is composed by Mexico, Central and South America.

Figure 3. EU's Total Trade with Latin America 1994-2007

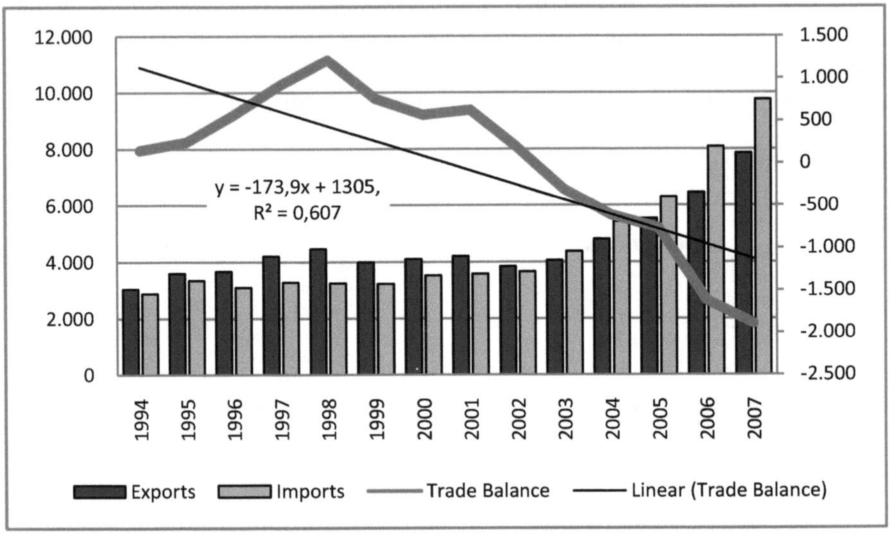

Source: Elaborated with data from the OECD.

Figure 4 shows the average distribution of trade between the EU and Latin America between 1994 and 2007. Brazil, Mexico and Argentina are the EU's three main trading partners in Latin America. Together these three countries receive 66.4% of the EU exports to the region and produce 63.6% of its imports. Brazil and Mexico are not only the most important trading partners for the EU but also, some of the most dynamic, in terms of growth. Over the 1994-2007 period, the EU exports to Brazil grew on average 11.2% per annum while its imports from the country rose 10.3%. Trade with Mexico has also evolved rapidly; throughout this period, imports from Mexico rose at an annual rate of 10.5% and 13.4% for exports.

Figure 4. EU's Average Trade Shares with Latin America (1994-2007)

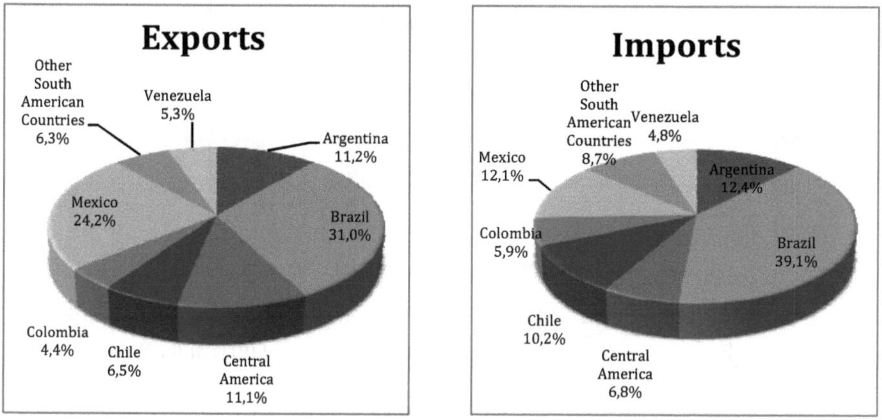

Source: Elaborated with data from the OECD.

During this period, Mexico contributed, on average, with 24.2% of the exports of Latin America to the EU and with 12.1% of the imports. In what follows, we examine the evolution of Mexico's trade with the EU in more detail.

2.2 *Mexico's total trade*

Figure 5 shows the evolution of Mexico's exports and imports to the NAFTA region, the European Union and to the rest of the world in 2005, constant US dollars. As expected, the most striking point in both figures is the dramatic increase in Mexican exports and imports to the US and Canada following the start of NAFTA. For any given year, Mexico's trade with the US and Canada considerably exceeded its trade with the EU. Nevertheless, looking at the rates of growth, the expansion results less dramatic. On average, total trade grew by 12.7% in the first nine years of NAFTA (14.5% for exports and 10.9% for imports), relative to 13.4% after the Mexico-EU agreement was enacted (14.2% for exports and 13.2% for imports). In aggregate terms, there is no evidence that this happened at the cost of lower trade with other particular regions, as Mexico's exchange of goods with Asia and Latin America also grew by 21.3% and 17.7%, respectively.

Figure 5. Mexico's Total Exports and Imports by Region

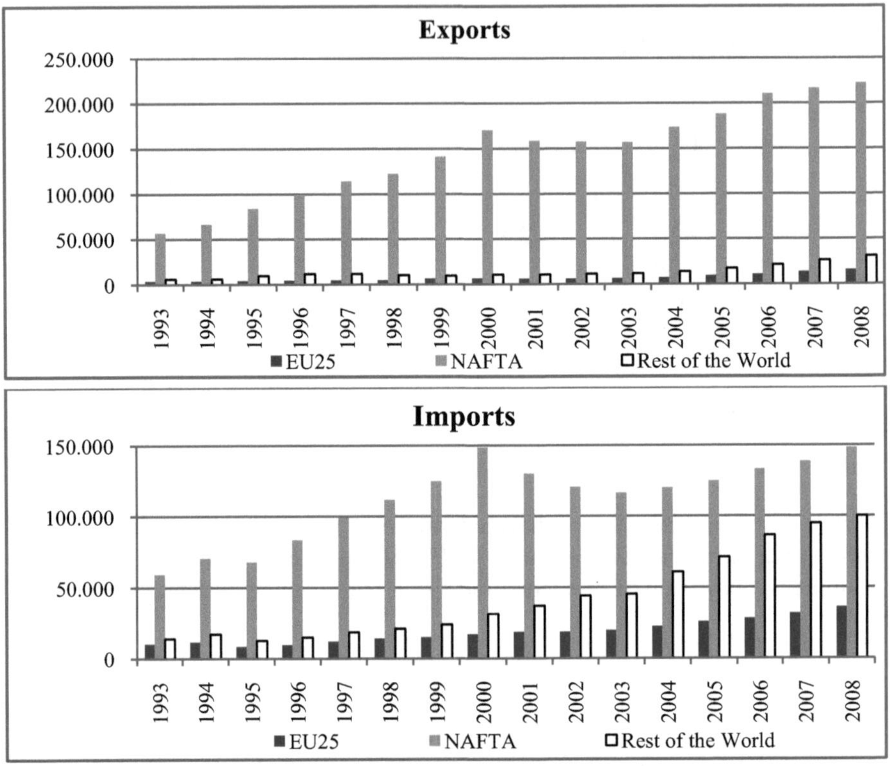

Source: Elaborated with data from the Instituto Nacional de Estadistica Geografia e Informatica (INEGI).

In the first eight years after the enactment of the EU-Mexico Agreement, average yearly exports from Mexico to the EU increased 2.37-fold (from USD3,979 million between 1993 and 2000 to USD9,466 million between 2001 and 2008) relative to the previous eight years. Imports increased 2.46-fold (from USD10,227 million to USD25,170 million) over the same intervals of time. This has led to a greater participation of the EU in Mexico's trade. As can be seen in Figures 6 and 7, the EU's share on Mexico's exports grew from 3.5% in 2000 to 5.9% in 2008. Meanwhile, the proportion of Mexican imports from the EU rose from 8.6% in 2000 to 12.7%. Over this same period, Mexico's trade with Asia expanded significantly; particularly in imports, where the share of Mexico's trade with Asia is higher than that with the EU.

Figure 6. Origin and Destination of Mexican Exports

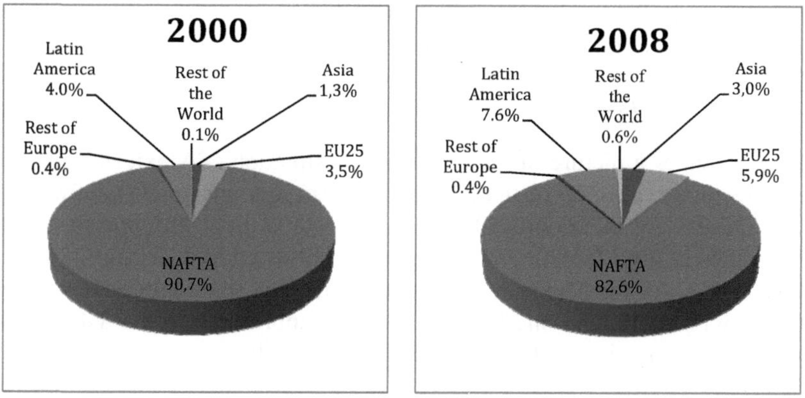

Source: Elaborated with data from the Instituto Nacional de Estadistica Geografia e Informatica (INEGI).

Figure 7. Origin and Destination of Mexican Imports

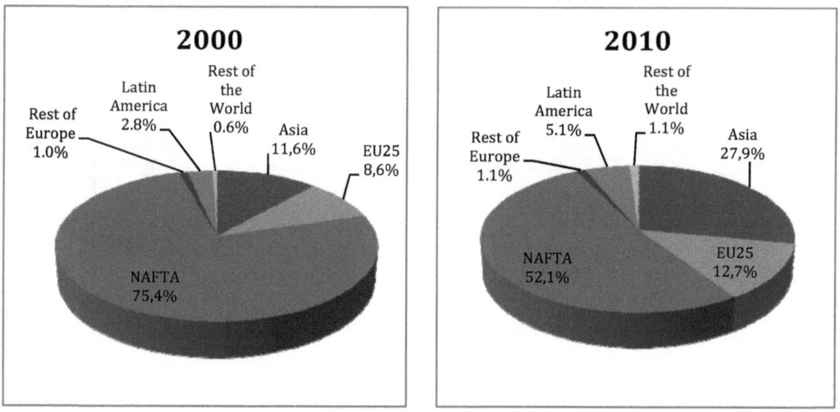

Source: Elaborated with data from the Instituto Nacional de Estadistica Geografia e Informatica (INEGI).

Another interesting point in Figures 6 and 7 is the overall diversification of Mexican trade since 2000. The proportion of Mexican exports and imports from Latin America, Asia and the EU rose between 2000 and 2008, while trade to the NAFTA region decreased.[5] This despite the expansion of trade with the latter

5 Indeed, Mexico's trade with other European countries, outside the EU, and with the rest of the world is also marginally raised.

region observed in Figure 5. Together, this data suggests that the EU agrement, as well as other bilateral agrements signed by Mexico, have promoted trade creation rather than trade diversion from the the NAFTA region.

2.3 EU-Mexico trade

Figure 8 provides a picture of the origin and destination of Mexican trade to the EU. Interestingly, only 10 of the 25 EU members account for 96% of Mexico's exports and 94% of its imports. On average, Spain is the main importer of Mexican products in the EU with 26% of the total, followed by Germany (24%) and the UK (12%). As for Mexican imports from the EU, the main EU exporter is Germany, with more than one-third of the total, approximately 35.8%, followed by Italy and Spain, with 12.9% and 11.5%, respectively.

Figure 8. Mexico's Trade with the EU 25 (1993-2008)

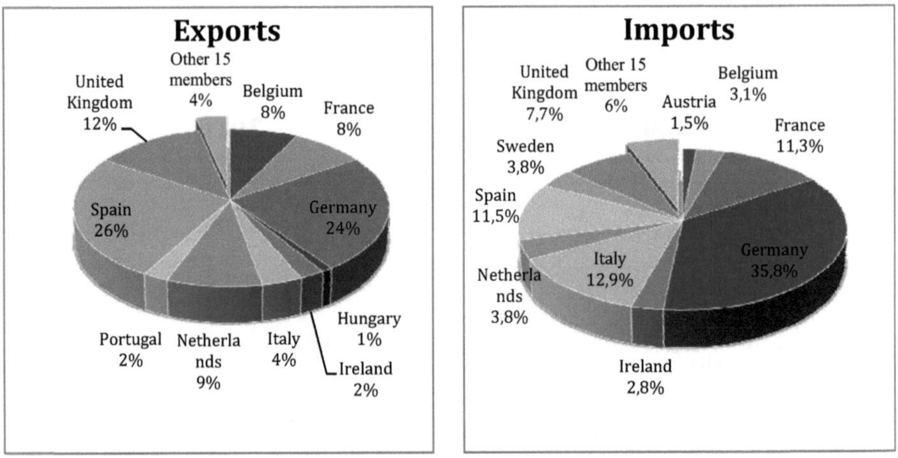

Source: Elaborated with data from the Instituto Nacional de Estadistica Geografia e Informatica (INEGI).

Table 1 disaggregates Mexico's imports and exports of goods from the EU by industry. It shows the most recent figures available for 2008 and the average participation of each industry over the 1993-2008 period. Looking at the shares, it can be observed that three industries concentrate nearly two-thirds, or 63.4%, of Mexico's exports to the EU. These are mineral products (28.5%), machinery and electrical equipment (22.8%), and transportation (12.1%), where the automotive industry is accounted. As for imports, again three industries account for 63.7% of Mexico's purchases from the EU: machinery and electrical goods (38.5%), chemical and allied industries (14.5%), and transportation (10.7%).

Table 1. Mexico-EU Trade by Industry

	2008 Millions of USD		Average Share (%) 1993-2008	
Industry	**Exports**	**Imports**	**Exports**	**Imports**
Total: All commodities	17,241.3	39,136.5	100	100
01-05 Animal & Animal Products	137.4	87.7	1.34	1.39
06-15 Vegetable Products	409.7	250.9	4.29	0.97
16-24 Foodstuffs	326.5	743.8	3.28	2.27
25-27 Mineral Products	4,692.4	6,148.8	28.49	3.33
28-38 Chemicals & Allied Industries	852.4	5,591.0	8.88	14.54
39-40 Plastics / Rubbers	375.9	1,616.2	2.03	4.09
41-43 Raw Hides, Skins, Leather, & Furs	35.8	173.9	0.42	0.46
44-49 Wood & Wood Products	36.7	840.3	0.43	2.78
50-63 Textiles	98.4	857.1	2.44	2.64
64-67 Footwear / Headgear	11.5	105.1	0.38	0.28
68-71 Stone / Glass	658.2	512.9	3.00	1.81
72-83 Metals	1,070.4	3,532.3	5.17	8.18
84-85 Machinery / Electrical	3,972.8	12,066.8	22.83	38.49
86-89 Transportation	3,862.5	3,792.5	12.09	10.67
90-97 Miscellaneous	665.5	2,195.8	5.02	5.63
98-99 Service	35.3	621.6	-	2.45

Source: Elaborated with data from the OECD.

Taken as a whole, we observe an increasing participation of the EU in Mexico's trade and vice versa; with industries, such as mineral products, transportation, machinery and electrical equipment, playing a more significant role. We see larger trade growth with the EU eight years after the agreement started, than with Canada and the US eight years after the start of NAFTA. There seems to be trade creation, rather than trade diversion, as a result of the expansion of aggregate trade between the EU and Mexico.

3. Foreign Direct Investment Flows

Besides the expansion of trade, the increase in capital flows has been another important goal of the EU-Mexico agreement. In this section, we look at the evolution of FDI, the most stable and significant form of foreign capital. Since the EU is significantly larger than Mexico, in terms of size, we pay particular attention to the flows of capital received by Mexico from the EU and exclude from the analysis the inconsequential flows of capital from Mexico to the EU. Instead, we briefly observe the destination of the EU's total outflows of FDI; this as a way of illustrating the potential source of capital flows that this economic block represents for the Mexican economy.

3.1 The EU's FDI

As with trade, the EU is an important source and destination of the world's capital investment, with intra-EU trade representing around 70% of total EU FDI (Eurostat, 2007). According to International Monetary Fund statistics, the EU25 contributes around 50% of the World FDI. Figure 9 describes the inflows and outflows of FDI from the EU between 1990 and 2008, as well as the EU's share of the world's total FDI. As can be observed, ever since Euro coins and notes started to circulate in 2001, inward and outward FDI flows rose to new record levels. Outward FDI went from 262.3 billion in 2002 to 823.5 in 2008 (26.1% annual growth rate), while inward FDI rose from 303.5 to 473.6 billion over the same period (19.9% annual growth rate). With the exception of 2002, the EU remains an overall net investor of long term capital.

Figure 9. EU 25 Inflows and Outflows of FDI (1980-2008)

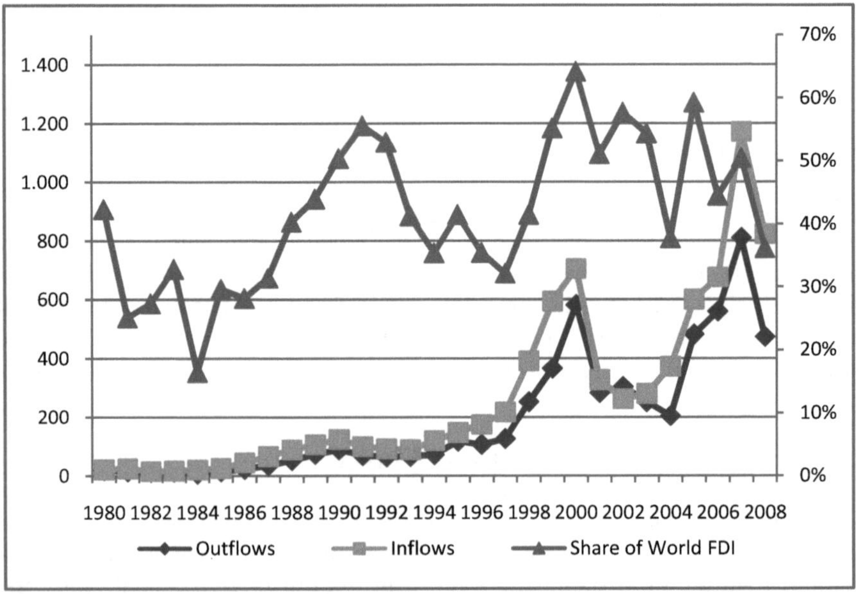

Source: Eurostat and IMF International Financial Statistics

Table 2 shows the distribution of extra EU's FDI; that is, FDI that does not have EU countries as its destination. We show 2007 because we consider it as a representative year; it is relatively recent and happened just before the world economic recession that began at the end of 2008 and continued during 2009. Table 2 also lists the destination of FDI by region, main countries in each relevant region and the proportions of the total FDI they received. Several interesting facts can be observed. First, North America is the first destination of the EU's FDI, with the US accounting for the most part. Nearly a third of the EU's total FDI has North America as its destination and about 75% of this region's FDI goes to the US. The European continent, excluding EU members, is the second largest receiver of FDI with almost 30% of the total, followed by Asia (13.3%), Central America (10.4%), South America (4.2%) and Oceania (1.1%).

Mexico merely represents roughly 1% of the EU's FDI; this is only about 2.5% of the total FDI received by North America every year. Interestingly, for the year 2007 Central America, a region mainly compose of small countries with a joint GDP smaller than that of Mexico, attracts, from the EU, more than 10 times the FDI received by Mexico. The other main destinations of FDI in Latin America are Argentina and Brazil (attracting 0.6% and 2.9% of the EU's total FDI, respectively), with the latter attracting by itself about three times the FDI received by Mexico. This data shows the significant source of FDI that the EU represents for Mexico and, along with the rest of the data shown above, the favorable effects that attracting more FDI from the EU could potentially have on the Mexican economy.

Table 2. Destination of Extra EU FDI in 2007

Destiny	Value	%
Total	977.0	100.0
Europe non EU	193.9	19.8
North America	392.4	40.2
USA	293.8	30.1
Canada	86.6	8.9
Mexico	12.1	1.2
Central America	184.2	18.9
South America	36.9	3.8
Argentina	3.2	0.3
Brazil	30.9	3.2
Asia	116.6	11.9
China	29.1	3.0
India	10.9	1.1
Japan	26.0	2.7
Oceania	13.5	1.4
Australia	13.9	1.4
Others	39.3	4.0

Source: Eurostat Statistics in Focus

As for the contribtion to the EU's total FDI, Figure 10 shows the economies with the highest average FDI outflows for the 2002-2008 period. From the 25 EU economies, France is the main contribuitor with 19.7% of the total, followed by the United Kingom (17.8%), Germany (13,7%), Spain (10.3%), the Netherlands (9.1%), Belgium (7.7%) and Italy (6.2%). Following, we explore in greater detail the FDI flows received by Mexico from the 25 EU economies.

Figure 10. Contribution to Outward FDI (2002-2008)

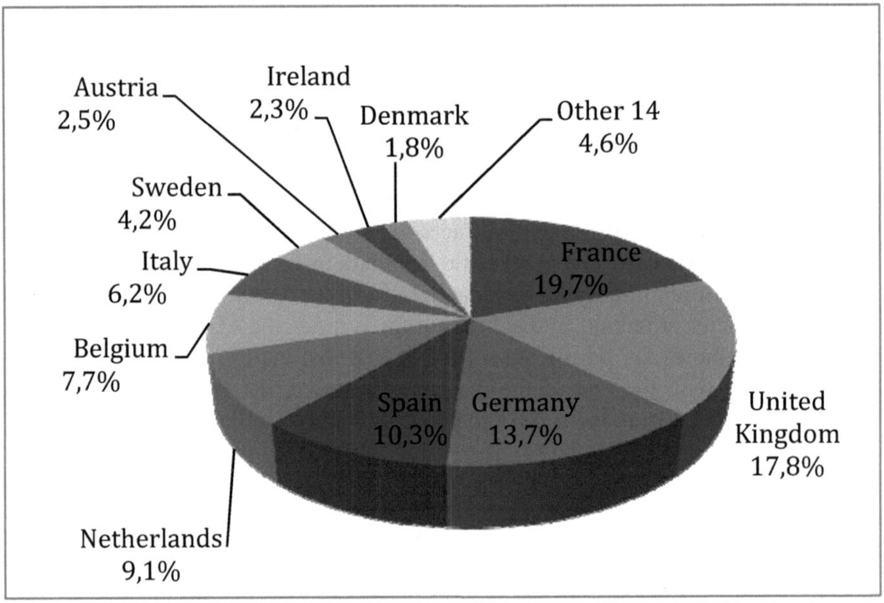

Source: Eurostat

3.2 Mexico's FDI inflows

Over the last three decades Mexico has become an important destination of foreign capital, particularly of FDI. Over the course of the 1990s, average yearly inflows of FDI rose to USD7,743 million, compared with USD2,387 million during the 1980s. Between 2000 and 2007, average FDI rose to an average level of USD22,566 million. The evolution of FDI can be better observed in Figure 11. From 1994 onwards, the figure 10 allows us to disaggregated FDI flows by region. It can be observed that, ever since the NAFTA agreement entered into effect, Mexico saw a considerable increase in long-term capital inflows. FDI reached its peak in 2001 with USD 29,785 million, a figure six times larger than before the enactment of NAFTA in 1993.

Figure 11. Mexico's FDI Inflows

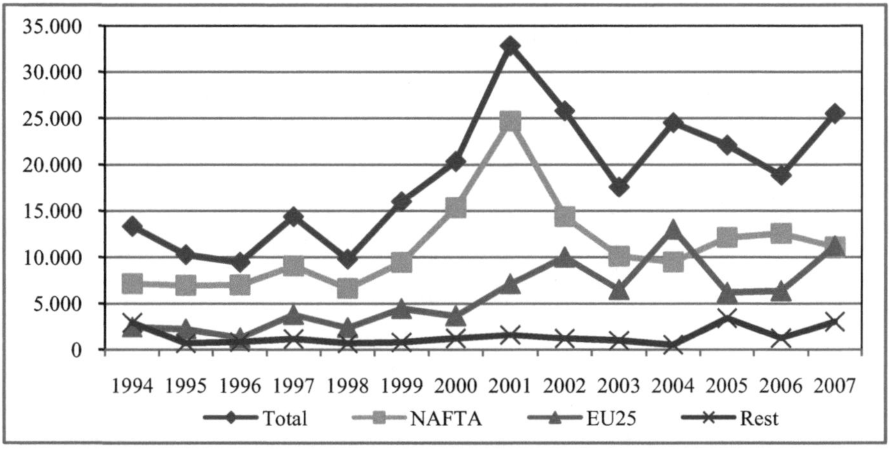

Source: Elaborated with data from the Instituto Nacional de Estadistica Geografia e Informatica (INEGI).

Over the last few years, FDI flows from the EU have also changed, both in size and behavior. By 2000, the year in which the EU-Mexico trade agreement entered into force, FDI from the 25 EU members reached USD3,259 million, this compared with USD1,964 million in 1994. Average annual FDI flows were only USD2,341 million between 1994-1999, compared with USD7,800 million between 2000 and 2007. Interestingly, direction-wise, the EU FDI flows have followed a very different pattern than those of the US in recent years. For the 2000-2007 period, the correlation coefficient between US and EU FDI is -0.33, compared with 0.91 for the 1994-1999 period. This, along with the picture portrayed by Figure 11, suggests not only an increasing contribution of the EU to Mexico's FDI total flows but also a complementary role of those capital flows to the FDI that Mexico receives from the US and Canada. Such complementarity benefits the Mexican economy by exerting a countercyclical force on FDI receipts from the US.

3.3 Mexico's reception of FDI by sector

Figure 12 shows the average sectorial destination of FDI received by Mexico. The manufacturing industry has historically been the main receptor of FDI in Mexico; for the period under analysis (1994-2007), it represents, on average, more than 50% of total FDI. The second largest receptor is the financial services sector with 19.6%. This industry was particularly dynamic between 2000 and 2003, a period in which the five largest commercial banks in Mexico were acquired by foreign financial institutions. For instance, in 2001, financial services accounted for more than 55% of total FDI inflows; this was the year in which, for instance, Citibank acquired Banamex, the largest Mexican private bank.

Figure 12. Distribution of Total FDI Inflows by Sector (1994-2007)

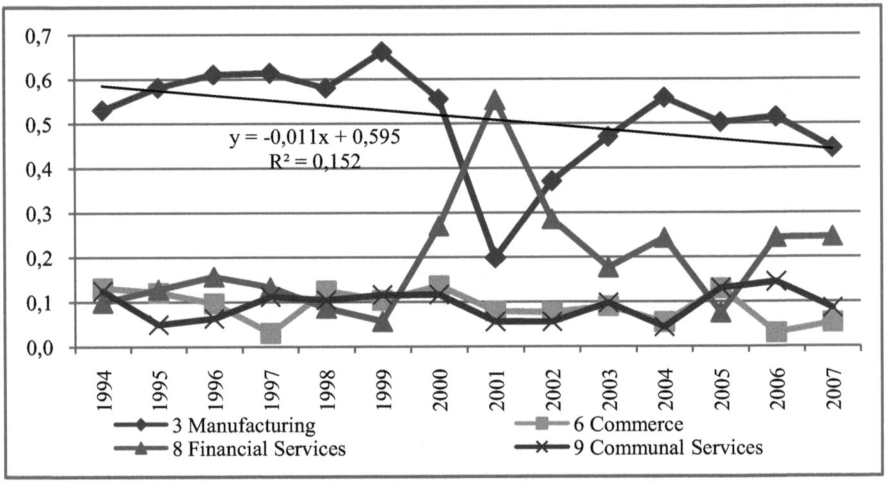

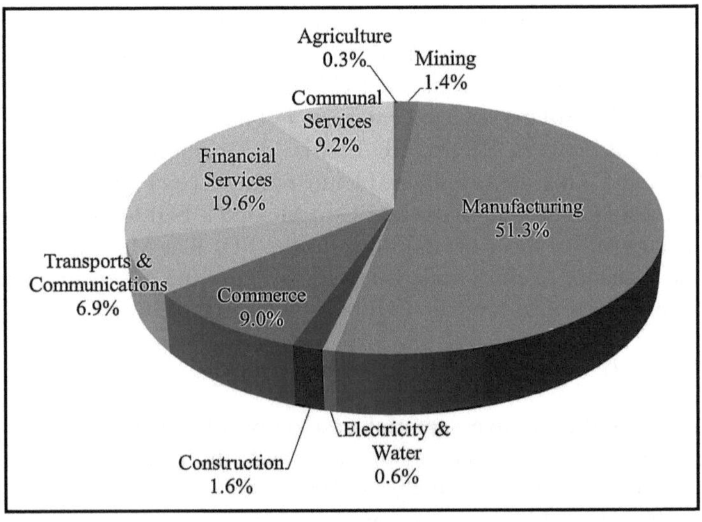

Source: Elaborated with data from the Instituto Nacional de Estadistica Geografia e Informatica (INEGI).

The right panel in Figure 12 shows the participation of the four sectors that attracted more FDI to Mexico during the 1994-2007 period. Together, these absorb 90% of the total flows. An interesting aspect of this figure is the declining participation of manufacturing in total FDI over recent years. Leaving aside the expansion of FDI in services caused by the privatization of commercial banks that took place between 1999 and 2001, on average, the manufacturing industry's participation in total FDI has been reduced by approximately 10%. This coincides with the diversification of trade and the more important countercyclical role of the EU's capital flows.

3.4 FDI flows from the EU

The dramatic change in the behavior of the EU's FDI outflows to Mexico observed in Figure 11 can be also traced to its sectorial composition. Figure 13 compares the distribution of the EU's FDI by sector in the years 1999 and 2007. It is clear from these two illustrations that manufacturing is also the largest recipient sector of FDI. Over the eight year period, however, the share of manufacturing has declined considerably from 62.2% of the total FDI inflows the year before the commencing of the EU-Mexico agreement to 40.9% in 2007, the last year for which we have information on FDI. The increasing role of financial services also seems to be contributing to the declining role of manufacturing in total FDI across the EU's flows. Indeed, this sector went from representing only 2.3% in 1999 to 26.4% in 2007. Construction is another sector that has grown considerable over the period observed, for it represented more than 15% of total FDI in 2007, compared with less than 2% in 1999.

Figure 13. Distribution of FDI by Inflows from the EU by Sector

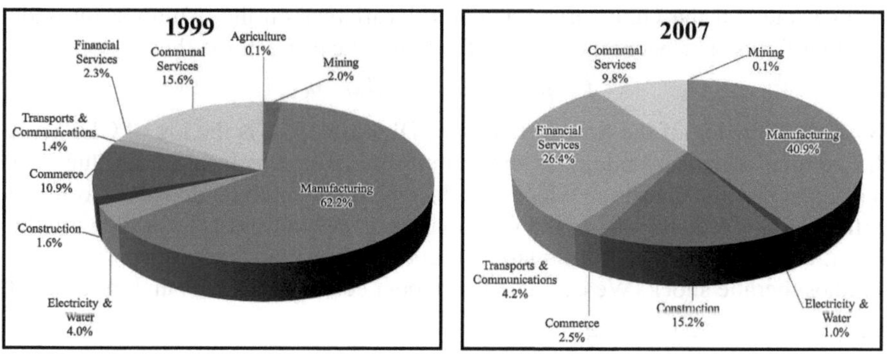

Source: Elaborated with data from the Instituto Nacional de Estadistica Geografia e Informatica (INEGI).

Overall, in this section we observed an increasing participation of the EU in Mexico's receipts of FDI. The FDI flows seem to have different favorable impacts in terms of sectoral diversification and as a countercyclical force to those flows of capital received from other countries, especially from the US. Despite this, we observe that the amount of FDI Mexico receives from the EU is relatively small as compared with the total EU capital outflows.

4. Trade and FDI determinants

We have observed the complimentary role and potential positive effects that trade and capital flows, to and from the EU, can have on the Mexican economy. However, the continuous flow of trade and capital strongly depend on the relative price of domestic goods and the performance of both economies. Following the logic of a restricted gravity model, in this section, we observe the role that economic activity and the exchange rate can have on Mexico's exports and imports from the EU, as well as on the arrival of the EU's direct investment into Mexico. Rather than employing a complete gravity model having the mass of both economies, measured by their GDP, and geographical distance as explanatory variables, we estimate a partial gravity model then control only for the mass (size) of the counterpart and nominal exchange rate effects.[6] This is because in our analysis, distance is a constant that does not vary over time from region to region. We include the nominal exchange rate to capture the effect of variation in relative prices. The specification proposed is estimated in logarithms so that we can obtain the elasticity (sensitivity) to trade and FDI with respect to GDP and the exchange rates.

We employed quarterly data to estimate an empirical model in which the exchange rate and the GDP served as control variables on the evolution on trade and FDI flows. The econometric specification to be estimates is thus:

$$f_t = \beta_0 + \beta_1 y_t + \beta_2 e_t + \beta_3 d_t + u_t$$

Where f_t is the log of the flow of trade or FDI at time t, y_t is the log of GDP, e_t is the nominal exchange rate, f_t is the dummy variable which takes a value of 1 starting at the first quarter in which a trade agreement entered into force (for trade with the US, d_t equals 1 from the first quarter of 1994 onward; for trade with the EU, it equals 1 from the third quarter of 2000 onward) and zero otherwise, u_t, is an idiosyncratic shock. We estimate this model considering trade and investment

6 For an introduction to the full specification of the gravity equation, see, for instance, Lazlo (1997). Particular applications of the full gravity model to analyze trade since NAFTA can be found in Gould (1998), Wall (2003) and Montenegro and Soloaga (2006).

from Mexico to the EU and the US. For trade, we have quarterly data since 1990 obtained from OECD Stat, while for FDI, we have data from Mexico's Ministry of Economy only since 1999.[7]

Table 3. Trade and Foreign Direct Investment Determinants

Variables	Mexican Exports from				Mexican Imports from				FDI inflows from	
	US		EU		US		EU		US	EU
	(1)	(2)	(3)	(4)	(5)	(6)	(7)	(8)	(9)	(10)
Log of US GDP	1.365***	2.068***							0.760	
	(0.137)	(0.191)							(0.987)	
Log of peso/dollar exchange	0.572***				0.532***	0.251			-3.209*	
	(0.112)				(0.125)	(0.447)			(1.802)	
Log of EU GDP			2.271***	1.059***						2.435
			(0.339)	(0.231)						(1.765)
Log of peso/euro exchange			-0.126				-0.181***	-0.201***		-0.700
			(0.146)				(0.050)	(0.043)		(1.218)
Log of Mexico GDP					0.717***	0.874***	2.106***	2.248***		
					(0.145)	(0.225)	(0.085)	(0.099)		
NAFTA dummy		0.507***				0.255				
		(0.171)				(0.422)				
EU-Mexico Agreement dummy				0.362**				-0.084**		
				(0.165)				(0.038)		
Constant	-14.039***	-24.624***	-30.045***	-11.012***	-2.099	-3.885	-21.543***	-23.424***	2.959	-30.646
	(2.062)	(2.942)	(5.166)	(3.662)	(1.854)	(2.607)	(1.085)	(1.289)	(12.988)	(26.445)
Adjusted R^2	0.948	0.960	0.844	0.783	0.871	0.871	0.982	0.983	0.144	-0.011
Observations	80	100	80	100	80	80	80	80	44	44

Note: Newey-West standard errors robust to heteroskedasticity and autocorrelation are reported in parenthesis below each coefficient.

7 A change in the methodology in which FDI is accounted prevents us from estimating the FDI model with data earlier than 1999.

Table 3 contains a summary of our empirical results. Columns (1) to (4) show the sensitivity of Mexican exports to the US and the EU with respect to the GDP and peso exchange rate of these two economies' currencies. For all these estimates, the empirical fit of the models estimates is fairly good, ranging from 0.783 to 0.960. In (1) and (3), we observe a greater sensitivity of Mexico's exports to the EU's GDP, a positive and significant effect of the peso/dollar exchange but no such effect from the peso/euro exchange. According to these results, a 1% increase in the US (EU) GDP increases Mexican exports to this point with 1.37% (2.27%). Meanwhile, a 1% depreciation of the Mexican peso relative to the US dollar leads to a 0.57% increase in exports. We conjecture that the insignificant effect of the exchange rate (peso/euro) on exports might be explained by the major intermediary role that the dollar plays in peso/euro exchange and the very limited role that the peso has on the exchange market. In columns (2) and (4), we include a dummy that captures the effect of NAFTA and the EU-Mexico agreement on Mexican exports. We do not control for the exchange rate in this estimations, as this variable becomes insignificant when we add the dummy variable. The results show a greater positive effect on Mexican exports after NAFTA than after the EU-Mexico agreement (coefficients 0.507 and 0.306, respectively). This might be as a result of the stronger economic ties prevailing between Mexico and the US.

Columns (5) to (8) analyze the sensitivity of Mexican imports from the US and the EU to the evolution of Mexico's GDP and the exchange rate parity in the same fashion as we did with exports in columns (1) to (4). Two very important results emerge from comparing columns (5) and (7). First, there is a considerably different response from EU and US exports to Mexico's GDP growth. A 1% increase in Mexico's GDP has a positive and significant effect on the EU's exports to Mexico, nearly three times higher than that of US exports (2.1% and 0.72%, respectively). Second, both, the peso/dollar parity and the peso/euro parity exert noteworthy effects on US and EU exports, though in opposite directions. For the US, a 1% depreciation of the Mexican peso relative to the dollar leads to a 0.53% increase in exports; meanwhile, a similar 1% depreciation of the peso relative to the euro leads, as expected, to a reduction in EU exports of 0.18%. The reason behind this contrasting result, particularly in relation to the US dollar, might be the cross border integration of the manufacturing sector between the US and Mexico, where a depreciation of the Mexican peso could also lead to greater exports production and thus a larger demand for imported inputs. Columns (6) and (8) provide a similar picture but with NAFTA exerting a significant effect on US exports and the EU-Mexico agreement having a rather small but negative effect on the EU's exports to Mexico, which is only significant at the 5% level.

Finally, in columns (9) and (10), we estimated the empirical model to observe the effect of GDP growth and the exchange rate on the FDI flows received by Mexico from the US and the EU. Except for a negative effect of peso depreciation on the FDI received by Mexico from the US (a 1% increase nominal depreciation of the peso/dollar exchange leads to a 3.2% decrease in FDI flows), we do not find concrete evidence that these two variables significantly affect the flows of capital into Mexico. Our intuition for this result is that we are not able to observe statistically significant effects of GDP growth and the exchange rate on FDI because this variable respond to long-run objectives rather than short-run fluctuations. Hence, we might need to employ larger time series or different econometric techniques to explore the impact of these variables on FDI.

Overall, in this section we encountered very different responses of trade with the EU and the US to economic growth developments and nominal exchange rate parities. These differences seem to be consistent with the behavior of trade and capital flows we found in the previous sections of this chapter.

5. Conclusions

In this chapter, we examined the effects of the EU-Mexico agreement on trade, after nearly 10 years of being in force, on the evolution of trade and capital flows, placing the North America Free Trade Agreement (NAFTA) as the benchmark. Our analysis suggests that the objectives of Mexico and the EU with respect to economic diversification and strengthening its presence in Latin America have been so far fulfilled.

In the first eight years after the enactment of the EU-Mexico agreement, average yearly exports from Mexico to the EU increased significantly in absolute terms and led to a greater participation of the EU in Mexico's trade. More importantly, we observed that the rate of growth of trade between Mexico and the EU was higher in its first eight years than that between Mexico and the NAFTA region for its corresponding eight-year period. Our analyisis suggests that the EU agrement, as well as other bilateral agrements signed by Mexico, have promoted trade creation rather than trade diversion from the NAFTA region.

In terms of investment, our examination of statistical data shows that over the last few years, FDI flows from the EU have also increased considerably. Interestingly, we observed that the direction of EU FDI flows has followed a very different pattern to those of the US in recent years. Our analysis suggests not only a significantly increasing contribution of the EU to Mexico's FDI total flows but also a complementary role of those capital flows to the FDI that Mexico receives from the US and Canada. We argue that such complementarity benefits the Mexican economy by exerting a countercyclical force on FDI receipts from North America. We also observe that despite the beneficial effects that EU FDI has on counteracting business cycles, Mexico has only a limited role in attracting FDI from the EU. Finally, exploring the effects of GDP growth and exchange rate parities on trade and capital flows, we find very different responses for flows with and from the US and the EU. These are, however, consistent with the unequal behavior of trade and capital flows previously described.

References

Eurostat. (2008). *European Union Foreign Investment Yearbook 2007*. Luxembourg: Office for Official Publications of the European Communities.

Gould, D. M. (1998). Has NAFTA Changed North American Trade? *Federal Reserve Bank of Dallas Economic Review, 1*, 12-23.

Hanson, G. (2004). *What has happened to wages in Mexico since NAFTA? Implications for hemispheric free trade.* In A. Estevadeordal, D. Rodrik, A. Taylor & A. Velasco (Eds.), *Integrating the Americas: FTAA and Beyond* (pp. 505-538). Cambridge, MA, USA: Harvard University Press.

Karkkaainen, A. (2009). EU Foreign Direct Investment in 2007. *Economy and Finance Eurostat Statistics in Focus* 19/2009. Retrieved from http://www.esf.be/new/wp-content/uploads/2010/01/Eurostat-Stat-in-Focus-FDI-in-2007-19-2009.pdf.

Lazlo, M. (1997). Proper Econometric Specification of the Gravity Model. *World Economy 20*(3), 363-368.

Lederman, D., Maloney, W. F., & Serven, L. (2005). Lessons from NAFTA. Palo Alto, CA, USA: Stanford University Press.

Mollick, A. V., & Cabral, R. (2009). Productivity Effects on Mexican Manufacturing Employment. *North American Journal of Economics and Finance 20*(1), 66-81.

Montenegro, C. E., & Soloaga, I. (2006). NAFTA's Trade Effects: New Evidence with a Gravity Model. *Estudios de Economía 33* (1), 45-63.

Nica, M., Swaidan, Z., & Grayson, M. M. (2006). The Impact of NAFTA on the Mexican-American Trade. *International Journal of Commerce & Management 16* (3/4), 222-238.

Ramirez, M. D. (2003). Mexico under NAFTA: A Critical Assessment. *Quarterly Review of Economics and Finance 43* (5), 863-892.

Wall, H. J. (2003). NAFTA and the geography of North American Trade. *Federal Reserve Bank of St. Louis Review 3*(3), 13-26.

Mexican-European Union Free Trade Agreement: Liberalization Process and Mexican Export Performance

Sergio Ortiz Valdés

1. Introduction

In recent years, Regional Trade Agreements (RTAs) have been multiplying and becoming an important trend in world economy (Ghosh C. & Yamarik. 2005). According to WTO, in 1990 only 107 RTAs were registered at the organization and by December 2008, 421 RTAs were notified. Of this number, 90% are partial-scope free trade agreements (FTA) and approximately 10% accounted for customs unions[1]. This proliferation of RTAs is influenced by the lack of substantial advances in the Doha Round of the World Trade Organization (WTO), given by the complexity processes to negotiate bilateral agreements as opposed to multilateral agreements.

The proliferation of RTAs has led to discussion based on the real impact on trade and well-being effect of these treaties. Robinson and Thierfelder (2003) argue that RTAs have had a positive effect on welfare, besides there is supporting evidence submitted by investigations that showed a dominance of trade creation over trade diversion. In contrast, Bhagwati and Kruger (1995) and Bhagwati and Panagariya (1996) question the efforts to negotiate increasing RTAs, but the real outcomes seem to be uncertain. This argument is consistent with the vision of Economics Nobel Laureate, Joseph Stiglitz who holds that Free Trade Agreements are meant to eliminate tariffs, quotas, restrictions and subsidies, but in reality things are different, and they are affecting some sectors in developing countries that benefit from other countries sectors as well.

In addition, he states that the real consequences in Latin America, are quite negative, because of the fundamental principle of non-discrimination that has been neglected, causing that Free Trade Agreements in the continent are neither free, nor fare (Stiglitz, 2006).

Entrepreneurship Institute Eugenio Garza Lagüera, Tecnológico de Monterrey.

1 In a regional integration process, the FTAs are considered a step behind custom unions, because FTAs are focused in the tariff and trade quotes elimination, and custom unions, besides reduction in tariffs and quotes elimination, involve a commitment to have the same commercial policy at least in tariffs and quotes among the countries involved. For more information see (Ball et al., 2006)

On the other hand, 2009 Economic Nobel Laureate, Paul Krugman argues that RTAs increase well-being and improve consumption capacity. They are crucial strategies to increase business competitiveness and therefore substantial improvements in industrial specialization in the countries involved (Krugman 1993). RTAs represent a "new regionalism" that complements the multilateralism where developing countries enter trade schemes traditionally dominated by developed countries (Ethier, 1998).

Mexico has been one of the countries particularly prolific in the negotiation and implementation of free trade agreements (FTA), transforming from one of the closest economies in the world, practically without any commercial agreements, to one of the economies with more free trade agreements worldwide. During the period of 1994-2005 Mexico signed 12 FTAs, including the Mexican-European Free Trade Agreement.

In terms of Mexican diversification exports, FTAs have not been successful tools as expected. The present chapter includes a portrayal of the Mex-EU FTA characteristics, including a description of the liberalization process for industrial and agricultural industries. Besides it is also analyzed the real commercial benefits for Mexico and trend examination of the Mex-EU FTA before and after the commercial agreement. Finally, this chapter will focus on detail in the agricultural sector.

2. General Characteristics of the Mexican – European Union Free Trade Agreement

According to the original text "Globalization for All: The EU and World Trade: Europe in Movement", published by the Directorate General of Press and Communication for the European Commission in 2002, the EU first 15 Members represent only 6 % of world population, and more than 20 % of international trade, making the EU one of the major commercial players in world trade. Given the economy's size and its consumption capacity, it is easy to visualize the importance of this region for Mexico.

In Brussels, on December 8 of 1997, the "Economic Association Agreement and Political Cooperation *(Acuerdo de Asociación Económica, Concertación Política y Cooperación)* was signed between Mexico and the 15 members of the European Union. However, it was not until February 23 in Lisbon and on February 24 in Brussels of 2000, that the European Council approved the agreement. In Mexico, the agreement was signed by the Senate Chamber on March 20 of the same year. In this document was stated that the Mexican-European Free Trade Agreement (Mex-EU FTA) would enter into force on July 1, 2000. This agreement replaced the Framework Cooperation Agreement *(Acuerdo Marco de Cooperation)* between Mexico and the European Community signed in Luxembourg on April 26, 1991.

By 2000, Mexico had already signed six FTAs including the North America Free Trade Agreement (NAFTA). However, with the European Union, Mexico negotiated a much broader agreement. Besides there are some aspects usually negotiated in FTA's such as the removal of trade tariffs, investment and the movement of capital, competition, national treatment to service providers, intellectual property, among others; this FTA included other features like economic and political cooperation topics, cooperation for scientific and technological research in different sectors, cooperation for the establishment and strengthening of small and medium-sized enterprises (SMEs), including the creation of funds for this purpose, also cooperation in the field of training and education and social affair, strategies to overcome poverty and finally cooperation on human rights, democracy and health.

Unlike previous FTAs signed by Mexico, this agreement dealt with economic and politic cooperation in an attempt for a stronger Mexican integration with the world. The negotiations of this agreement, contemplated three elements: (1) trade of goods and services, (2) economic cooperation for development, and (3) political cooperation and democracy. Because of the latter two elements, this agreement is considered an "Agreement of Economic Partnership" (*Acuerdo de Asociación Económica*) in which, the FTA is only one of the three components of the Mexican-European Union Agreement of Economic Partnership. Nevertheless, the purpose of this work is to describe and analyze the commercial component, focusing on the analysis of the commercial performance, particularly the Mexican Exports to the EU.

Mexican and European Union representatives, agreed to establish a free trade area within a maximum of ten years since the entry into force of the agreement. In spite of this period established in the Mexican-EU FTA negotiation, the EU eliminated most of the customs tariffs on imports from Mexico in 2003, while Mexico eliminated most of the custom tariffs on imports from the EU in 2007. For the European Union, the benefits of the agreement should be the same, as those established with the NAFTA partners.

Commercial Treaty	Partner Countries	Governmental News Paper Publication (*Official Journal*)	Entry into force
GATT membership	GATT Members	December 20, 1984	January 1, 1985
NAFTA	United States and Canada	December 20, 1993	January 1, 1994

Commercial Treaty	Partner Countries	Governmental News Paper Publication (*Official Journal*)	Entry into force
G3 FTA (TLC-G3)[2]	Colombia and Venezuela	January 9,1995	January 1, 1995
Mexico–Costa Rica FTA	Costa Rica	January 10, 1995	January 1, 1995
Mexico-Bolivia FTA	Bolivia	January 11, 1995	January 1, 1995
Mexico-Nicaragua FTA	Nicaragua	July 1, 1998	July 1, 1998
Mexico–Chile FTA	Chile	July 28, 1999	August 1, 1999
MEX-UE FTA	**UE** (15 members)	**June 26, 2000**	**July, 2000**
Mexico–Israel FTA	Israel	June 28, 2000	July 1, 2000
Mexico–NT FTA (North Triangle FTA)	Salvador, Guatemala and Honduras	March 14, de 2001	March 15, 2001 with Guatemala and Salvador. June 1, 2001 with Honduras.
Mexico–EA FTA (Mexican-European Association of Free Trade Agreement	Island, Norway, Liechtenstein and Switzerland	June 29, 2001	July 1, 2001
Mexico-Uruguay FTA	Uruguay	Jul 14, 2004	July 15, 2004
Mexico-Japan FTA	Japan	March 31, 2005	April 1, 2005

Source: Mexican Secretary of Economy (Secretaría de Economía de México), 2009

Nonetheless, in other cases of FTAs, a Joint Council (JC) was established between the two governments of this agreement; it was charge of negotiating and monitoring processes. In addition, the JC elaborated eleven chapters as core references for different interest groups in Europe and in Mexico. These chapters became the main framework for the negotiation process due to the domestic concern expressed by both parts involved. It is important to mention, that the JC also established different bi-national commissions, such as agriculture, auto parts and electronic among others. Nevertheless, in any other FTA, the Commission based the product liberalization process on the Harmonized System (HS)[3].

2 Since November 19 of 2006, Mexico and Colombia are the only two participant of the G-3 FTA, g, due to the no-recognition of the agreement by Venezuela's President.

3 The Harmonized Commodity Description and Coding System (HS), is an internationally standardized system for trade products classification, developed and maintained by the World Customs Organization (WCO) and accepted by member countries of the World Trade Organization WTO. The HS entered into force in 1998, and is composed of 22 sections, 98 chapters and 1241 headings. For more information visit http://www.wcoomd.org/

Here are presented the chapters of the Mexico-European Union Free Trade Agreement:

1. Market access
2. Rules of origin
3. Technical norms
4. Sanitary norms and certification
5. Safeguards
6. Investment and related payments
7. Services trade
8. Government purchases
9. Competitiveness
10. Intellectual property
11. Dispute settlement

For the trade liberation process, the Mexican-European bi-national commissions conducted an analysis of the Harmonized System (HS) classification to address categories for each product. These categories were represented by numbers and letters for all products subject to trade between the European Union and Mexico. Industrial products were categorized by letters; and agricultural, farming and fishery products by numbers. Depending on the situation, this classification and product analysis was made according to economic and political interests of the parties, besides it serves as the basis to negotiate the tariffs and in most cases its elimination. In the case of Mexico, its representatives established letters "A", "B", "B +" and "C" to categorized all industrial, manufactured and mineral products; in other words, this classification was used for all those products that are not cataloged ad agricultural and fishery products.

For those products (industrial, manufactured and mineral products) European representatives established only two categories: "A" and "B". Therefore, in the European market, all products not classified as agricultural, farming or fishery goods, have only two schemes of tariff reduction, while in Mexico they have four.

The first four sections of the HS refer to agricultural and farming products, including chapters 1 to 24. These products were classified into seven categories, also listed by numbers. As it can be seen there are more categories in this kind of products due to their important political influence, complex negotiation process, and classification possibilities that respond to different economic and political sensitivities.

GENERAL CHARACTERISTICS OF THE MEXICAN-EU FTA.
General objective: To create a commercial space in the context of multinational integration through the establishment of a free trade zone for the opening of external development opportunities. **Service Trade** Unrestricted access to the operative or community service providers. Enjoy preferential treatment for being the most favored nation. Consolidation of trade liberalization according to the national laws. Contemplates the provision of cross border services and investment, excluding audiovisual, air transport and maritime operations.
Dispute Resolution System Establishment of a mechanism for consultation and dispute resolution with several procedures (This was the first time EU incorporates this discipline in a commercial Treaty). Granting conciliation first option, prior arbitration panel; Mexico maintains its right to ask WTO intervention. **Institutions** Creation of a Joint Council, integrated by ministerial level representatives from the European Council, European Commission and Mexican Government. Establishment of joint committee, as a joint council support organism. **Government Purchases** Granting better access conditions with respect to other trading partners of the EU. Consolidation of openness and modifying existing sector legislation. Entry validation of the services chapter until statistics delivery of disaggregated of UE governmental purchases at least 150 public EU companies.

Source: Mexican Ministry of Economics (Secretaría de Economía)
http://www.economia-snci. gob.mx/ 2008

In the agricultural, farming and food industry, categories represent different treatments for planning custom tariffs elimination. In general terms, in the text treaty, products under lower number categories like 1 or 2 mean early custom duties elimination, as compared to categories with numbers 3 or 4, in which custom duties relief were made in a longer process, or even numbers 6 and 7, with minimal custom duties reduction. Also, it is important to mention that products categorized under number 5 did not get any commercial benefit in this agreement. For instance, products classified under category "1" had a total elimination of custom duties when the agreement entered into effect. Products classified with the numbers "2", "3" or "4" should have their custom duties eliminated in the following years, and products classified under category 4, would have the longer process of custom duty relief. Besides these classifications, an extra category with the letter

"O" was defined, which refers to products with an "origin denomination", like champagne, cognac, some specific wines like Bordeaux, and other liquors like Tequila. These products were given the same treatment as intellectual property rights.

It is important to notice, that for each part, different products have different impact on domestic industry or political sensitivity, although they may be classified under the same chapter and even under the same title or subtitle. Also, the original document of the Mexican-EU FTA Annex I contain the European Union classification of products imported from Mexico, while Annex II has the imports coming from the European Union.

Although, both parties classified their products into two broad concepts (agricultural food products and manufacturing products), however, between the countries involved, there is a big difference in the classification of such products owing to their economic and political interests, as well as in the reduction of tariffs and quota schemes, therefore, letters and numbers were used in each category. For example, Mexico imposed quotas on chewing gum imports, classifying this product under Category 6, whereas Europe classified the same product under Category 1. Likely, the EU imposed quotas on egg imports, classifying this product under Category 6 while Mexico assigned it to Category 5, this in turn means that Mexico did not offered any commercial concession in this specific case, like these examples there are many others along the list of products. Moreover, under the tariff reduction scheme (Annex I of the Mex-EU FTA) dairy products, like powdered milk and butter are classify in different categories, even though they belong to the same chapter of the HS. In reference to industrial products, for instance, Chapter 85, alludes to heaters for cooking, which was classified under Category "A" and kitchens under category "C", despite being in the same industrial branch. This type of differentiation was applied considering that those goods deserved different treatment due to their tariff relief and according to national interests.

3. Mexican-EU FTA Tariff Elimination Scheme for Mexican Products

Based on the categories of products already mentioned, exports from Mexico to the European Union classified under Category A were exempt from any custom duty from the moment the agreement entered into effect. With respect to products classified under category B, European custom duties have been removed in four equal stages; the first one began with the entrance into force the Mexican-EU FTA (July 1 of 2000) while the other three phases began on January 1 of each year thereafter. This scheme means that customs duties for products classified in this category should have been completely eliminated by January 1, 2003.

Trade tariffs elimination scheme for products with category B+

Original Tariff	2000	2001	2002	2003	2004	2005
20	18	12	8	5	2.5	0
15	13	10	7	5	2.5	0
10	8	6	4	4	2	0
7	5	4	3	2	1	0
5	4	3	2	2	1	0

Source: MEU-Free Trade Original Document

Mexico eliminated all customs duties for products classified under Category A (Annex II Mexican-EU FTA) once the commercial agreement entered into force. Similarly, the custom duties of manufactured products from the EU that Mexico classified under Category B were eliminated in four equal stages as the ones that had been mentioned before. Therefore, products under this classification were also free of trade tariffs by January 1, 2003. However, besides these two categories, Mexico addressed another two product classifications; B+ and C. Regarding products within category B+, tariffs would start to reduce in January 1 of each year (except 2000, since the FTA entered into force on July 1 of that year), being totally eliminated by January of 2005.

For products classified under Category C, tariffs on imports from the EU to Mexico were fully eliminated on January 1, 2007, according with the following calendar:

Trade tariffs elimination scheme for products with category C

Original Tariff	2000	2001	2002	2003	2004	2005
20	18	12	8	5	5	4
15	13	10	7	5	5	4
10	8	6	4	4	4	3
7	5	4	3	2	2	2
5	4	3	2	2	2	1

Source: MEX-EU Free Trade Agreement, Original Document

4. MEX-EU FTA Commercial Liberation for Mexican Food Products

Agricultural and food products (known as agro-food products) correspond to the HS first 24 chapters. These products suffer a more difficult negotiation process, including a longer tariff reduction scheme. Regarding international trade, the agricultural and farming products have had always a complicated negotiation process same that is reflected in the problems presented by the agricultural sector in the Doha agenda. In the Mexican-EU FTA, agro-food products (tariff fractions) of these 24 chapters were classified in seven categories, reduction and elimination of custom duties in these goods had different periods, including tariff trade variations depending on the year season, like tomato and avocado, just to mention some examples.

For products classified under Category 1, the European Union eliminated all custom duties from Mexico at the moment the agreement entered into force. For the following categories, a tariff relief scheme was designed on the basis of the existing custom duties prior to the Mexican-EU FTA, but regardless of existing trade tariffs, custom duties would be reduced gradually. Depending on the product classification, only a percentage of the previous tariff was applicable, therefore customs duties would be reduced with the same scheme every year.

European Community samples of market access for Mexican agricultural products

Immediate and progressive tariff elimination process in a maximum 10 year period.

Existence of a waiting list for agricultural products which would have production support for exports and import quotas.

Export preferential access for 95 % of Mexican agricultural products.

Immediate elimination of import tariffs (at the moment the FTA entry into force) for products such as: coffee, chickpea, tequila, beer, mangoes and guavas, benefits for a wide quota with preferential access for orange juice and avocado, which in 2008 had seasonal zero tariff import window.

Since 2003, free access for lemon, grapefruit and since 2008 elimination of custom duties in grapefruit juice.

Since 2003, tariff elimination of 88 % for fishery products, and granting a quota with preferential access to canned tuna.

Establishment of norms, standards and government requirements for consumer protection, environment, human, animal and plant health.

Source: Mexican Ministry of Economy *(Secretaría de Economía de México:*http://www.economia-snci.gob.mx), 2008

For the products listed under Category 2, EU removed customs duties according to the following scheme:

Before July 1, 2000	July 1, 2000	January 1, 2001	January 1, 2002	January 1, 2003
100% of tariff	75% of the tariff	50% of the tariff	25% of the tariff	0% of the tariff

Source: Self compiled base on Mexican European Union Free Trade Agreement original document

For the products listed under Category 3, EU removed customs duties according to the following scheme:

Before	July 1,	January 1,							
July 1, 2000	2000	2001	2002	2003	2004	2005	2006	2007	2008
100%	89%	78%	67%	56%	45%	34%	23%	12%	0%
of the tariff									

Source: Self compiled base on Mexican European Union Free Trade Agreement original document

For the products listed under Category 3, EU removed customs duties according to the following scheme:

Before	July 1,	January 1,							
July 1, 2000	2003	2004	2004	2005	2006	2007	2008	2009	2010
100%	87%	75%	62%	50%	37%	25%	12%	0%	0%
of the tariff									

Source: Self compiled base on Mexican European Union Free Trade Agreement original document

Products classified under category 5 did not receive any tariff or quota concession. However, it was negotiated that no later than 2003, EU will review this list, but without any modification at the time it entered into force. In spite of this negotiation, and until August of 2011, these products were included in the so called "waiting list", and still do not have any commercial concession since the signing of the Mexican-EU FTA.

While, products classified under category 6 are subject to the application of custom duties and quotas; which means that these products have specific quotas in addition to a custom duty. Still, these products have preferential access. Products classified under this category, would have only 50% or the lower applicable tax at the time of importation under the code of the Most Favored Nation (MFN) or the Generalized System of Preferences (GSP) code[4]. In any case, the products classified within this category, regardless of applicable trade tariff, had the custom

4 The Most Favored Nation principle is a concept created by the World Trade Organization and the United Nations. The Generalized System of Preferences is the system used by the European Union. Both systems are commonly used to give commercial concessions to developing countries.

duties benefits, since it could be applied 50 % of the lowest tariff between MFN and GSP at the time of import.

On the other hand, products classified under Category 7 did not receive an *Advalorem* trade tariff, yet specific taxes were imposed. Specific taxes, means to apply specific custom duties to a determined amount of a given product. For example, in the terms of commercial concessions, goods related with the egg, milk or sugar industry are very controversial, noting that all these products received specific quotas.

Agro-Food Products Classification in the MEXICAN-EU FTA

CATEGORY	DATE FOR ELIMINATION OF TARIFFS TRADE
1	July 2000
2	January 2003
3	January 2008
4[a]*	January 2009
4	January 2010
5	"Waiting List"
6	Quotas and Custom Duties
7	Specific Tariffs on quotas

* This category is applied to a few amounts of products.

Source: Self compiled based on information from Mexican Ministry of Economy *(Secretaría de Economía de México) 2005.*

Some trade agreements negotiated by the EU have important limitations in different industries and products; this condition reduces potential benefits for others commercial agreements. Still, in the case of Mexico, Chile and Turkey, FTAs can be seen as more complete commercial agreements. For example, Mexican-EU FTA considers a commitment which covers the majority of products, with notable reductions of tariff rates including agricultural sector (Francois, McQueen y Wignaraja, 2005).

As we will see later, in terms of Mexican exports, the HS code with corresponds to section IV (processed food industry). This segment represents over 40% of all Mexican agro-food exports. Because of the relevance of chapters 16 to 24, it is important to analyze at least the most important parts regarding trade which includes chapters 17, 20, 21 and 22. In section 17, products are mainly classified under categories 5 and 7. Whereas section 20, contains products classified under categories 2, 3, 4, 5, 6 and 7. However, in the same chapter, goods with greater export volume to the EU are in the heading number 2009 of the HS. This heading (2009), consists in products related with fruit and vegetable juices unfermented and unsweetened, also it represents 60% of the total sales of the section. Besides, are classified over 90 products; most of them under the category 5, six under category 2, nine under category 3 and thirteen under category 6. This condition means that almost 70% of the products of the heading number 2009 in the chapter 20 of the HS did not obtain any benefit from the Mexican-EU FTA.

Moreover, chapter 21 includes various food preparations (infusions, broths, different sauces, soups and condiments), most of the located in heading 2103, which refers to products related with sauces and condiments. It is important to mention, that for the past seven years, it represented almost 70% of the exports of this section (69.2 per cent). In the same heading, the EU classified seven products (associated to its tariff fractions); three as category 1, three as category 2, and one as category 7, so in this case, it can be observed clear tariff benefits for Mexican exports to the EU.

Likewise, in chapter 22, most products were classified under Category O. However, the most important good of the section is malt beer, and is by far the Mexican product with more exports in all agro-food industry, at least in the analyzed period. In the Mexican-EU FTA, beer and malt beer were classified under category 1, which means that this product could and should be introduce to the European market without any customs duty since the entry into force of the commercial agreement.

Along this segment and as it can be seen, all agro-food industry, given its complications, is the economic sector with most commercial restrictions, including quotes and longer custom duties reduction schemes. In spite of this, most Mexican agricultural goods (95% of products according to the Mexican Ministry of Economy), present benefits or preferential access to the EU. Besides customs duties reduction, many commercial quotas increase at the moment the commercial agreement enter into force. However, as shown further, when comparing statistics monthly data for agricultural products, prior to the Mexican-EU-FTA and five years after; products without or with clear commercial benefits in terms of custom duties and quotas, did not change their export behavior, neither the normal trend nor the long term trend analysis. This is important information because Mexican exports to EU are comparatively low before and after the Mexican-EU-FTA, at least with respect Mexican agro-food exports to the United States.

E.G. OF EU QUOTAS NOT USED BY MEXICAN AGRICULTURAL PRODUCERS (2007)
Melon – 0 % of export quota
Bananas and tropical fruits: 0 % of export quota
Frozen strawberries: 0 % of export quota
Pineapple juice: 0 % of export quota
Concentrated orange juice: equivalent to 23.3% of export quota
Avocado: equivalent to 22% of export quota

Source: Foreign Commerce Mexican Bank (Bancomext) and Mexican Ministry of Economy (Secretaría de Economía de México) 2008

Mexico's presence in the vegetable exports to the UE (2007)
Garlic: 2%
Asparagus: 2%
Avocado: 21%
Mango: 2%
Lime: 4%
Grapefruit: 2%
Products where Mexican presence is non-existent: broccoli, onions, bananas, and strawberries.

Source: Foreign Commerce Mexican Bank (Bancomext) and Mexican Ministry of Economy (Secretaría de Economía de México) 2008

5. Mexican Exports to European Union before and after the Mexican-EU-FTA

According to the Mexican Agency of Information and Statistics *(INEGI),* the total of Mexican exports to the EU went from $ 2,700 billion USD in 1993 to 10,800 billion in 2006. In spite of this apparently explosive increase of 300 per cent over 13 years, the relative weight of Mexican exports to the EU in this period decreased from 13.2% to 4.3%. The above should be taken into account that the purchasing power and magnitude of the EU market in comparison to the Mexican exports to the EU are really low. The major European buyers during this period were Spain, Germany, United Kingdom and Netherlands. In the last 10 years, 75% of all Mexican products entering the EU were distributed among these four countries. From 1999 to 2006, 28% of Mexican exports were sent to Germany, 26% to Spain, 13% to United Kingdom and 13% to Holland. Germany and Spain together represent the main destinations with 54% of all Mexican exports. Yet, in the first six years of the Mexican-EU FTA, Spain became the first purchaser of Mexican exports. Probably, this phenomenon is associated with cultural factors, expressed in the ideas of authors like Bilkey (1982), Ditch, Koeglmyer & Muller (1990) Cadogan, Diamantopoulos, & de Mortanges (1999), Solberg & Durrieu (2006) correlate cultural proximities with international trade.

Similarly, we can see that there have been various impacts on Mexican exports to the EU as a result of the trade agreement; this is due to the analysis made before and after the signature of the FTA, that involved the total exports, including the agro-food sector. Manufactured products are the most important Mexican exports to the European Union. This very common in the export structure of many countries, since the manufacturing sector comprises the largest number of tariff fractions of the HS. However, Mexican manufactured exports to the European Union have not had the significant growth, it has been expected, because in absolute and relative terms, from 1995 to 2006, it has shown a growth from 70% to 90%.

MEXICAN EXPORTS TO THE EUROPEAN UNION (SECTION IV)										
YEAR	TOTAL S. IV	CHAPTER 16	CHAPTER 17	CHAPTER 18	CHAPTER 19	CHAPTER 20	CHAPTER 21	CHAPTER 22	CHAPTER 23	CHAPTER 24
1995	120.859.535	2.873.652	25.032.010	3.240.591	87.917	24.663.317	4.859.403	41.650.756	4.262.506	14.189.383
1996	108.915.486	3.240.124	24.866.273	1.663.721	311.672	10.164.537	4.983.887	43.219.071	6.015.680	14.450.521
1997	105.758.341	540.977	18.283.451	3.597.688	498.388	6.261.551	5.404.640	50.298.991	4.162.757	16.709.898
1998	130.061.623	46.482	19.150.996	1.523.538	375.908	18.136.243	4.151.486	63.443.550	6.852.454	16.380.966
1999	120.606.011	132.807	9.838.309	698.309	268.747	12.162.102	4.550.427	69.077.763	5.743.508	18.033.788
2000	153.099.130	11.342	11.371.671	542.492	581.578	13.680.135	5.854.317	95.376.633	7.169.461	18.511.501
2001	179.591.969	318.540	8.173.999	223.313	736.295	18.161.994	6.357.064	119.250.794	6.746.212	19.623.758
2002	195.266.944	879.893	8.873.427	288.042	1.359.019	30.866.186	5.850.193	120.869.697	7.115.957	19.164.530
2003	159.726.120	303.104	4.730.154	734.720	755.155	15.111.307	4.900.328	109.214.964	7.061.332	16.915.056
2004	152.644.701	168.823	8.682.348	1.585.052	808.488	15.061.098	3.202.866	104.631.608	6.475.446	12.028.972
2005	262.593.719	88.022	15.531.356	8.731.858	680.159	33.799.377	4.928.139	165.734.108	4.166.042	9.226.758
2006	271.842.300	24.236	5.726.340	3.983.236	740.804	34.391.008	6.415.829	182.971.938	5.355.376	12.661.493

Source: Self compiled based on information from Mexican Institute of Statistics, Geography and Informatics (INEGI) 2008

% OF MEXICAN EXPORTS TO GERMNAY AND SPAIN 1993-2006					
	TOTAL EXPORTS	GERMANY	SPAIN	GERMANY %	SPAIN %
1993	2.696.979	430.195	877.309	16%	33%
1994	2.869.714	394.673	909.423	14%	32%
1995	3.353.488	515.434	796.878	15%	24%
1996	3.509,837	640.885	906.941	18%	26%
1997	3.988.073	718.786	939.031	18%	24%
1998	3.889.766	1.151.579	714.066	30%	18%
1999	5.323.266	2.093.100	943.016	39%	18%
2000	5.593.275	1.543.915	1.503.001	28%	27%
2001	5.349.396	1.504.062	1.270.692	28%	24%
2002	5.524.641	1.590.129	1.393.734	21%	25%
2003	6.116.592	1.715.218	1.512.434	28%	25%
2004	6.699.191	1.689.129	2.026.904	25%	30%
2005	9.006.578	2.289.415	2.954.097	25%	33%
2006	10.774.984	2.972.607	3.270.119	28%	40%

Source: Self compiled based on information from Mexican Institute of Statistics, Geography and Informatics (INEGI) 2008

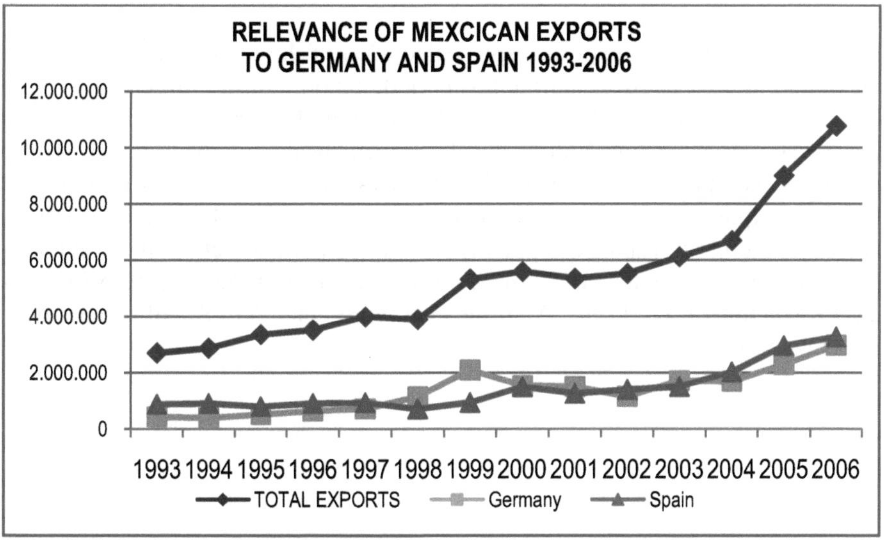

Source: Self compiled based on information from Mexican Institute of Statistics, Geography and Informatics (INEGI) 2008

TOTAL MEXICAN EXPORTS TO THE EU VS MEXICAN MANUFACTURING EXPORTS TO THE EU (Thousand Euros)						
Year	Total Exports to the EU	Oil Exports	Total Exports without oil	Manufacture Exports	% of oil exports	% manufacture exports (without oil)
1995	3,165,505	603,853	2,561,652	2,016,870	19.08%	78.73%
1996	3,096,969	593,179	2,503,790	1,935,650	19.15%	77.31%
1997	3,743,826	849,455	2,894,371	2,221,187	22.69%	76.74%
1998	3,926,319	654,517	3,271,802	2,647,314	16.67%	80.91%
1999	4,606,224	851,369	3,754,855	3,203,661	18.48%	85.32%
2000	6,922,275	1,736,734	5,185,541	4,485,441	25.09%	86.50%
2001	7,302,666	1,552,468	5,750,198	5,037,814	21.26%	87.61%
2002	6,194,944	1,536,820	4,658,124	4,014,394	24.81%	86.18%
2003	6,175,833	1,337,886	4,837,947	4,234,292	21.66%	87.52%
2004	6,652,270	1,688,547	4,963,724	4,356,013	25.38%	87.76%
2005	8,967,055	2,667,043	6,300,012	5,601,455	29.74%	88.91%
2006	10,195,627	2,575,989	7,619,638	6,834,503	25.27%	89.70%

Source: Self compiled based on information from the European Information Agency, EUROSTAT, 2007

From 2000 to 2006 oil exports, represented 25% of the total exports reaching a maximum of 30% in 2005. During this period, the oil industry presented a considerable growth in its weight probably influenced by the increase of oil price over those years. Also, section XVI of the HS, (mechanical equipment, boilers, parts; machines, equipment and electrical appliances), represented 29% of the total Mexican exports to Europe. Next in line was section XVII (vehicles, aircraft, vessels and other transport equipment) (with an important weight of the automotive industry) represents 11.5% of Mexican sales to Europe. The agro-food industry, (sections I, II, III and IV of the HS) represented 6 to 8% of exports over the same period.

DISTRIBUTION OF MEXICAN EXPORTS TO ERUPEAN UNION APPLYING THE HARMONIZED SYSTEM SECTIONS 1993-2006. EU SECTIONS SADCM 1993-2006-15 COUNTRIES	
SECTION I (LIVE ANIMALS AND ANIMAL PRODUCTS)	1.3%
SECTION II (VEGETABLE PRODUCTS)	3.5%
SECTION III (FATS, OILS AND THEIR CLEAVAGE PRODUCTS)	0.1%
SECTION IV (FOOD PRODUCTS, BEVERAGES, SPIRITS, VINEGAR AND TOBACCO PRODUCTS)	2.9%
SECTION V (MINERAL PRODUCTS, INCLUDING OIL)	23.5%
SECTION VI (PRODUCTS OF THE CHEMICAL OR ALLIED INDUSTRIES)	7.6%
SECTION VII (PLASTICS, RUBBER AND ARTICLES MADE FROM THESE MATERIALS)	2.3%
SECTION VIII. (RAW HIDES, SKINS, LEATHER)	0.3%
SECTION IX. (WOOD AND WOOD ARTICLES, CORK, STRAW AND OTHER PLAITING MATERIALS)	0.0%
SECTION X (WOOD PULP, PAPER AND PAPER ARTICLES)	0.8%
SECTION XI (TEXTILES AND TEXTILE ARTICLES)	1.7%
SECTION XII (FOOTWEAR, HEADWEAR, UMBRELLAS, CANES AND SIMILAR ACCESSORIES)	0.2%
SECTION XIII. (GLASS, GLASSWARE; ARTICLES OF CERAMICS, STONE AND SIMILAR MATERIALS)	0.6%
SECTION XIV (PEARLS, PRECIOUS METALS OR STONES, COINS AND JEWEL-LERY)	1.6%
SECTION XV (BASE METALS AND ARTICLES OF BASE METAL)	4.4%
SECTION XVI (MACHINERY; MECHANICAL, ELECTRICAL AND ELECTRONIC APPLIANCES OR EQUIPMENT)	28.6%
SECTION XVII (VEHICLES, AIRCRAFT, VESSELS AND OTHER TRANSPORTA-TION EQUIPMENT)	11.5%
SECTION XVIII (CLOCKS, WATCHES AND SPECIALIZED INSTRUMENTATION)	6.5%
SECTION XIX (ARMS AND AMMUNITION)	0.0%
SECTION XX (MISCELLANEOUS MANUFACTURED ARTICLES)	1.1%
SECTION XXI (WORKS OF ART, COLLECTOR's PIECES AND ANTIQUES)	0.1%
SECTION XXII (NOT CLASIFIED PRODUCTS)	1.3%

Source: Self compiled based on information from the European Information Agency, EUROSTAT, 2007

The following graph shows the long term trend adjusted for the total Mexican exports to the EU. It is possible to notice that there is a long term component with a positive trend, except for years 2001 and 2002, where it shows a fall in Mexican sales to this region. This leaning change could be explained by the global economic recession during that period of time; however things change favorably, having a positive trend in 2002. Nonetheless, since the Mexican-EU FTA entered into force on July 1, 2000, it cannot be observed any important change in a long term trend basis. Thereby, it could be imply that the signing of the trade agreement between Mexico and the European Union did not incite a change in the long term pattern of Mexican exports to the EU.

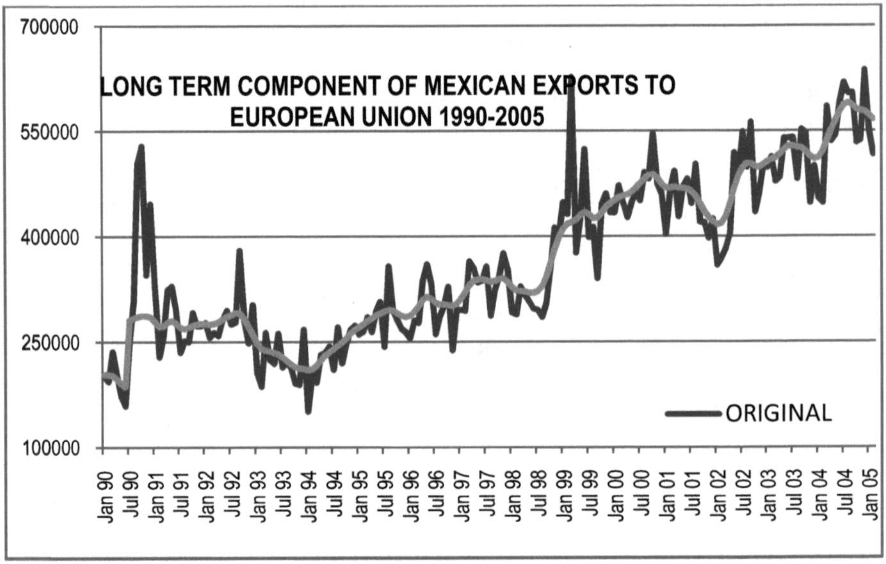

Source: self-compiled based on statistical series the Mexican Agency for Statistics and Information, INEGI

Similarly, agro-food Mexican exports to the EU have not shown any increase in the long term trend. On the contrary, there has been a decreasing or stagnating trend in the last four years of the analyzed period. In this way, the physical distance between Mexico and Europe seems to be an inhibitor of Mexican exports, as it has been suggested by different authors like Kaynak & Kothari (1984), Bauerschmidt, Sullivan & Gillespie (1985) Stöttinger & Schlegelmilch (1998), Verwaal & Donkers (2002), and Bernard & Jensen (1999) among others.

Source: Self compiled based on statistical series the Mexican Agency for Statistics and Information, INEGI

As stated before, Spain is the largest buyer of Mexican exports to the EU in the observed period, showing an important increase in 1999 and 2000. Nevertheless, is important to mention, that this trend had a decrease in the preceding years of the Mexican EU FTA beginning, probably caused by the world's economic recession in those years. In spite of the information presented in this graph, it cannot be conclude that there was a change in the long term trend of Mexican exports to Spain as a result of the mentioned commercial agreement.

In the case of Germany, the following graph shows a marginal positive trend but with many fluctuations, the most important in 1999. In any circumstance, it can be observed that the long term trend of Mexican exports to EU did not change as a result of the Mexican-EU FTA. The graph also suggests a behavior that varies between stagnation and the negative trend in the long term component of the Mexican exports to Germany, still any change has been observed as a result of the entry into force the Mexican-EU FTA.

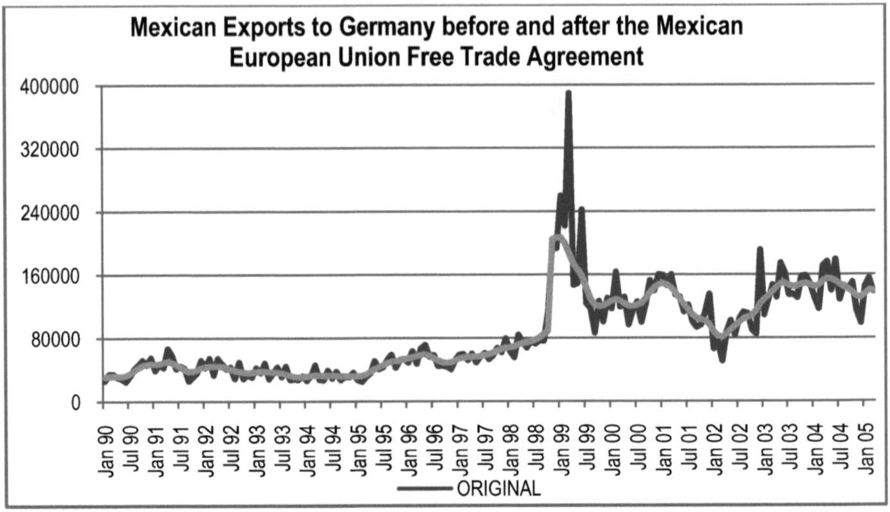

Source: Long term trend adjust self-compiled based on statistical series the Mexican Agency for Statistics and Information, INEGI

Regarding the analysis, it can be suggest that the Mexican-EU FTA had no significant impact on the Mexican exports to the European Union. However, it is possible that agreement had more positive impact on some specific sectors or industries, like the so called agricultural products. Therefore, the next part of this chapter would show a more specific analysis of this sector.

6. Agro-Food Mexican Exports to the European Union

According to EUROSTAT data, in the period from 1997 to 2006, agro-food products represented about 8% of Mexican exports to the EU (7.8 %). During these years, those exports went from 383 million Euros in 1995, (around 444 million USD historical exchange rates) to 557 million Euros in 2006, (around 700 million USD historical exchange rates). Likewise, it is important to mention as well, that corresponding to the United States Secretary of Commerce in 2006, that Mexican agro-food export to the US reached 10,000 million USD. Based on this numbers and the purchasing power of the euro zone, sales of agricultural products from Mexico to the EU are marginal and far beyond of the potential market.

AGRO-FOOD MEXICAN PRODUCT EXPORTS TO THE EUROPEAN UNION (HS SECTIONS) (EUROS)					
YEAR	SECTION I of the HS	SECTION II of the HS	SECTION III of the HS	SECTION IV of the HS	TOTAL
1995	57,005,622	183,760,345	7,048,227	134,955,982	382,770,176
1996	97,680,974	179,690,521	2,006,825	113,291,112	392,669,432
1997	120,946,082	302,097,030	1,765,232	109,288,794	534,097,138
1998	85,040,539	215,094,468	4,656,602	139,374,834	444,166,443
1999	70,252,113	193,245,329	4,222,917	129,051,864	396,772,223
2000	66,694,142	237,583,767	5,369,042	163,837,212	473,484,163
2001	70,392,658	231,760,682	3,640,459	186,872,880	492,666,679
2002	90,597,008	179,439,664	3,206,856	202,473,587	475,717,115
2003	66,256,941	194,275,158	8,948,009	177,622,137	447,102,245
2004	67,108,631	185,668,417	11,724,431	176,411,375	440,912,854
2005	61,485,415	180,608,074	9,853,950	262,593,719	514,541,158
2006	47,932,845	226,938,847	9,786,020	271,842,300	556,500,012

Source: Self compiled based on information from the European Information Agency, EUROSTAT, 2007

WEIGHT SECTIONS I, II, III AND IV (HS) IN RESPECT TO THE TOTAL AGRO-FOOD MEXICAN EXPORTS TO THE EU 1995-2006				
YEAR	SECTION I of the HS	SECTION II of the HS	SECTION III of the HS	SECTION IV of the HS
1995	14.9%	48.0%	1.8%	35.3%
1996	24.9%	45.8%	0.5%	28.9%
1997	22.6%	56.6%	0.3%	20.5%
1998	19.1%	48.4%	1.0%	31.4%
1999	17.7%	48.7%	1.1%	32.5%
2000	14.1%	50.2%	1.1%	34.6%
2001	14.3%	47.0%	0.7%	37.9%
2002	19.0%	37.7%	0.7%	42.6%
2003	14.8%	43.5%	2.0%	39.7%
2004	15.2%	42.1%	2.7%	40.0%
2005	11.9%	35.1%	1.9%	51.0%
2006	8.6%	40.8%	1.8%	48.8%

Source: Self compiled based on information from the European Information Agency, EUROSTAT, 2007

Between 1997 and 1998, Mexican agro-food exports to the EU had a significant increase. Still, agro-food exports (sections I, II, III and IV of the HS) remained marginal and without change in the long term trend with the entry into force of the Mexican-EU FTA.

Reviewing the exports of each section of the Harmonized System separately, there is a difference in their behavior. Section I (meat and seafood), drives a strong increase in Mexican sales to Europe, from 1995 to 1997, but after this period, that trend changed, decreasing its relative weight in respect with the total agricultural exports to the EU from 14.9% in 1995, to 8.6% in 2006. The following graph also shows Mexican exports to the EU corresponding to section III (edible oils and fats), which is just over 1% of Mexican agro-food exports to the EU (1.3%). The previous is not representative, therefore has little impact in Mexican food, agricultural exports to the EU and elsewhere in the world.

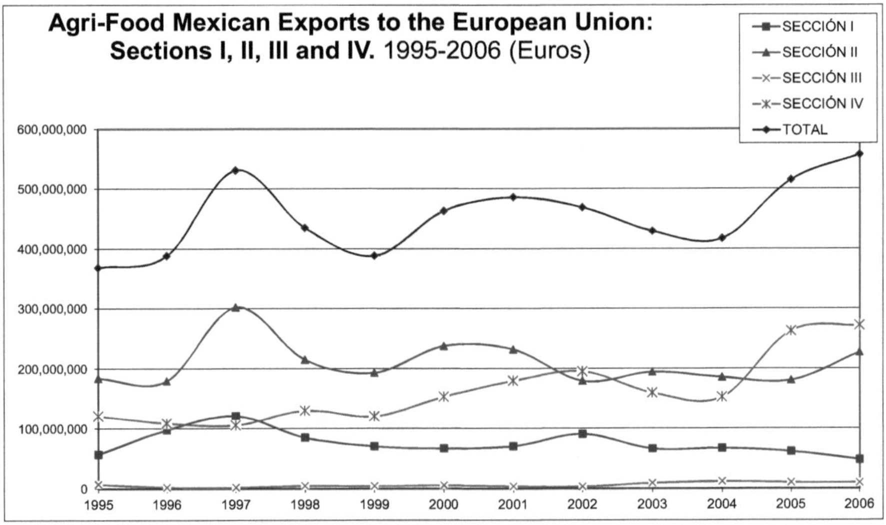

Source: Self compiled based on information from the European Information Agency, EUROSTAT, 2007

As it can be seen, this graph demonstrates that section II (vegetable products) and section IV (processed food products, beverages, spirits, vinegar and tobacco) have the most significant weight in Mexican agricultural exports to the EU. Besides, it showed an important increase from 184 million Euros in 1995 to 227 million Euros in 2006; in spite of this rise in absolute terms, it also has a tendency to decrease its relative terms, by changing from 48% in 1995 to 41% in 2006. Since 2004, section IV is the most important sector in terms of Mexican agro-food exports to EU overpassing section II. Among all sections of the agro-food sector, section IV had the most significant increase in sales to the EU during that period, growing from 135 million in 1995 to 172 million Euros in 2006, increasing its relative weight of agro-food exports from 35% in 1995 to 49% in 2006. Despite the relatively low volume of Mexican agricultural exports to the EU (sections I, II, III and IV of the HS), section IV presents the greatest dynamism and propensity to increase its sales to the EU.

According to data from the Mexican Agency for Information and Statistics, (INEGI), agro-food Mexican exports are 15 times lower than exports to the United States. This information suggests that Mexican agro-food exports to the European Union presented a slower dynamism than the agricultural exports to the United States. In any case, section IV represented the greatest increase in Mexican sales to the EU in the same period. Also, this section is composed by industrial food products, (processed foods and processed drinks), which has presented a positive and constant long term trend. Besides, it represents the greatest trend to export growth to the EU.

Besides, the monthly and annual data suggests that the tendency of Mexican agro-food exports to Europe does not change with its beginning (July of 2000). Though, Mexican food exports showed a decreasing trend in 1997 and a growing one in 2004, not enough to explain the trend under institutional changes. Nevertheless, exports of these goods to the US market have flourished quickly, caused by a reorientation of Mexican trade or deviation effect, typical of a free exchange market.

7. Mexican exports of processed food to the European Union (Section IV of the HS) before and after the Mexican-EU-FTA.

To avoid seasonal tendencies and to visualize a long term component in the mentioned FTA effect in Mexican exports to EU, simple trend and ARIMA method were used. In both cases, monthly statistical information was used from the European Agency for Information, EUROSTAT.

According to the following two charts, it is possible to make a difference among chapters of section IV. Of all nine chapters of this section, in the analyzed period, chapters 17, 20, 22 and 24 represent in average 90% of section IV exports, highlighting the importance of chapters 20 and 22 in the last five years. In 2006, these two chapters fairly represented 80% of the entire section IV; mainly chapter 22, which itself only had an average weight of 61% exports in this period, and more than 67% in 2006.

MEXICAN EXPORTS TO THE EUROPEAN UNION (SECTION IV)

YEAR	TOTAL S. IV	CHAPTER 16	CHAPTER 17	CHAPTER 18	CHAPTER 19	CHAPTER 20	CHAPTER 21	CHAPTER 22	CHAPTER 23	CHAPTER 24
1995	120,859,535	2,873,652	25,032,010	3,240,591	87,917	24,663,317	4,859,403	41,650,756	4,262,506	14,189,383
1996	108,915,486	3,240,124	24,866,273	1,663,721	311,672	10,164,537	4,983,887	43,219,071	6,015,680	14,450,521
1997	105,758,341	540,977	18,283,451	3,597,688	498,388	6,261,551	5,404,640	50,298,991	4,162,757	16,709,898
1998	130,061,623	46,482	19,150,996	1,523,538	375,908	18,136,243	4,151,486	63,443,550	6,852,454	16,380,966
1999	120,606,011	132,807	9,838,309	698,309	268,747	12,162,102	4,550,427	69,077,763	5,743,508	18,033,788
2000	153,099,130	11,342	11,371,671	542,492	581,578	13,680,135	5,854,317	95,376,633	7,169,461	18,511,501
2001	179,591,969	318,540	8,173,999	223,313	736,295	18,161,994	6,357,064	119,250,794	6,746,212	19,623,758
2002	195,266,944	879,893	8,873,427	288,042	1,359,019	30,866,186	5,850,193	120,869,697	7,115,957	19,164,530
2003	159,726,120	303,104	4,730,154	734,720	755,155	15,111,307	4,900,328	109,214,964	7,061,332	16,915,056
2004	152,644,701	168,823	8,682,348	1,585,052	808,488	15,061,098	3,202,866	104,631,608	6,475,446	12,028,972
2005	262,593,719	88,022	15,531,356	8,731,858	680,159	33,799,377	4,928,139	165,734,108	4,166,042	9,226,758
2006	271,842,300	24,236	5,726,340	3,983,236	740,804	34,391,008	6,415,829	182,971,938	5,355,376	12,661,493

Source: Self compiled based on information from the European Information Agency, EUROSTAT, 2007

In addition, chapter 22 exports reflect the most important increase in both absolute and relative terms. The exports ranged from 42 million Euros in 1995 to 183 million Euros in 2006, representing more than 330% growth. Its relative weight also increased notoriously, since it went from 34.5% 1995 to more than 67% in 2003. This means that chapter 22 increased twice its relative weight in section IV in less than ten years.

PERCENTAGE OF MEXICAN PROCESSED FOOD AND BEVERAGES TO EUROPE (HS SECTION)

	Chapter								
Year	**16**	**17**	**18**	**19**	**20**	**21**	**22**	**23**	**24**
1995	2.38%	20.7%	2.68%	0.07%	20.4%	4.0%	34.5%	3.5%	11.7%
1996	2.97%	22.8%	1.53%	0.29%	9.3%	4.6%	39.7%	5.5%	13.3%
1997	0.51%	17.3%	3.40%	0.47%	5.9%	5.1%	47.6%	3.9%	15.8%
1998	0.04%	14.7%	1.17%	0.29%	13.9%	3.2%	48.8%	5.3%	12.6%
1999	0.11%	8.2%	0.58%	0.22%	10.1%	3.9%	57.3%	4.8%	15.0%
2000	0.01%	7.4%	0.35%	0.38%	8.9%	3.8%	62.3%	4.7%	12.1%
2001	0.18%	4.6%	0.12%	0.41%	10.1%	3.5%	66.4%	3.8%	10.9%
2002	0.45%	4.5%	0.15%	0.70%	15.8%	3.0%	61.9%	3.6%	9.8%
2003	0.19%	3.0%	0.46%	0.47%	9.5%	3.1%	68.4%	4.4%	10.6%
2004	0.11%	5.7%	1.04%	0.53%	9.9%	2.1%	68.5%	4.2%	7.9%
2005	0.03%	5.9%	3.33%	0.26%	12.9%	1.9%	63.1%	1.6%	3.5%
2006	0.01%	2.1%	1.47%	0.27%	12.7%	2.4%	67.3%	2.0%	4.7%

Source: Self compiled based on information from the European Information Agency, EUROSTAT, 2008

Chapter 20, also represents an important weight in section IV (11.4% on average in the 10 year period presented), at the same time, it can be observed that the same chapter represents a less dynamic trend than chapter 22.

During the period of 1995-2006, chapters 20 and 22 were approximately 67% of section IV of Mexican exports to European Union, but during 2005 and 2006, these two chapters represented nearly 80% of the exports of the entire section. In the following graph, it is possible to observe that the behavior of section IV is similar to the export conduct of chapters 20 and 22. These brief calculations reflect the important influence of both chapters; nevertheless chapter 22 has more significance. For the past four years, those chapters represented about 80% of section IV exports. Given the importance of these parts it is presented an analysis using the long term component of the mentioned chapters.

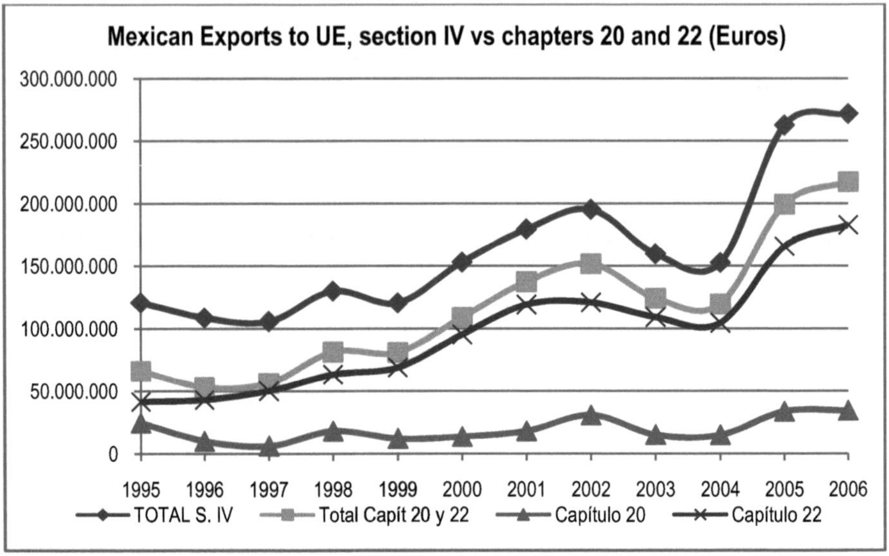

Source: Self compiled based on information from the European Information Agency, EUROSTAT, 2008

Under chapter 20, in respect with vegetables, fruits and plants exports, the following graph shows an increase in year 2000. This is consistent with the annual natural trend presented before, where exports of the same chapter goes from 12 million Euros in 1999, (year before the commercial agreement entrance in force), to 31 million USD in 2002. In spite of this notorious increase, this trend changed dramatically in 2003, decreasing to the same level it had before the trade agreement. Similar to total exports and agricultural exports, this information suggests that there is no important modification in the long term trend in Mexican exports to European Union in the products presented for this section as a result of the free trade agreement.

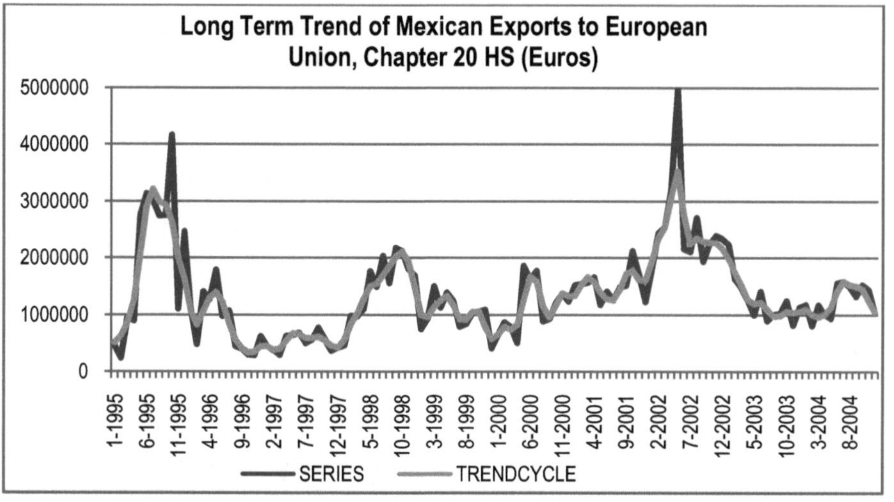

Source: Long term trend adjust self-compiled based on statistical series of European Agency for Information, EUROSTAT

Chapter 22 is composed by nine branches or headings representing products related with different prepared beverages, including the ones with natural and mineral water, beer, vinegar, tequila, mezcal, etc.

In order to give context to this analysis, it is needed a brief explanation of the HS. There are 22 sections in the Harmonized System, all agro-food products are classified in sections I, II, III and IV, and in these four sections are 24 chapters. Among all these 24 parts, number 22 is the most important chapter in terms of Mexican agro-food exports to the EU. The following graph represents the long term trend of Mexican exports to the Europe; as well, it represents the monthly exports five years before and after Mexican-EU FTA. Although it is possible to perceive an increasing trend in the exports to the EU in chapter 22, the change in trend is observed in early 1999, a year and a half before the entry into force of the commercial agreement. No to mention that the constant and positive trend is affected in year 2002 and since that year, it can be observed a period of stability in the long term trend, but without visible changes as a result of the entry into force the Mexican-EU agreement.

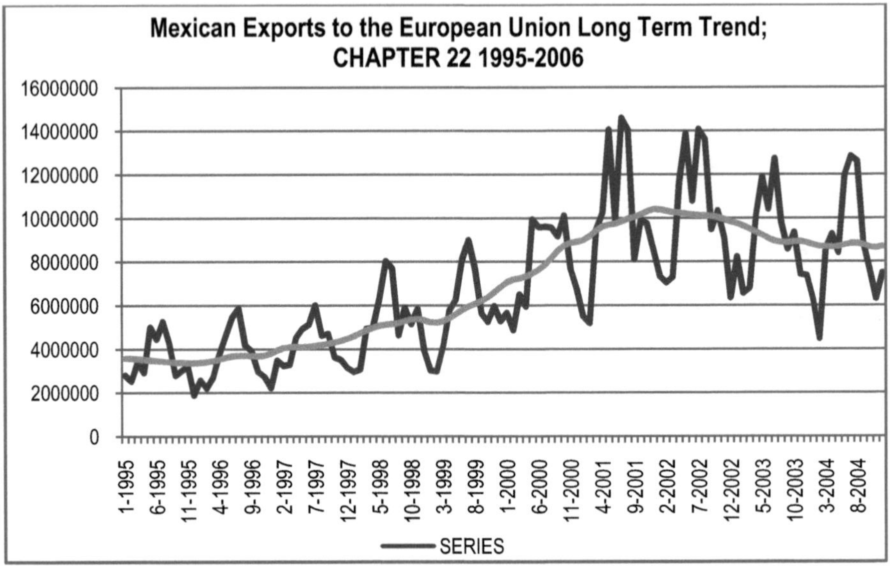

Source: Long term trend adjust self-compiled based on statistical series of European Agency for Information, EUROSTAT

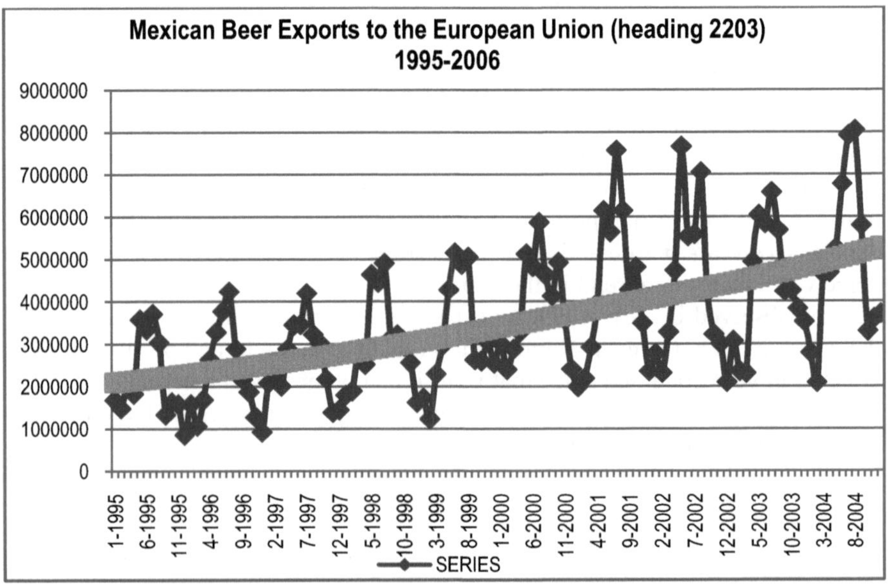

Source: Long term trend adjust self-compiled based on statistical series of European Agency for Information, EUROSTAT

In the chapter 22, the product with more weight in terms of sales to the EU corresponds to malt beer (branch or heading number 2203), considering that this good, is the most important Mexican agro-food product for exportation. The next graph, presents the long run trend component for this specific product.

This chart suggests a constant positive trend in Mexican beer exports to the EU. However, at the same time, the long term trend component of this product does not change from the entry in force of the Mexican-EU FTA, remaining this ongoing trend before and after the treaty. Therefore, it can be observed that there is no positive or negative change in the long term trend component, in other words, this calculations does not reflect any impact on the commercial agreement, not in all agro-food exportation, neither in the section IV, nor Chapter 22, or specifically in beer exports. It can be said that the most important agro-food product in terms of exportation to the EU or any other country, are the ones that have been eliminated from them, all custom duties since the entry into force of the Mexican-EU FTA.

8. Conclusions

The Economic Association Agreement and Political Cooperation between Mexico and the European Union entered into force in July 1, 2000, representing a step beyond of Mexican integration to world economy. The arrangement implied not just the commercial arena, but rather an economic and political cooperation, in which the Free Trade Agreement was one of the three elements of the economic partnership. As a result of the announced benefits of the commercial component of the agreement, was logical to expect that Mexican exports to the EU would increase.

Along this chapter was presented a description of benefits and liberalization scheme of this commercial agreement based on the Mexican-EU FTA original document. In addition, it is presented a simple and long term trend analysis of the total Mexican exports to the EU, agro-food exports in particular. Section IV of the HS, as well as some of the most representative chapters and branches of the agro-food sector, being the most important agro-food product in terms of exportation, malt beer. Moreover, in this chapter is showed natural annual trend and long term trend component before and after of the entry in force the Mexican-EU FTA. Both analysis were based on monthly statistical series taken from European Agency for Statistics and Information EUROSTAT and Mexican Agency for Statistics and Information INEGI. The main objective of this investigation was to notice whether there was any significant change in the exports trend as a result of the trade agreement in any of the studied levels.

In the original Mexican-EU FTA document, it is possible to observe that the commercial benefits for Mexico were mainly for industrial products. Not all agricultural products received commercial benefits or tariff reductions as a result of the agreement; in fact, some goods, did not have any benefit and were placed until this date, in a so-called "waiting list". However, many of the agro-food products obtained tariff benefits immediately, removing all customs duties at the entry into force the Mexican-EU FTA, such as the case of the malt beer. The lack of real commercial benefits could be a possible explanation of the marginal Mexican exports to the EU, particularly in the agricultural sector. In any case, this analysis suggests that neither those products which obtained significant tariff reductions or quota benefits, nor those which did not obtained any commercial benefit, present a significant increase in the trend of Mexican exports to the EU, at least in products, chapters and sections studied in this research.

In the case of the total exports, including the 22 sections and 98 chapters of the Harmonized System, the natural annual trend and the long-term trend component of Mexican exports to the EU, did not suggest any significant impact in the increase of exports to Europe as a result of the FTA between the involved parts.

The agro-food sector includes the sections I, II, III and IV of the Harmonized System. These four sections are compound by the first 24 chapters of this classification. Section IV corresponds to processed food and beverage industry, being chapters 16 to 24. This explanation is relevant because section IV, is the most dynamic part in terms of agricultural exports. Besides, it is considered the most positive and dynamic section in terms of export to the European Union.

Furthermore, chapter 22 corresponds to processed beverages being the most relevant part in section IV. Only this chapter, from 2001 to 2006 represents 67% of the exports of the entire section. In addition, the most important product in terms of Mexican exports to EU by far is malt beer, representing in the same period, more than 60% of the 22 chapter total exports. In all these levels of analysis, it cannot be appreciated any significant change or trend increase in the Mexican beer exports to the EU associated to the entry into force the Mexican-EU FTA. This situation is similar to the total Mexican agro-food exports to the EU, as well as the chapters and products analyzed.

Even though that this trade treaty could had a short term for an assessment; the data analyzed since the agreement entered in force in 2000 until 2006, suggests that the Mexican-EU FTA has not been an effective tool, neither to increase Mexican exports in general nor to increase agro-food Mexican exports in particular. This conclusion reveals that distance between the Mexican producers and the European market has not been reduced because of the FTA. In addition, it can be seen a clear success achieved by Mexican beer manufacturers, who have been able to increase their participation in one of the most competitive markets worldwide, while Europe seems not to be related to the benefits of this commercial agreement.

Therefore, it is important to deepen the analysis of the relationship of the European market with a longer term perspective. This topic is linked with the internationalization of the Mexican companies, nevertheless it is important to identify in the business reality, why Mexican products in the European market has not taken an advantage that seem to be an interesting opportunity.

References

Ball, A.B.; McCulloch, W.H.; Frantz, P.L.; Geringer, J.M. & Minor, M.S. (2006): *International Business: The Challenge of Global Competition*, 10ª Ed., Nueva York: McGraw Hill.

Bauerschmidt, A.; Sullivan, D.; Gillespie, K. (1985): "Common Factors Underlying Barriers to Export: Studies in the U.S. Paper Industry", *Journal of International Business Studies,* otoño, pp. 111-123.

Bernard, A. y Jensen, B. (1999): "Exceptional Exporter Performance: Cause, Effect, or Both?", *Journal of International Economics,* vol. 47, pp. 1-26.

Bhagwati, J. y Krueger, A. (1995): "The Dangerous Drift to Preferential Trade Agreements", *AEI Press,* Washington DC.

Bhagwati, J. y Panagariya, A. (1996): "The Economics of Preferential Trade Agreements", *AEI Press,* Washington DC.

Bilkey, W.J. (1982): "Variables associated with export profitability", *Journal of International Business Studies,* Otoño, vol. 13, núm. 2, pp. 39-55.

Cadogan, W.J.; Diamantopoulos, A. y de Mortanges, P.C. (1999): "A Measure of Export Market Orientation: Scale development and Cross-cultural Validation", *Journal of International Business Studies,* 4th Quarter, vol. 30, núm. 4; pp. 689-707.

Dichtil, E.; Leibold, M.; Koglmayr, G. y Muller, S. (1990): "International Orientation as a Precondition for Export Success", *Journal of International Business Studies,* vol. 21, núm. 1, pp. 23-40.

Francois, McQueen & Wignaraja (2005): "Regional Trade Agreements: Performance Evaluation and Research Agenda", Elaine Plant, La Trobe UniversityMehdi Taghian, Deakin University. http://www.anzmac2008.org/_Proceedings/PDF/S10/Plant%20and%20Taghian%20S9%20S6%20P2%20.pdf.

Ghosh, S. y Yamarik, S. (2005): "Are Regional Trading Arrangements Trade Creating? An Application of Extreme Bounds Analysis": *Journal of International Economics.* Vol. 63, num.2 julio, pp. 369-395.

Kaynak, E. y Kothari, J.E. (1984): "Export behavior of small and medium-sized manufactures: Some policy guidelines for international marketers", *Management International Review,* vol. 24, núm. 2, pp. 61-69.

Krugman, P. (1993): "Regionalism versus Multilateralism: Analytical Notes, in Melo, J. and Panagariya, A. (*Eds*.), *New Dimensions in Regional Integration*, Cambridge: Cambridge University Press.

Ortiz, S. (2008): "Análisis de los Factores Críticos y Propuesta de un Modelo de Valor para Fomentar las Exportaciones Mexicanas a la Unión Europea: Una Aplicación al Sector Agropecuario". Doctoral Dissertation, Universidad Antonio de Nebrija, Madrid, Spain.

Robinson, S. y Thierfelder, K. (2003): "Trade Liberalization and Regional Integration: the Search for Large Numbers", *The Australian Journal of Agricultural and Resource Economics,* 46, 4, pp 585-604.

Solberg, C.A. y Durrieu, F., (2006): "Access to Networks and Commitment to Internationalization as a Precursors to Marketing Strategies in International Markets", *Management International Review,* vol. 46, núm. 1, pp. 57-83

Stöttinger, B. y Schlegelmilch, B.B. (1998): "Explaining export development through psychic distance: enlightening or elusive?", *International Marketing Review,* vol. 15, núm. 5, pp. 357-372.

Stiglitz, J. (2006), *Como hacer que funcione la globalización.* Editorial Taurus, Ciudad de México.

Verwaal, E. y Donkers, B. (2002): "Firm Size and Export Intensity: Solving and Empirical Puzzle", *Journal of International Business Studies;* vol. 33, núm. 3, pp. 603-613.

Acuerdo de Asociación Económica, Concertación Política y Cooperación entre los Estados Unidos Mexicanos y la UE y sus Estados Miembros, (Mexico-European Union Free Trade Agreement). June 26 of 2000. Diario Oficial, México D.F.

Banco de Información del Instituto Nacional de Estadística, Geografía e Informática: http://www.inegi.gob.mx/inegi/ 2008

Centro Empresarial México-Unión Europea,
http://www.cemue.com.mx/apps/sitemgr.nsf/portada/1

Dirección General de Prensa y Comunicación de la Comisión Europea, "*Europa en movimiento 2002"*. http://europa.eu, 2005.

"Economagic" web page: http://www.economagic.com/

EUROSTAT: *The Statistical Office of the European Comission.* http://europa.eu

Secretaría de Economía, Negociaciones Comerciales Internacionales http://www.economia-snci.gob.mx/

United States of America Department of Commerce, 2008. http://www.commerce.gov/
World Trade Organization: http://www.wto.org/
World Customs Organization: http://www.wcoomd.org/

Mexican Firms' Entry Strategies to the European Union Market

Laura Zapata Cantú , Mariela Quiroga[†] *& Ana Luisa Cabrera*[‡]

1. Introduction

As noted by Bauman (2006), globalization has created a new way of perceiving the world in order to live in it. During the eighties, the term "global" meant a new way to compete, "compete aggressively" in the words of Prahalad (1998). Since then and until today, "global" means to compete aggressively for a market share of nearly 8,000 million people in the world.

Moreover, globalization has shown asymmetric economic growth, mainly due to multinational companies whose headquarters are in Western countries. This trend began to change in the nineties with the emergence of multinationals, mainly from Asian countries and particularly from India.

Given this irreversible fact, most countries of the world participate in treaties or trade agreements that facilitate the export and import of goods and services. Thus, this chapter presents an exploration of how several Mexican companies have entered the European market, with some having the auspices of the Free Trade Agreement (FTA) between the European Union and Mexico. While other companies started trading with the European Union long before the creation of the FTA.

2. The European Union and Mexico Free Trade Agreement

Mexico is one of the two largest economies in Latin America, with a population of over 110 million and a per capita income of almost US $10,000. Mexico has been a member of the North American Free Trade Agreement (NAFTA) since 1994 and has concluded a set of free trade agreements (FTA) with its major commercial partners. At present it is one of the few emerging countries to have an FTA with the US, the EU and Japan (Commission of the European Communities, 2008).

A major asset for Mexico is its strategic geographical position of bordering the US. Mexico is a significant political, economic and cultural actor in Latin America, and forms a cultural, political and physical "bridge" between North

EGADE Business School, Tecnológico de Monterrey.

† Department of Business and Human Resource Management, Tecnológico de Monterrey.

‡ Social Science PhD Program, Tecnológico de Monterrey.

America and Latin America. Mexico's "bridging" position is one of its main assets in the context of a progressive multilateral and multicultural international community. A closer relationship with Mexico could also facilitate the development of consensus on key regional issues between the EU and its Latin American partners (Commission of the European Communities, 2008).

Since the early nineties, Mexico was considered to be the main market for the European Union in Latin America. Thus, the Free Trade Agreement between the European Union and Mexico had as its main objective to strengthen Mexico's relations with Western Europe. In 2008, the EU represented Mexico's second largest trading partner and the second largest source of foreign direct investment (Ministry of Economy, 2009). This is shown in Table 1, which presents how in 2008, total trade between Mexico and the EU reached MXN$59,640 billion, an increase of 222% from 1999. This growth has been gradual since the beginning of EU-Mexico FTA. Trade statistics show that both Mexican imports and exports have registered strong growth since the FTA enforcement date. It is also true that Mexico buys from the EU twice as much as the bloc purchases from Mexico (Ministry of Economy, 2010).

Figure 1. EU-Mexico Total Trade (1999-2008)

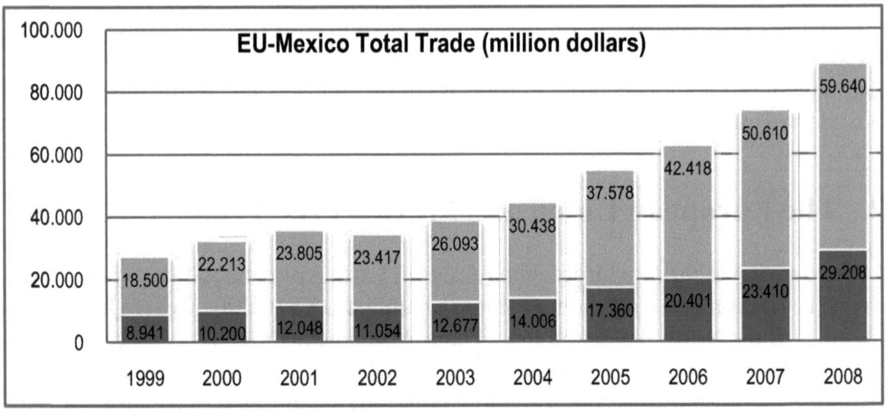

Source: Mexican Ministry of Economy with data from Banco de Mexico (Banxico)

In 2008, 82.5% of Mexico's trade with the EU was with Germany (28%), Spain (23.8%), United Kingdom (11.2%), Netherlands (11.1%) and Belgium (8.4 %). However, in recent years, Mexico has been losing its position as the Latin American buyer of EU products, despite the significant growth of Mexican imports.

Since the beginning of the Free Trade Agreement between the European Union and Mexico, which came into effect on July 1, 2000, both sides committed to the principles of international law, multilateralism, international cooperation for development and peace, and international security. The Coordination and Cooperation Agreement with Mexico was signed in 1997 and entered into force in 2000. The Agreement has three main pillars: political dialogue, trade and cooperation. It also allowed the EU to reinforce its economic and commercial positions in Mexico, which had been under considerable pressure since NAFTA's enforcement in 1994.

Indeed, the EU and Mexico recognize that multilateralism and the strengthening of coordination and cooperation on global issues are an important part of the strategic partnership. This strategic partnership strengthens bilateral and regional cooperation between these two regions. Some of the main points of the Executive Plan of the strategic partnership relate to cooperation in economic, environmental, development, scientific and cultural.

Economic cooperation, particularly trade facilitation, is described in the Programme Facilitation of the Free Trade Agreement EU-Mexico (commonly known by its Spanish abbreviation PROTLCUEM) which aims to support Mexico's efforts to improve competitiveness and promote economic, trade and business between Mexico and the EU. In socioeconomic issues, these refer to development policy, investment and social responsibility, innovation and intellectual property rights, open markets, social policies, decent work/social protection, migration, poverty, global macro-financial stability, good governance in the tax area, energy security, sustainability and improved efficiency, food prices, fisheries, maritime policy and ocean governance, and transport issues of common interest (Commission of the European Communities, 2008).

3. Mexican Imports from the European Union

A review of the sectors in which major product acquisitions are concentrated shows that Mexican imports from EU are inputs and consumer goods. This indicates that, in large part, Mexico is using its strategic geographical position as an export platform to the United States (US) market. EU companies established in Mexico import inputs, transform them into finished goods in Mexico, and, in many cases, export them to the US market. This process generates productive investment in Mexico, which translates into more jobs.

4. Mexican Exports to the European Union

From 1999 to 2007, Mexican exports to the EU increased at an average annual rate of 58.7%. Mexican sales to the EU increased in virtually all sectors and Mexican exports are relatively concentrated (see Table 1).

Table 1. Mexican Exports to the EU in 2008

Main Products	USD millions	%
Total	**20,307**	**100**
Crude oils obtained from bituminous minerals	4,494.6	22.1
Motor cars and other motor vehicles to transport people	3,524.9	17.4
Electrical apparatuses for line telephony or line telegraphy	1,655.4	8.2
Appliances used in medical, surgical, dental or visual veterinaries	1,285.4	6.3
Machines for processing data and their units	640.1	3.2
Intermediates of iron or non-alloy steel	537.0	2.6
Petroleum oil	241.7	1.2
Parts and accessories of motor vehicles of headings	225.8	1.1
Parts for use solely or principally by the engines under headings 84.07 or 84.08	200.3	1.0
Molybdenum ores and concentrates	177.8	0.9

Source: Ministry of Economy (2009)

The sectors that have achieved greater participation in 2008 are oil, vehicles, machinery and electrical equipment, nuclear reactors, pearls and precious stones, and optical instruments and appliances. Oil is the main export to the EU, representing about 29% of Mexican sales to this trading bloc, with more than USD$27 million during the first half of 2008. Regarding non-oil exports, its composition is purely industrial. With the exception of beer, the first fifteen non-oil products exported to Mexico are manufactured goods (automotive, steel, electronics, medical devices and communication) (Ministry of Economy, 2009).

With reference to the Mexican non-oil exports, in some cases these final goods are cars, computers or syringes. For example, the establishment of Mexico as the production platform of some car models for a German company, as is the case of the "New Beetle", explains the significant inflow to that country (Table 2).

Table 2. Mexican Exports to the EU by Sector in 2008

Sector (SITC V.4)	Exp.	%	Imp	%
	20,307	**100**	39,333	100.0
Food and live animals	707.9	3.5	464.0	1.2
Beverages and tabacco	293.1	1.4	385.9	1.0
Minerals except fuel	554.3	2.7	394.0	1.0
Mineral fuels and lubricants	4,784.6	23.6	6,047.5	15.4
Oils, fats and animal or vegetable waxes	22.0	0.1	57.9	0.1
Chemicals and related products	928.8	4.6	6,317.1	16.1

Sector (SITC V.4)	Exp.	%	Imp	%
Manufactured goods classified by material	1,382.5	6.8	5,611.5	14.3
Machinery and transport equipment	9,098.3	44.8	16,016.6	40.7
Miscellaneous	2,181.4	10.7	3,409.6	8.7
Unclassified products	343.7	1.7	1.4	0.0
Rule 8a	0.0	0.0	627.5	1.6
Gold and currency	10.7	0.1	0.0	0.0

Source: Ministry of Economy (2009)

There are important Mexican input exports to the EU that reflect the economic integration promoted by the presence of EU companies in Mexico. For example, the establishment of a Finnish company in Mexico drives Mexican sales of phone parts to Finland.

Mexican exports to the EU appear to be concentrated on a limited number of products, which can be confirmed by reviewing the products that have contributed to the growth of Mexican exports to the trading bloc after the treaty's enforcement. This data shows that there are still great challenges in terms of penetration of Mexican exports into the European market. While the composition of sales from Mexico to the EU shows a significant level of sophistication, the presence of Mexican product industries and those with higher surplus value have not yet managed to expand into most sectors of the EU economy.

5. Chapter objectives

Therefore, the big questions that arise are: What have Mexican firms done to enter and have a presence in the European market? What are the key organizational elements when Mexican firms are considering entry into this market? Thus, the main objectives pursued by this study raised in this chapter are: (1) to identify the main strategies used by Mexican firms to enter and have a presence in the European Union, and (2) to know the traditional motivators for Mexican companies to enter the European Union.

The literature review is the starting point of this chapter, explaining how firms use different entry strategies based on coordination and integration needs and differences, as well as the local differentiation degree. An exploratory methodology has been useful to identify how Mexican firms have been entering the EU market and what motivators influence these strategies. Our sample is composed of 14 firms: eight are large firms, four are medium firms and three are small. All of them represent the dominant segments of the economy: services, manufacturing and merchandising.

6. Literature Review: International Strategies

Over the past thirty years, there have been major changes in the world system. Globalization is one of them, characterized by the intention to develop a global market for production, trade, and political and cultural interaction[1].

The concept of globalization can be described as a process that creates links and transnational social spaces, reassesses local cultures, and brings third cultures to the forefront[2], according to Salman Rushdie, quoted by Ulrich Beck in his book *What is Globalization?* (1997). Europe, which already has a trajectory in its unification project, has been an example for fcother world regions and has managed to generate trade agreements outside its geographical space, including the treaty signed with Mexico during the government of Dr. Ernesto Zedillo Ponce de León (1994-2000).

Currently, the singularity of the globalization process lies on the ramification, density and stability of the regional-global relationship networks creation (Hirst and Thompson, 1996). This resulted in the generation of an environment for the technological transformation, characterized by the introduction of automated machinery and information technologies as an organizational factor of productive tasks. This led to a sort of revolution in firms' administrative processes in order to reduce costs and boost productivity (Roberston, 1992), thus generating a network of organizational structures to support operational efficiency and achieve activities with greater surplus value. In Mexico, just a few companies anticipated this to be the path to triumph in the new arena, and managed to face the new business reality established in Mexico at the end of the eighties.

Consequently, Mexico increased its debt during this period; it had mounting financial needs and the opportunity of a spontaneous supply of international capital[3], which helped to address a growing international competition. This resulted in the search for competition schemes different from those that had already existed in the country.

In the nineties, the founding idea of the global productive system suggested that the previous production system – based on the predominance of vertically integrated corporations, which were the prototype of the large Mexican firms of the seventies and eighties – tended to be replaced by an international subcontracting

1 Globalization, understood as knowledge of new markets and cultures, has a long history. Aldo Ferrer traces its origins back to the year 1050 in his book *Historia de la globalización*, (1996)

2 Salman Rushdie mentions "a bit of this, another bit of that, which is the way new things come into the world."

3 Unfortunately, they did not use this capital to invest in new industries or expand their technological capacity but spent it on diversifying their activities and intensifying their sales in the traditional sectors, due to the internal market boom during the seventies.

model that increasingly incorporated first, second and third order suppliers located in different countries (Farjoom, 1994). In this context, the future of a country was considered to depend on the capacity of its productive sector to form links with the new international subcontracting system. Mexican firms played this role through strategic alliances with foreign partners. These alliances constituted entry channels into the country of foreign direct investment[4] and intangible goods, such as technology and information, among others; they operated as mechanisms for integrating the companies into international markets.

In that era, the neoliberal policy of the Mexican government appeared to adhere faithfully to the recommendations of the World Bank's financial analysts who back then indicated that:

> The capacity to attract foreign financial investment is related to the beneficial impact of a wide range of structural reforms, legislative and economic ones. As governments have liberalized or eliminated capital restrictions, they have improved the flow of financial information and strengthened investors' protection mechanisms. In other words, investors have seen a chance to make more money and to take their profits back home. They choose countries that have a trustworthy capital market institutional regulation framework and avoid the rest. (World Bank, 1995)

The association of Mexican companies with foreign capital, that started as a defensive strategy against the opening and imminent arrival of new competitors, later became the spearhead of their expansion strategy and the principal means for accessing international markets. Obviously, strategies are not selected from a set of options, but are gradually constructed according to very particular circumstances, such as: the attractiveness of the industry (Porter, 1985), the analysis of its resources (Barney, 1991; Barney, 2001; Barney, Wright and Ketchen, Jr., 2001), and capacities (Teese, 1982; Grant, 1996; Hayes and Pisano, 1994; Hamel and Prahalad, 1995), as well as the degree of cooperation and/or competition in the industrial sector in which the company contends (Brandenburger and Nalebuff, 1996).

7. Traditional Motivators in International Trade

What motivates firms to expand their operations internationally? Although at times the motives might be completely idiosyncratic, such as a CEO's desire to spend some time in Mexico or Europe (Madhok, 1997), a large number of research suggests more systematic guidelines. One of the first motivations that led

4 It must be stressed that foreign direct investment is conducted by transnational corporations, and in general, it is defined as an investment that implies the administrative control of a company or local entity of a country by another one headquartered in another country. The control could be total or shared in different proportions with local businesspeople.

firms to invest overseas was the need to ensure the key supplies for their production processes.

Another strong motivator for internationalization could be described as market search behavior. This motivation is particularly important in the companies that have had some sort of intrinsic advantage, normally related to their technology or brand recognition, which gives them a competitive advantage in international markets (Hitt and Ireland, 1985). Although at first these firms' moves were opportunistic, later the firms realized that the additional sales generated both economies of scale and of scope, thus providing a source of competitive advantage over their internal rivals. This was a particularly strong motivator for some European multinationals whose markets were too small at home to withstand the intensive production volume. Companies like Nestlé expanded internationally, mainly in search of new markets (Fernandez, 1993).

The next traditional and important trigger for internationalization has been the desire to access low-cost production factors. In particular, countries like those in Europe, for which labor represents a significant cost, discovered that their products were at a competitive disadvantage with imports. In response, a number of firms in sectors, such as the textile, electrical appliance, domestic appliances and watchmaking industries, among others, sought labor outside their borders, in order to produce components or entire product lines. It soon became obvious that labor was not the only productive factor that could bring cheaper costs overseas. For example, the availability of lower cost capital (perhaps through an investment subsidy from the host nation's government) also became a powerful force for internationalization (Barlett, Ghoshal a Birkinshaw, 2004).

These three motives were the main traditional driving forces for multinationals' international expansion. The way in which these motivators interact to prompt companies to turn into multinationals are explained in the product cycle theory developed by Professor Raymond Vernon (1996).

8. New Motivators

After establishing international sales and production operations, the multinationals have gradually changed their perceptions and strategic motivations. The typical initial attitude was that overseas operations were caused by strategic and organizational motives and therefore, should be managed in an opportunistic manner. Nevertheless, managers gradually realized that a more integrated direction was needed. In this process, the forces that originally instigated their international expansion often became secondary and gave way to a new set of motivations that underline their new global strategies (Barlett, Ghoshal and Birkinshaw, 2004).

The first set of actions consists of increasing the economies of scale, investing more resources in research and development, and shortening products' lifecycles. This transformed many industries and caused the abandonment of national structures worldwide, as well as the acknowledgement that for certain industrial activities, the global scope was not a matter of choice but an essential requirement for survival (Eriksen and MIikkelsen, 1996).

A second factor that made firms' international strategy vital – though it did not become the principal motivator – was the need to generate learning and knowledge at an international level. When a company manufactures its products overseas, it must be able to guarantee the supply of its raw materials, which is why companies are aware of the existence of alternative low cost production sources worldwide and are tempted by market opportunities generated by new technologies or market needs that stimulate the development of innovative products. The very nature of the presence of a multinational offers an enormous advantage over the information that could be gathered in the search of more efficient sources or more advanced products and process technologies. Therefore, a company whose international strategy was generated by a technological or marketing advantage could increase its advantage through the exploration and the potential learning inherent to its global operating network (Kauffman, 1995).

A third benefit that soon surfaced was that multinationals had significant competitive positioning advantages over national firms. Cross-subsidization across markets is undoubtedly the most controversial of the many strategic competitiveness actions adopted by multinationals over the past few years (Friedman, 2006).

9. The Meaning of Internationalization: Prerequisites and Processes

After exploring the reason why companies aspire to international expansion, or their motivation, it's needed to understand how they do so by examining the meaning of internationalization. Apart from the desire to expand outside its borders, a company needs to possess certain competencies – the attributes that become prerequisites – if it wants to succeed in foreign markets. The firm must be capable of putting into practice its desire to expand outside the national market through a series of decisions and commitments that define the internationalization process (Barlett, Ghoshal and Birkinshaw, 2004).

Prerequisites for internationalization. In each domestic market, an international firm is to some extent disadvantaged compared to its local competitors, at least at first. Local firms have a huge advantage being familiar with the national culture, industrial structure, government requirements and other matters related to doing business in the country. Their relationships with the relevant consumers, suppliers and regulators, amongst others, give them an additional advantage over the foreign company that has to offset this with a specific and unique strategic capacity. An advantage of the foreign firm consists of its knowledge and superior skills in technology or specific competencies regarding the value chain processes (Foster and Kaplan, 2001).

However, on their own, the strategic advantages, including knowledge, are insufficient to justify internationalizing operations. A firm can, as we have seen, sell or license technology to foreign producers, franchise its international brand name or sell its products overseas through local distributors, without having to configure its own operations (Barlett, Ghoshal and Birkinshaw, 2004).

The other prerequisite for a company that is considering becoming a multinational is that it must have the organizational capacity to exploit its subsidiaries' strategic assets effectively, instead of doing so through contractual relations with third parties. If superior knowledge is a multinational's main source of competitive advantage, it must, for example, have an organizational system that allows for greater profitability in the expansion and exploitation of its knowledge through direct foreign profitability operations that it might obtain from selling or franchising knowledge licenses (Morabito, Sack and Bhate, 1990).

In short, three conditions must be met for a multinational to exist. First of all, some foreign countries must offer particular location advantages in order to provide the necessary motivation for the company to invest in them. Secondly, the firm must have some of the strategic competencies or ownership of the specific advantages to offset the disadvantages of its ignorance in relation to foreign markets. Thirdly, the firm must have the organizational capacity to gain better returns, making the most of its strategic advantages rather than external market mechanisms, such as contracts or licenses. Understanding these prerequisites is important not only because they explain why multinationals exist, but also because they help to define the strategic options for competing in business on a global level.

The internationalization process. The process of developing these organizational strategies and characteristics is the core of the internationalization process through which each firm constructs its position in the global marketplace. The process is usually based on a combination of rational analysis, opportunism and pure luck. Nevertheless, it is still possible to highlight some of the general behavioral guidelines that companies usually follow.

The best known internationalization model was developed during the 1970s by two Swedish academics from Uppsala University, Jan Johanson and Jan-Erik Vahlne. This model describes the entry of a firm into a foreign market as a learning process. The firm makes an initial commitment of resources in the foreign market and thus, gains knowledge of the local market regarding customers, competitors and the regulatory conditions. On the basis of this market knowledge, the firm is able to assess its current activities and to expand its resource agreement with the commitment, perhaps, to buy from its local distributor or invest in a local factory that will allow it to develop its market knowledge. Gradually, through several investment cycles, the firm develops the necessary level of local capacity and market knowledge to become an effective competitor in the foreign country (see Figure 2).

Figure 2: Internationalization Learning Model

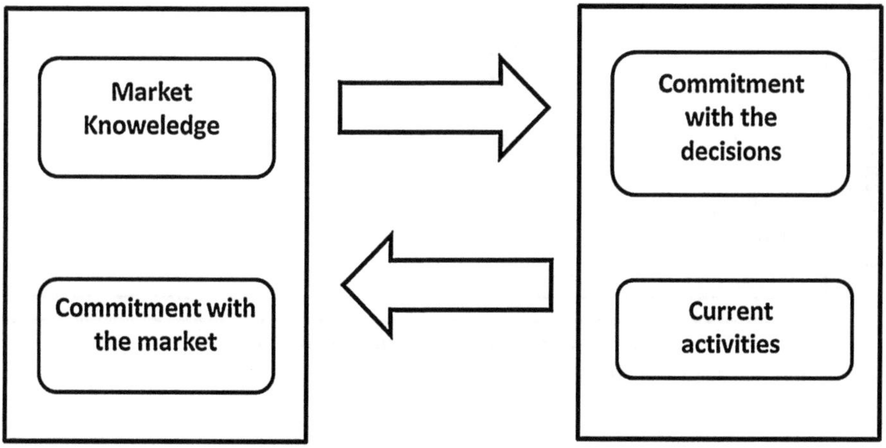

Although many firms internationalize in the manner described by the Uppsala model, many others do not. Some companies invest in acquisition or look for local partners to facilitate the process of constructing its knowledge of the local market. Others prefer to reduce their local presence to a minimum by subcontracting to local partners. An important set of factors includes the assimilation of knowledge of the local market by the subsidiary, as suggested by the Uppsala model. But other, equally important factors for the multinational are its overall level of commitment to the selected foreign market, the necessary control level of the foreign operations, as well as the timing of its entry. In order to understand these factors, it helps to think about the different ways of operating overseas according to two factors: the level of market commitment and the level of control (Barlett, Ghoshal and Birkinshaw, 2004). (See Figure 3)

Figure 3: Entry Approaches to Foreign Markets

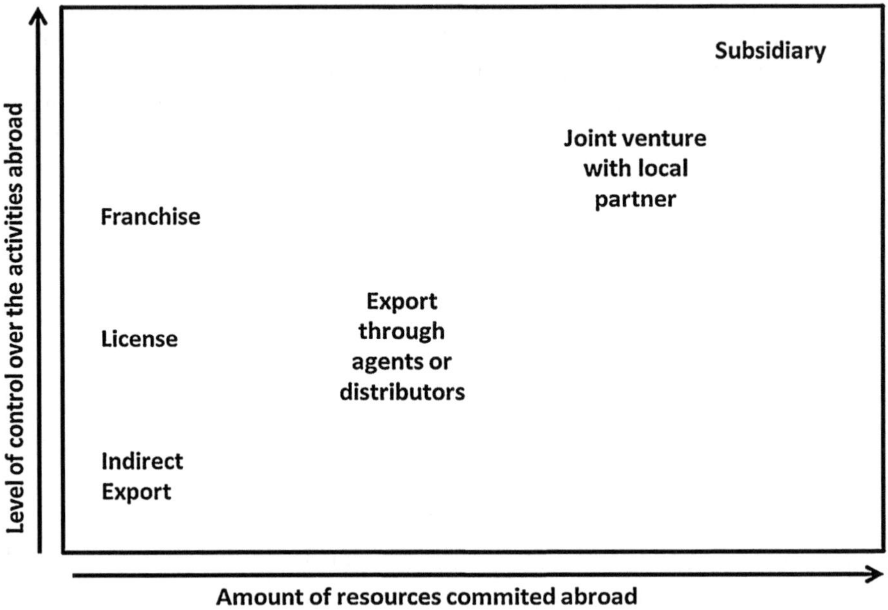

Source: Barlett, Ghoshal and Birkinshaw (2004)

10. The evolution of a mentality: from an international strategy to a transnational strategy

Even after the brief description of the changes in motivation and the meanings of internationalization, a gradual evolution in the strategic role of international operations played by multinationals can be observed. This evolutionary pattern can be classified in four stages and visualized as the way in which administrative thinking has developed over time, as well as the changes that have taken place in the international setting (Barlett, Ghoshal and Birkinshaw, 2004).

International strategy. In the first phases of internationalization, numerous managers from the companies that wish to compete internationally tend to think that the function of foreign operations is to support the domestic parent company in diverse ways, such as contributing to increasing national production sales. This is known as the international strategic mentality. Products are developed for the internal market and only later are sold overseas; technology and other knowledge are transferred from the headquarters to the international operations; and international production is seen as a means of protecting the firm's domestic market.

Firms with this mentality see themselves basically as a local firm with some overseas branches.

Multinational strategy. The organization's opening to foreign locales and the growing importance of sales and earnings from these sources gradually convince managers that international activities can provide opportunities that are more than just marginal. Increasingly, they also realize that in order to support these opportunities they must do more than send old equipment, technology or product lines that have been developed for the local market. Local competitors in foreign markets and the host governments often speed up the learning process of firms that maintain an international mentality that has been stagnant for a long time. A strategic multinational mentality is developed as managers begin to recognize and emphasize the differences between domestic markets and operational environments.

Global Strategy. Although the multinational mentality typically leads to satisfaction with products that adapt to the tastes and preferences of the diverse domestic markets, it is also true that it generates an increase in the inefficiency of the manufacturing infrastructure within the firm. Plants are constructed to supply local marketing advantages or to improve political relations, rather than to maximize productive efficiency. At the same time, the proliferation of products designed to satisfy the local market also contributes to a general loss of efficiency in design, production, logistics, distribution and other functional tasks.

In a market setting that seeks to improve transportation and communication facilities, as well as to counteract the tariff barriers, some firms adopt a very different strategy to face up the international market. This type of firm thinks in terms of creating products for a global market and therefore, manufactures on a global scale in highly efficient plants, often counting on a headquarters.

This is the strategic global mentality, since it views the world as its unit of analysis. It understands that national tastes and preferences are more similar than different. From another point of view, this mentality provides the world with standardized products at affordable prices and with a higher quality than the options offered by its local competitors (Levitt, 1983).

Transnational Mentality. During the eighties, many global enterprises began to believe that they were invincible. They managed to surpass not only the local firms, but also their international and multinational competitors in a setting that was being rapidly globalized through new manufacturing and information technologies.

For instance, for many host governments, these global firms became a greater threat than the firms with a strategic international mentality. Many of these governments increased restrictions and demands, calling for the transfer of technology (Fahy, 1996).

Customers also contributed by rejecting the homogenization of global products and reaffirming their national preferences. Although they did not ease their expectations regarding the high levels of quality and low costs that global products had offered (Farjoom, 1994). Finally, the growing volatility in the international economic and political scenario, particularly the rapid changes in currency exchange rates, also had a negative effect on the effectiveness of this centralized global approach.

As a result of these processes, many firms worldwide recognized that the demand to respond to the local market and political needs, and the pressures to develop efficiency on a competitive global scale were simultaneous, though, at times, controversial. In these circumstances, the attitude reflected by both the multinational firms and the strategic global mentalities were increasingly inappropriate. It became evident that companies had to become more sensitive of local needs, while maintaining their global efficiency. This emerging management approach is what we call the strategic transnational mentality.

The companies whose resources and capacities are not centralized in the parent company, but are not decentralized in the subsidiaries either, can perform their tasks with a local base. In this case, the resources and capacities are dispersed but, at the same time, specialized, so that both efficiency and flexibility can be achieved. It is important to point out that these resources and capacities are integrated into a dynamic network composed of interdependent firms spread out in different regions and, in order to operate efficiently, each firm is located in the region that offers it a competitive advantage according to its specific function within the network (Morabito, Sack and Bhate, 1999).

This results in the need of intensive coordination throughout the organization, as well as shared decision making, which implies that this is a much more sophisticated and subtle management approach than multinational management.

However, it must be made clear that, depending on the industry, the strategic positions of the individual firm, the diverse needs of the host nations and a variety of other factors, a firm could reasonably operate with any of these strategic mentalities.

Figure 3 illustrates how these four strategies are positioned according to the dimensions of the need for global coordination and a degree of local difference and differentiation.

Figure 4: International Strategies

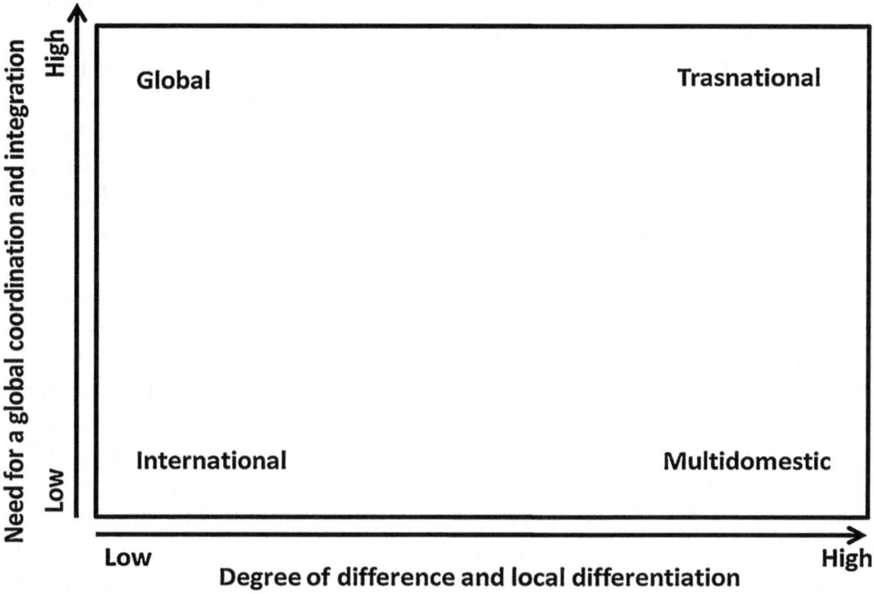

Source: Barlett, Ghoshal and Birkinshaw, 2004

The following section describes the entry strategies into the European market by 14 Mexican firms.

11. The mode of entry strategies into the European Union by Mexican firms

Over the years, Mexican companies have endeavored to expand their markets towards the Old Continent. For this, diverse strategies have been implemented with varying commitments of resources and operational control, as well as global coordination and differentiation in the goods and services they offer, from the export of purely Mexican products to the creation of factories in the European Union and to strategic alliances and the sale of franchises and licenses. The following is a description of few Mexican companies with international operations. The selection was made according to the different entry strategies and the information available.

Grupo Bimbo started out as a baker's shop in Mexico City in 1945 and has been present in the Czech Republic and Austria since 1998, thanks to the acquisition of the Park Lane confectionery. It also operated in Spain from 1964 to 1978 when that country's bakery broke away from the Mexican company, although it still bears the same name (Grupo Bimbo, 2010).

Cemex has been a paradigmatic case. It has been ranked as one of the leading cement producers in the world. At the end of the last century, with the purchase of Spain's Valenciana and Sansón, it began to expand internationally. In 2004, it acquired the cement company RMC and currently operates in Great Britain, Germany, Austria, Finland, France, Hungary, Ireland, Latvia, the Netherlands, Poland, the Czech and Sweden. It also entered into an alliance with Lafarge in Spain and Portugal that was terminated in 2005 (CNN Expansion, 2010).

The ups and downs of the Mexican economy are reflected in companies like *Vitro*. After being a diversified enterprise, the Monterrey-based company had to focus on its product that had the greatest comparative advantage. As far back as 1965, Vitro entered into an alliance with Pilkington in the UK to produce float glass, a strategy that also involved a technological alliance. In 1992, it acquired the English firm Aci America (Pozas, 1998:167). In 2001, it acquired 60% of the shares of the Spanish firm Cristalglass (Vitro, 2003) and has plans to buy the remaining 40%, but the economic situation has postponed this operation. In 2005, Vitro entered into a technological alliance with Allied Glass Containers in the UK and in 2008, took over the French firm Verre & Glaces d'Epinay (*El Semanario*, 2008, May 2).

Grupo Alfa, with its four business groups, has diverse operations in the European Union. Since 1975, it has been a partner of BASF in Germany through Alpek. Together with Himont from Italy, it created the Indelpro plant in 1989. That same year, and also in Italy, Nemak obtained an equity interest and technology alliance with Teksid and created the Galvamet plant with Metecno in 1992. It also formed a partnership with Fiat to manufacture auto parts (Pozas, 1998:147). Its interest in Hylsa (which was dissolved in 2005) associated it, in 1996, with Man GHH in Germany, Galvamet Galvac in Italy and NV Bejaert in Belgium. Also in 1996, Sigma gained presence in France thanks to its association with Sodima. The alliance with AkzoNobel established its presence in Holland and Sweden and through Indelpro, with the Italian enterprise Montell. In 2003, Nemak opened its plant in the Czech Republic and in 2005, acquired Rautenbach (Pozas, 2007).

As the largest corn flour and tortilla manufacturer in the world, *Gruma* opened its offices in England in 1997 and its plant in 2000. In 2004, in Italy and Holland, it purchased the company Ovis Boske (Gruma, 2010).

A particularly noteworthy firm is *FEMSA Cerveza*, the division that was sold to the Dutch Heineken at the beginning of this year in exchange for 20% of the latter's stock. This not only permitted the expansion of the Mexican beer market to Europe but also, the presence of the Monterrey-based group on that continent (Kesmodel and Cimilluca, 2010, January12).

With regard to franchises, *Kidzania*, the children's entertainment center, has had a park in Lisbon since 2009. The firm's founders decided to operate in other countries through franchises, since their strategy consists of finding partners to invest in the park's design, know-how and staff training, in order to achieve international positioning with a view to robustly penetrating the US market (González Lara, s/a). *Sushi Itto*, which began in Mexico City in 1994, opened the first restaurant in Spain in 2000, where it now has four branches (Sushi Itto, 2010). The Mexican coffee franchise *Punta del Cielo* began operating in Spain in 2008 (Alonso, 2008, July 25).

The export of *Grupo Modelo's* Mexican products has been very successful, which has been present in European Union countries since 1985, including countries with a strong beer-drinking tradition, such as Holland, Germany and Belgium (Grupo Modelo, 2010). Citrofrut from *Grupo Proeza* exports to Holland, the UK and Switzerland (Lara, 2002). *L. A. Cetto*, the renowned wine producer from Baja California, exports to the UK, Holland, Switzerland, Belgium, Germany, Italy, Finland, Sweden, Poland and France (L. A. Cetto, 2010).

After exporting its products to Europe, the newly created brand *Fulanitos* returned to Germany, Portugal and Spain in 2006 with licenses. Its next goal is to sell franchises on this continent (Rosas, 2006, 2 November). *Distroller* has also begun to expand by selling its products in the Spanish market (Morales, 2007, March 13).

Table 3: Summary of Entry Strategies for Mexican Firms

Enterprise	**Strategy (year)**	**European countries**
Bimbo Group	Plant (1964-1978)	Spain
	Acquisition of Park Lane (1998)	Czech Republic and Austria
Cemex	Acquisition of Valenciana y Sansón (1992)	Spain
	Acquisition of RMC (2004)	Great Britain, Germany, Austria, Finland, France, Hungry, Irland, Latvia, Netherlands, Poland, Czech Republic y Sweden
	Strategic Alliance with Lafarge (2005)	Spain and Portugal
Vitro	Strategic Alliance with Pilkington (1965) Acquisition of Aci América (1992) Strategic Alliance with Allied Glass Containers (2005)	England
	Partial Acquisitions of Cristalglass (2001)	Spain
	Acquisition of Verre & Glaces d'Epinay (2008)	France

Enterprise	Strategy (year)	European countries
Alfa Group	Strategic Alliance with BASF (1975) Strategic Alliance with Man GHH (1996) Acquisition of Rautenbach (2005)	Germany
	Strategic Alliance with: Himont (1989) Teksid (1989) Metecno (1992) Galvamet Galvac (1996) Fiat (1989) Montell (1992)	Italy
	Strategic Alliance with NV Bejaert (1996)	Belgium
	Strategic Alliance with Sodima (1996)	France
	Strategic Alliance with AkzoNobel (1962)	Holland and Sweden
	Plant (2003)	Czech Republic
Gruma	Subsidiary (1997) Plant (2000)	England
	Acquisition of Ovis Boske (2004)	Italy and Holland
Femsa	Merger Femsa Cerveza and Heineken(2010)	Holland
Kidzania	Franchise (2009)	Portugal
Sushi Itto	Franchise (2000)	Spain
Punta del Cielo	Franchise (2008)	Spain
Modelo Group	Export (1985)	European Union
Proeza Group	Export (s/a)	Holland, England, Switzerland
L. A. Cetto	Export (s/a)	Germany, Belgium, Finland, France, Holland, Italy, Poland, United Kingdom, Switzerland and Sweden
Fulanitos	Export (s/a) License (2006)	Spain
Distroller	Export (s/a) License (s/a)	Spain

As it can be seen, the aforementioned companies have enjoyed a significant presence in the European Union. However, they penetrated the European markets without the backing of an agreement, since, for the most part, their participation in the EU dates back to years and even decades before the EU-Mexico FTA.

Considering this information and according to the dimensions of the need for global coordination and the degree of local difference and differentiation, the aforementioned firms would be placed as follows:

Figure 5: Mexican Firms International Strategies

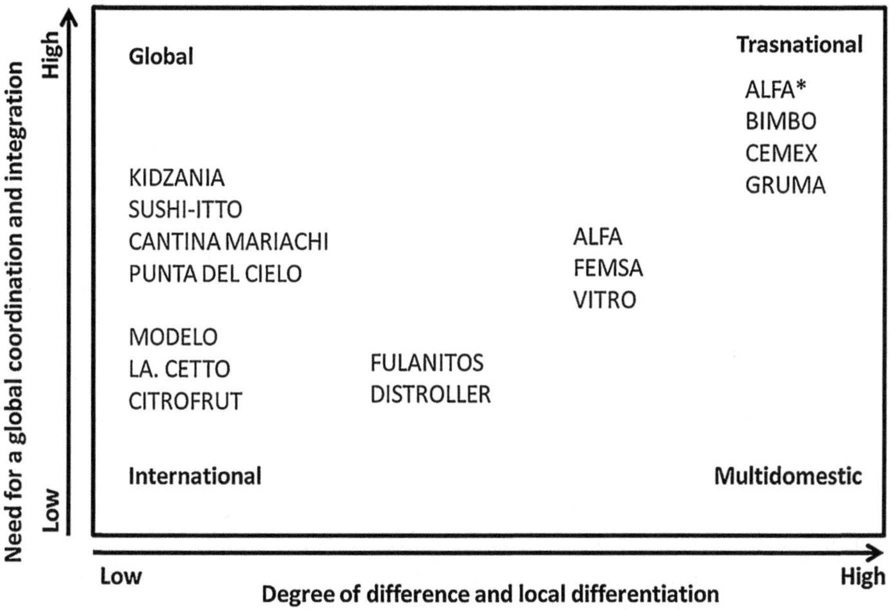

Figure 5 presents a diagram of the diverse entry strategies into the European Union used by Mexican firms. The transnational strategy is the most commonly used by manufacturing companies, unlike service firms that have opted for a strategy with a low level of differentiation and a mid-level coordination, as exemplified by the licenses and franchises.

This figure shows that six of the sample companies have a low level of local differentiation, since they export their products or sell licenses or franchises. In addition, the amount of resources committed is low, since the importer or buyer pays for placing the product or service overseas. Only four of the firms have invested strongly in the European Union, mainly through strategic alliances that have facilitated their entry to the market. Moreover, these six firms use global coordination and integration that allows them to achieve a higher level of control in their activities in the EU.

The EU is Grupo Modelo's second largest export market. It is the leading firm in the non-European bottled beer category and has accomplished outstanding results in England, Ireland, Denmark, Scotland, Greece and Sweden, "Thanks to the efforts of the importers in those regions". (Grupo Modelo, 2008)

An investment of approximately 15 million Euros was needed for the Kidzania park in Lisbon. For this firm, cultural differences have not implied a greater expense, since the concept handled is universal. Nevertheless, the firm does adapt to the country in which it sets up its parks, working with the franchise buyer to understand and adapt the country's licenses and regulations (Notifranquicias, 2009).

Café Punta del Cielo, which is growing at an annual rate of 30%, began operating in Spain in 2008, with the vision of opening another franchise in France. According to its directors, they selected Europe rather than the United States because they have enjoyed a better response from the European than the US market. Even though the chain is well positioned in Mexico, and even sells inside supermarkets and is distributed to hotels and airlines, annual coffee consumption in Mexico is just one and a half kilos per person, while in Finland or the United States it exceeds 10 kilos (Alonso, 2008, July 25).

After exporting, the Fulanitos brand arrived to Europe in 2006 with licenses and franchises. The firm increased the number of licenses rather than the number of its own stores to boost the franchise. Fulanitos observes a strong potential in Europe and the United States and goes on gift trade fair tours to negotiate franchises and licenses (Rosas, 2006, 2 November).

The acquisition of RMC by Cemex was a determining factor for its participation in the EU. Cemex's previous strategy was to favor rapidly growing emerging markets, "with a great deal of large construction projects", however, Cemex required a greater market share in Europe, in order to compete with its two greatest rivals (Lafarge and Holcim) (Tricks, 2004, September 28). Moreover, Gruma's expansion to the Old Continent increased its capacity to serve its growing client base in the region, leading it to purchase firms that were already established locally (Gruma, 2006).

Enterprises like Grupo Bimbo expand by means of strategic associations, for they acquire sector firms and plants in other regions due to the limited Mexican market (Rivera and Osterroth, 2001).

The main motivations in the case of these Mexican firms, apart from the conditions of a globalized scenario, are the search for new markets and the attainment of advantages over their competitors. Mexican companies regularly turn to Spain, since it offers the advantage of the language. In the countries in which market entry is more difficult, firms first seek a strategic alliance that would reduce international participation costs, even if this means sacrificing operational control. Evidently, many companies are adopting an international mentality. However, there is still a long road ahead towards the global and transnational paradigm to which large enterprises with a solid organization and global participation strategy can more easily aspire.

12. Conclusions

Globalization has been a catalyst for trade relations between different countries. It also led the European Union and Mexico to see the urgency of working out a trade agreement and later on, a strategic association.

However, even though the exchange of goods and services between Mexico and the EU has gradually increased over the years, it can be observed that, in the case of the sample presented in this work, Mexican operations in the European Union did not stem from the agreement but rather, date back to years, even decades, before it existed.

As mentioned beforehand, the association of Mexican firms with foreign capital began as a defense strategy against liberalization, well into the nineties, and would later become the principal means of access to the international marketplace. The motives would lie in a larger market, cheaper resources and the company's very survival.

Signing treaties facilitates an exchange between countries. Nevertheless, this is not in itself a motivator for operating internationally. The treaty with the EU has not been a motivator for Mexican companies either, despite the fact that the EU is Mexico's second most important partner after the United States.

Therefore, it can be concluded that the possibilities of this treaty should be further exploited, especially as the political relations and cooperation efforts of the Global Agreement accompany them.

Likewise, Mexico must reinforce its presence in the EU. Its historical competitor for leadership in Latin America, Brazil, is being signaled out by the EU as a growing influence in the region, as well as for its role as a stable, emergent economic power, while Mexico's political and socioeconomic changes are acknowledged as being significant, though with huge challenges still ahead (European Commission, 2007a).

A greater participation of Mexico in the EU would lessen its dependence on the United States. Nevertheless, for this to be possible, the country needs to work on issues such as social cohesion, governance, human rights, safety, drug trafficking, competitiveness, telecommunications and tax reforms, all of which have been indicated as important by the EU and some of which are included in the Global Agreement (European Commission, 2007b).

Finally, in studies on trade activities, as is the case here, it will be necessary to consider the 2008-2009 crisis, although its effects have not yet been documented in the EU-Mexico statistics, since it is highly likely that the economic crisis would have modified trade and investment exchanges between both parties (European Parliament, 2010). Furthermore, firms might have adapted their operations and strategies overseas in order to survive the crisis.

References

Aleda, R.; Tsay, A.; Pullman, M.E. and Gray, J.V. (2008). Unraveling the Food Supply Chain: Strategic Insights from China and the 2007 Recalls. Journal of Supply Chain Management , vol. 44, num. 1, pp. 22-40.

Alonso, R. (2008, July 25). "Llega a Europa una Punta de Cielo mexicano". *El Universal* online, available at: http://www.eluniversal.com.mx/articulos/48164.html.

Barlett, C. A.; Ghoshal S. and Birkinshaw J. (2004). Transnational Management. McGraw Hill.

Barney, J. (1991). Firm resurces and sustained competitive advantage. Journal of Management , vol. 17 (1), pp. 99-120.

Barney, J. B. (2001). Resurce-based theories of competitive advantage: A ten year retrospective on the resource-based view. Journal of Management, vol. 27, pp. 645-650.

Barney, J.; Wright, M. and Ketchen, D. J.Jr. (2001). The resource-based view of the firm: Ten years after 1991. Journal of Management, vol. 27, pp. 625-641.

Bauman, Z. (2006). La globalización: Consecuencias humanas. Fondo de Cultura Económica, México.

Beck, U. (1997). ¿Qué es la globalización? Falacias del globalismo, respuestas a la globalización. Barcelona, España: Paidos.

Brandenburger, A. and Nalebuff, B. (1996). Co-opetition. Nueva York: Currency Books.

CNN Expansión (2010). Cemex S. A. B. de C. V. *Cemento*. CNN Expansión online, available at: http://www.cnnexpansion.com/empresas/cemex-s-a-b-de-c-v.

Commission of the European Communities (2008). Communication from the commission to the council and the European parliament. Towards an EU-Mexico Strategic Partnership. COM/2008/447.

El Semanario (2008, 2 de mayo). "Compra Vitro francesa Verre et Glaces d'Epinay". El Semanario online, available at: http://www.elsemanario.com.mx/news/news_display.php?story_id=6525.

Eriksen, B. and MIikkelsen J. (1996). Competitive Advantage and the Concept of Core Competence. En N. J. Foss, & C. Knudsen (Edits.), Towards a Competence Theory of the Firm, pp. 54-74, Londres: Routledge.

European Commission (2007a). Brazil. Country Strategy Paper 2007-2013. E/2007/889.

European Commission (2007b). Mexico. Country Strategy Paper 2007-2013. E/2007/1063.

European Parliament (2010). European Parliament recommendation to the Council of 12 March 2009 on a EU-Mexico Strategic Partnership. Retrieved: http://www.europarl.europa.eu/sides/getDoc.do?pubRef=//EP//TEXT+TA+P6-TA-2009-0141+0+DOC+XML+V0//EN.

Fahy, J. (1996). Competitive Advantage in International Services: A Resource-based View. Competitive Advantage in International Services: A Resource-based View, 26 (12), pp. 24-37.

Farjoom, M. (1994). Beyond Industry Boundaries: Human Expertise, Diversification and Resource-Related Industry Groups. Organization Science, vol. 2, pp.185-199.

Fernandez-Rodriguez, Z. (1993). La organización interna como ventaja competitiva para la empresa. Papeles de Economía España, vol. 56, pp. 178-193.

Ferrer, A. (1996). *Historia de la globalización: orígenes del orden económico mundial*. Buenos Aires: FCE.

Foster, R. and Kaplan, S. (2001). Creative Destruction. Nueva York: Currency.

Friedman, T. (2006). La Tierra es Plana: Breve Histria del Mundo Globalizado del siglo XXI. México: M. R. Ediciones.

Grant, R. M. (1996). Prospering in Dynamically-competitive Environments: Organizational Capability as Knowledge. Organization Science, vol. 7, num. 4, pp. 375-387.

Gruma (2006). Gruma International Foods. Gruma online available at: http://www.gruma.com/vEsp/NuestrasEmp/nuestras_empresas-grumaAO.asp.

Gruma (2010). Historia. Acerca de Gruma. Gruma online, available at: http://www.gruma.com/vEsp/Acerca/acerca_historia.asp.

Grupo Bimbo (2010). Comunicados de prensa. Relación con inversionistas. Grupo Bimbo online, available at: http://www.grupobimbo.com/relacioninv/pressrelease.php?id=39.

Grupo Modelo (2010). "Historia de Grupo Modelo". *Grupo Modelo online, available at*: http://www.gmodelo.com.mx/index-1.asp?go=historia.

Hamel, G. and Prahalad C. K. (1995). Compitiendo por el futuro. Barcelona: Ariel.

Hayes, R.H. and Pisano, G.P. (1994). Beyond World-Class: The new manufacturing strategy. Harvard Business Review 72(1): 77-84.

Hirst, P. and Thompson, G. (1996). Globalization in Question. Cambridge: Cambridge Press.

Hitt, M. A. and Ireland, R. D. (1985). Corporate Disructive Competence, Strategy, Industry and Perfomance. Strategic Management Journal, vol. 6, pp. 237-293.

Kauffman, S. (1995). At home in the universe: The Search for Laws fo self-organization and complexity. New York: Oxford University Press.

L. A. Cetto (2010). "Exportaciones". *L. A. Cetto online*, available at: http://www.lacetto.com.

Lara, J. A. (2002, 3 de junio). "Logran mérito exportador". Economía y negocios. *El Norte*, p. 12.

Levitt, T. (1983). The Globalization of Markets. Harvard Business Review, pp. 92-102.

Madhok, A. (1997). Cost, Value and Foreign Market Entry mode: The Transaction and the Firm. Strategic Management, vol. 18, pp. 39-61.

Ministry of Economy (2010). http://www.economia-snci.gob.mx.

Morabito, J.; Sack, I. and Bhate, A. (1999). Organization Modeling: Innovative Architectures for the 21st. Centuy. Upper Sadle River: Prentice-Hall, Inc.

Porter, M. E. (1985). Ventaja competitiva: creación y sostenimiento de un desempeño superior. Buenos Aires: Rei Argentina.

Prahalad (1998). Managing Discontinuities: The Emerging Challenges. Research Technology Management, June, pp. 14-22.

Roberston, R. (1992). Globalization: Social Theory and Global Culture. Londres: Sage.

Rivera, E. Y Osterroth, M. (2001, 17 de mayo). "Grupo Bimbo: estrategia inconsistente". *Reforma.*

Rosas, F. (2006, 2 de noviembre). "Fulanitos triunfan en Europa". *El Universal online, available at:* http://www.eluniversal.com.mx/articulos/35712.html.

Teece, D. J. (1982). Toward and Economic Theory of the Multiproduct Firm. Journal of Economic Behavior, vol. 3, pp. 39-63.

Tillmann Wagner, Richard J. Lutz, y Barton A. Weitz. (2009). Corporate Hypocrisy: Overcoming the Threat of Inconsistent Corporate Social Responsibility Perceptions. Journal of Marketing, vol. 73, 77-91.

Vernon, R. (1996). The manager in the international economy. Upper Saddle River, N.J.: Prentice-Hall.

The EU-Mexican FTA and Art. XXIV GATT

Gerhard Niedrist

1. Introduction

Both the European Union and Mexico have concluded numerous preferential trade agreements with a variety of partners in the world. According to the most recent data from the WTO, the European Union currently has 27 preferential trade agreements in force and Mexico eleven (WTO, 2011). The most notable agreements include the European Economic Area between the EFTA states and the EU, the agreements between the European Union and its neighbors in the Mediterranean region, and in the case of Mexico the North American Free Trade Agreement (NAFTA) with Canada and the United States from 1994.

However, the Free Trade Agreement between the European Union from 1997 is also noteworthy for several reasons. Firstly, it grants the European Union preferential access to the NAFTA region and is therefore strategically very important to the European Union. The agreement is also Mexico's first preferential agreement after the conclusion of the North American Free Trade Agreement (NAFTA) in 1994 and represents an important step in the process of liberalization and economic opening of the country since the late nineties. Finally, the EU-Mexican FTA is worldwide one of the first cases of a cross-regional preferential agreement. That means it involves not just neighboring countries (and is thus a regionalist policy), but establishes free trade between different continents. As a consequence, the EU-Mexican Free Trade Agreement can also be seen as in important piece in a general proliferation of free trade agreements. While in the early nineties only about 50 FTAs were in force, according to the WTO 228 free trade agreements are currently in force, many of them of a cross-regional nature. (WTO, 2011).

This development of intensified bilateral liberalization must be analyzed in the multilateral context of the WTO. As multilateral liberalization seeks to reduce barriers regardless of the parties involved, it naturally has a tense relationship to bilateral free trade agreements which liberalize trade only between the parties to them and leave the outside world with a comparative disadvantage. This tension is reflected in Art. XXIV GATT, which recognizes in general "the desirability of increasing freedom of trade by the development, through voluntary agreements, of closer integration between the economies of the countries

EGAP Gobierno y Política Pública, Tecnológico de Monterrey.

parties to such agreements" (Art. XXIV:4 GATT). On the other hand, Art. XXIV GATT sets several conditions that FTAs must meet in order to be consistent with the multilateral regime of the WTO. Art. XXIV:5b GATT requires,

> "that the duties and other regulations of commerce maintained in each of the constituent territories ... shall not be higher or more restrictive than ... prior to the formation of the free-trade area". Moreover, Art. XXIV:8b GATT requires that "the duties and other restrictive regulations of commerce ... are eliminated on substantially all the trade between the constituent territories".

This tension in Art. XXIV GATT is of a legal nature and must therefore be distinguished from the economic debate about whether free trade agreements have a positive or negative effect on trade liberalization. In this chapter, the EU-Mexican Free Trade Agreement will be discussed from this legal perspective and an attempt will be made to answer whether it is consistent with the multilateral concept of the WTO and Art. XXIV GATT. For a better understanding, we will firstly describe the basic economic theory on free trade agreements, mainly based on the works of Jacob Viner. We will then analyze the meaning of "substantially all the trade" as the central legal term of Art. XXIV GATT. Finally, we will analyze the EU-Mexican FTA in the light of Art. XXIV GATT and the corresponding analytical material of the WTO and trade data available from a World Bank Trade Database.

2. Trade creation vs. trade diversion

The terms "free trade" and "preferential agreements" have a positive connotation, imply something good and indicate unlimited, liberalized trade. But in a free trade area such as that between the European Union and Mexico, trade is not only liberalized but might also be diverted and have protectionist effects on the world as a whole. As a consequence, many political economists see free trade agreements as a threat to the multilateral system of the WTO and speak of discriminatory agreements or in terms of protectionism. Some authors (Bhagwati, 1991 ; Panagariya, 1999) even see in the proliferation of preferential zones the risk that at the end of the development two or three highly integrated trading blocs will face each other within a weakened WTO. These trading blocs would grant themselves free trade via bilateral agreements, but would confront each other within the WTO with a protectionist high tariff policy. In these terms, preferential agreements would be stumbling blocks for a multilateral system of trade liberalization. However, other authors (e.g. Krueger, 1999) see in preferential agreements building and not stumbling blocks for the multilateral trade system. Pascal Lamy (2002) even sees in regional agreements the possibility to deepen multilateral liberalization via the facilitation of additional trade (WTO-plus).

Nearly all considerations start with Jacob Viner's (1950) analysis of custom unions, which was the first economic investigation of the possible trade diverting effects of preferential trade agreements. Imagine a simplified world with three countries A, B and C. A produces product P more expensively than B, but because A's tariff policy is P within A cheaper than P produced in B. The formation of a free trade agreement between A and B abolishes the tariffs between A and B and the production of P shifts from A to the more cheaply producing B. C, representing the world outside the FTA, is not affected. The FTA between A and B creates trade, although the gain could be even higher if we assume that C produces P even more cheaply than B.

The situation changes if it is assumed that P is not produced within A but is imported from the outside world C. Through the creation of an FTA between A and B, the price of P as produced in B drops due to the abolition of the tariffs charged by A. As the products from C still have to carry the burden of the tariffs from A, B gains a comparative advantage over C and the demand for P in A shifts from C, which produces more cheaply, to the more expensive B. This results in trade diversion and in protectionism on the part of A and B against the outside multilateral world C (Viner, 1950).

Viner (1950) has summarized the effects of the two examples: If trade creation is present, one of the two countries necessarily benefits from the FTA, and both may actually benefit, while the world outside the FTA (C) loses in the short term and only gains in the long term via the secondary effects of more prosperous trade within the FTA. If, however, trade diversion is dominant, at least one of the participants of the FTA will lose trade, the other partner might also lose trade and both will lose in terms of their trade with each other. The countries outside the FTA will lose too, as will the world as a whole.

Viner's analysis, however, only represented the starting point of the extensive economic debate on preferential agreements; his simple model has been extended and expanded continuously. Kemp and Wan (1999a; 1999b), for example, have proven that theoretically some agreements do not show any trade diverting effects at all. They do not, however, provide information on how such agreements must be designed and have been criticized as too theoretical (Venables, 2003).

That the issue of trade creation versus trade diversion not only involves economic but also political issues can easily be seen in the following example: Imagine that the US – immediately after the conclusion of NAFTA – started to displace an inefficient industry in Mexico. This would be desirable for the both for US and outside world companies, who could participate more easily in the Mexican market. The result would be trade creation as meant by Jacob Viner. But the decline of an industry not only represents a shift in trade but also involves rising unemployment and social problems. Mexico, bound by its obligations under

NAFTA and the WTO, cannot just simply raise its tariffs to establish a protectionist policy. But in order to resolve its internal social-economic issues, Mexico could raise other non-tariff barriers to international trade, which are much more technical and whose legality would have to be determined at the institutions for dispute settlement, which would last at least several years. During this period, Mexico would remain relatively untouched, shifting the trade related parts of the problem back to the US and to the outside world. Trade diversion would be the result (Baldwin & Venables, 1995; Baldwin, 1997). However, empirical studies have shown that preferential agreements are, in the vast majority of cases, trade-creating and very unlikely to lower living standards in their member countries (Baldwin, 1997; Venables, 2003).

For the following legal considerations, Jacob Viner's basic concept of the economy of free trade will be sufficient. For further and much more detailed analyses in the economic literature, please consult the compilation of Bhagwati, Krishna and Panagariya, who summarize the key contributions in one volume, (Bhagwati et. al, 1999; de Melo & Panagariya 1993), or for analyzing the EU-Mexican FTA in particular the works of Rene Cabral and Daniel Villarreal Cabello within the present book. (See above, page 39).

3. Art. XXIV GATT

Art. XXIV GATT is the key provision of the WTO regarding preferential trade agreements. This relatively long and detailed article is divided into twelve paragraphs, of which the first three only regulate territorial issues. Paragraphs nine and eleven deal with historical questions which are no longer of significance today, and paragraph twelve stipulates the general obligation of the signatories to GATT to apply the provisions of Art. XXIV GATT. Paragraph ten concerns the possibility of exceptions to Art. XXIV GATT, but as the general rules for waivers within GATT are less restrictive than exemptions from free trade agreements, it is very rarely used (Then de Lammerskötter, 2004).

Paragraph 4 of Art. XXIV GATT states generally that closer integration between the members of GATT via customs unions and free trade agreements is desirable. On the other hand, the same provision stipulates that preferential agreements shall not be used to raise or establish trade barriers against third countries outside the customs union, which is of particular significance remembering the basic economic considerations of Jacob Viner. The exact meaning of this ambiguous provision was discussed very controversially for a long time, especially if Art. XXIV:4 GATT requires an economic trade diverting test as defined by Jacob Viner for new FTAs and CUs. Recently, this question has been resolved by the WTO Dispute Settlement Body, which stated that Art. XXIV GATT does not involve an economic test and "merely" requires a legal interpretation (WTO, 1999a; WTO, 1999b; Mathis, 2000). This result seems logical, as Viner's first considerations on the diverting effects of free trade agreements arose in 1950, three years after the formation of the GATT in 1947, and therefore could not be part of the motivation and legal reasoning that led to the formulation of paragraph 4. Consequently, the main criteria which a preferential agreement must meet to be consistent with the GATT can be found in paragraphs 5-8 of Art. XXIV, requiring both internal and external criteria.

Paragraph 5 sets out the conditions which a preferential agreement must meet towards third countries, in other words it establishes the external criteria of a preferential agreement. Paragraph 5 concerns in particular the regulation of new restrictions, which means trade diversion as defined by Jacob Viner which may result from the formation of a new preferential agreement. The provision distinguishes between customs unions, free trade agreements and interim agreements, and determines for each of these different types of economic integration the requirements to be met.

Article XXIV:6 GATT provides rules of compensation if one country entering into a customs union has to raise its bound tariffs under the WTO. Examples of such compensation may be found during the third, fourth and fifth enlargements of the European Union, but are irrelevant for the EU-Mexican FTA (Then de Lammerskötter, 2004). Paragraph 7 deals with procedural aspects, especially the obligation of all members to notify the WTO of the formation of a preferential agreement. Article XXIV:8 GATT provides a legal definition of a customs union and a free trade agreement and establishes the requirements that those preferential agreements must meet internally. This paragraph is – together with paragraph 5 – of crucial importance, because both must be met in order to establish a bilateral exception to the multilateral rules of the GATT. Below we will examine the EU-Mexican FTA based on those external and internal criteria.

4. The external criteria: Art. XXIV:5b GATT

Article XXIV: 5 is the key provision on the criteria to be met by preferential agreements with third countries (Berrisch, 2003). According to the Appellate Body in the Turkey-textiles case, the basis of paragraph 5 is Article XXIV:4 GATT, according to which no additional trade barriers shall be established upon the formation of a free trade zone. Article XXIV:5 GATT requires an economic test which must be based on effectively applied and unbound tariffs. (Marceau & Reimann, 2004; WTO, 1999a; WTO 1999b)

Regarding free trade agreements, Article XXIV:5b GATT states:

> "(b) with respect to a free-trade area, [...], the duties and other regulations of commerce maintained in each if the constituent territories and applicable at the formation of such free-trade area [...] shall not be higher or more restrictive than the corresponding duties and other regulations of commerce existing in the same constituent territories prior to the formation of the free-trade area,[...]"

Article XXIV:5b of the GATT provides that the duties and other regulations of commerce in each of the partner states of the FTA shall not be higher or more restrictive than before its formation. This has to be understood as an absolute prohibition, which means that none of the partners of the FTA may raise their tariffs against third countries. However, and unlike custom unions where the different external tariff regimes must be harmonized (please see Art. XXIV:5a for custom unions), this criterion does not cause major problems regarding free trade agreements, where the external tariffs usually remain unchanged. As a consequence, the practically relevant problems regarding free trade areas can be found internally within the free trade area itself, especially in relation to the criterion to liberalize substantially all the trade (SAT) of Art XXIB:8b GATT. (Then de Lammerskötter, 2004)

5. The internal criteria: Art. XXIV:8b GATT

Beside that, the provisions contain almost identical wording, as?? Art. XXIV: 8 GATT distinguishes between customs unions and free trade agreements. In paragraph b we can find a definition of free trade areas, including the internal criteria to be met by the FTA:

> "(b) A free-trade area shall be understood to mean a group of two or more customs territories in which the duties and other restrictive regulations of commerce (except, where necessary, those permitted under Articles XI, XII, XIII, XIV, XV and XX) are eliminated on substantially all the trade between the constituent territories in products originating in such territories."

From this provision it is clear that in order to be consistent with the GATT, free trade agreements must abolish duties (tariffs) and other restrictive regulations on commerce (ORRC) and on substantially all the trade (SAT). While the meaning of "duties" does not cause major problems and has never been subject to major discussion in the GATT, ORRC and especially SAT require further clarifications.

The first discussions regarding SAT arose during the creation of the European Union in 1957. The debates on the SAT problem took place in the sub-group D, which examined the relationships between the countries in the newly created customs union of the six founding EU states and their overseas territories. The EU argued that only 1.4% of its trade with overseas countries was subject to duties. However, the EU was heavily criticized by the other parties of the GATT, because the amount provided by the European Union was not just based on the EU-overseas trade at issue but also included the internal trade within the six EU states. The other member states of GATT required clear and accurate data. This demand was rejected by the EU on the grounds that first the GATT had to agree on a precise definition of SAT before they could provide such data. Otherwise, the working group could have adapted the definition to the already known EU trade data and hindered EU-overseas trade. As the GATT working group could not agree on a definition of SAT, the only official statement was the unilateral EU definition that a trade liberalization of 80% within a free trade zone meets the requirement of abolishing duties on "substantially all the trade" (GATT 1947, 1957).

Because of the unclear wording in Art. XXIV of GATT as well as due to the inadequate specification of the term 'SAT' by working groups of the GATT, substantially all the trade has been interpreted in various ways. Regarding the quantitative degree of liberalization, values from 51% to 99% have been argued in the academic literature (Roselieb, 1961; Haight, 1972). According to Hipold (1993; 2003), values between 80% and 90% seem to have the greatest acceptance, as was argued in the working group during the foundation of the EU.

But the definition of SAT is not only a quantitative problem. For example, upon the establishment of EFTA in 1960, trade in almost all industrial products was liberalized, while the agricultural sector was excluded as a whole (GATT 1947, 1960). To avoid such a problem, Australia has proposed in the recent debate on Art. XXIV GATT that 95% of the six-digit harmonized system of tariffs (HS) should be liberalized between the parties of a preferential agreement (WTO, 1998a & 1998b). While several Asian states supported the Australian initiative, it was rejected by the USA and the EU. Both emphasised that such a clarification and legal definition of SAT could not cover all of the possible situations of preferential agreements, as they are very different in their characteristics (WTO, 1998c & 1998d).

Due to different trade policy interests, the WTO members have so far not been able to agree either on a quantitative criteria or on qualitative elements of SAT. At least part of the qualitative problem was resolved by the WTO Dispute Settlement Body (DSB) in the Turkey-textiles case. While the case did not require a general statement on quantitative elements, the DSB (WTO, 1999a, paragraph 9.148) stated generally:

> "The ordinary meaning of the term 'substantially' in the context of sub-paragraph 8(a) appears to provide for both qualitative and quantitative components. The expression 'substantially the same duties and other regulations of commerce are applied by each of the Members of the [customs] union' would appear to encompass both quantitative and qualitative elements, the quantitative aspect more emphasized in relation to duties."

Subsequently we will analyze the EU-Mexican FTA on the basis of the term 'SAT'.

6. The EU-Mexican FTA in the light of Art. XXIV GATT

6.1 The CRTA

Art. XXIV:7 GATT establishes the obligation to notify the other WTO members of the formation of a new preferential agreement. The 1994 Understanding on Art. XXIV GATT makes it clear that this obligation serves as a basis for a multilateral review process of the agreement (Tevini, 2011).

Based on a decision of the WTO General Council from 1996, this task was carried out by the Committee on Regional Trade Agreements (CRTA) (WTO, 1996). The examination of the FTAs in the CRTA started with a brief presentation of the agreement by the parties. This was followed by several sessions of questions and answers in which the other WTO members were able to address either oral or written questions to the parties. The CRTA lacked the possibility to issue specific measures or recommendations to the parties of the agreement and must therefore be seen much more as an instrument which is only able to reflect critical issues and concerns of an FTA, but not to determine whether a preferential agreement meets the criteria of Art. XXIV GATT.

Thus, for example, in the very first session in the evaluation of EU-Mexico the representative of Australia expressed his concerns about the degree of liberalization in the agricultural sector (WTO, 2001). According to the response by the European Union, at the end of the transitional period of the EU-Mexican agreement, 62% of agricultural trade and 97% of total trade should be duty free (WTO, 2001). However, the discussion in the CRTA did not bring forth new aspects of the FTA between the EU and Mexico and especially no data to prove the allegations over the degree of liberalization which had been carried out. Finally, the parties got stuck in lengthy formal and informal discussion, which typically led to a stalemate (Crawford, 2007).

Starting 2003, the WTO members increasingly sought to improve the revision of preferential agreements, which in 2007 ended up in an RTA transparency mechanism (WTO, 2006a). The focus lies much more on the publication of the basic information of the agreements, e.g. via the publication of fact sheets and not so much to come to a joint conclusion. The EU-Mexican FTA was not assessed by this new transparency mechanism, but following its spirit, in 2006 both parties provided more detailed tariff data of the FTA.

According to the newly provided trade data, both the EU and Mexico assumed high degrees of liberalization under their agreement. 98.1% of the total EU imports from Mexico are to be liberalized, which equals 94.9% of the total products in the HS-6 tariff classification. 80.9% of the agricultural products are to be liberalized, which equals 68.1% of the products in the 6-digit HS tariff system. However, it is important to note that agricultural trade only accounts for 3.6% of the total trade volume from Mexico to the EU. (WTO, 2006b).

On the Mexican side, at the end of the transitional period 98.1% of the total trade volume is also to be fully liberalized, which represents 95.3% of HS-6 products. The agricultural sector will reach a liberalization of only 56%, representing 58.2% of the products listed in the HS 6-digit tariff code. (WTO, 2006b).

The ambiguity of Article XXIV GATT and the lack of possible consequences on the part of the CRTA means that the revision process of preferential agreements is ultimately toothless. The weakness of the CRTA may be seen from the fact that it has been inactive for more than five years in the analysis of the agreement between the European Union and Mexico. As a result, only some critical questions from traditional agricultural countries such as Australia remain, and over twelve years after the entry into force of the EU-Mexican agreement no final report has been adopted.

6.2 Trade Data

If we compare these statements with the actual existing trade data obtained from the World Bank WITS database[1], we can see that the trade agreement between the EU and Mexico has actually brought decisive tariff liberalization. Thus, the average EU duties for Mexican products from 2000 to 2010 have dropped by 90% from an already low 1% to just 0.1%. And it is equally important that at the HS-2 tariff level 91.6% of the product groups are now duty free, while at the time of the entry into force of the agreement in 2000 only 34% of the HS-2 products exported from Mexico to the European Union were completely exempt from tariffs. At the HS-6 digit level the percentage of exempted products is even higher. In 2000, 67% of the tariffs from Mexico to the EU were liberalized, while under the free trade agreement this amount increased to 98% in 2010.

It is also noteworthy that under the HS-2 digit system the EU charges tariffs over 1% on just four Mexican product categories. These are obviously the most sensitive areas for EU trade policy, like dairy products (HS-04, 17.6% in 2010),

1 All trade data has been obtained from the Tariff and Trade Analysis from the World Bank WITS Database (http://wits.worldbank.org/wits/) and represents effective applied weighed average preferential tariff rates according to UNCTAD method I.

flour products (HS06, 6.04% in 2010), vegetables (HS20, 7.89% in 2010) and miscellaneous edible preparations (HS 21, 1.16% in 2010).

The impact of the free trade agreement becomes clear when we compare this data with the tariffs of the EU with third countries. While the average tariff applied by the EU to third countries decreased from 2.12% in 2000 to 1.61% in 2010, it is important to notice that Mexico's comparative advantage increased in the same period. The difference in the HS-2 tariff line is even more clear, where in 2010 only 8.33% of third country products were completely liberalized (2000 6.25%). At the HS 6-digit tariff level, 27.59% of the products imported from third countries were exempted from EU tariffs in 2010, compared to 20.18% in 2000.

On the Mexican side, the agreement has brought extensive trade liberalizations too. At the entry into force of the agreement in 2000, Mexico had an average tariff level of about 10% against the European Union, which was reduced to just 0.23% in 2009. On the HS-2 tariff line, no group of products was completely exempted from tariffs in 2000, while in 2009 80% (77 out of 97 commodity groups) could already enter Mexico from the EU duty free. The results for the HS 6-digit tariff line are quite similar. In 2009 for example, 96.64% of all Mexican HS 6 tariff rates had already been fully liberalized by the EU, compared to 0.67% in 2000.

If we compare these data with those duties that Mexico has applied for the same period against third countries, it is clear that the Free Trade Agreement establishes extensive trade liberalization for EU products against products from third states. Mexico in general established significant tariff reductions from 2000 to 2009, where the average tariff rate dropped from 15% in 2000 to about 2% in 2009. At the HS-2 tariff level, in 2009 only 7% of all 97 commodity groups were completely exempted from Mexican duties. At the HS 6 digit tariff level, about 21% of Mexican imports from third countries were exempted from tariffs in 2009 compared to only 0.67% in 2000.

Like the European Union, Mexico has also excluded some agricultural commodity groups from liberalization. These Mexican sensitive areas are, according to the HS-2 tariff system, meat products (HS 02, 9.36% in 2009), dairy products (HS 04, 50% in 2009), coffee and tea (HS 09, 36%), flour and starch products (HS 11, 16%), sugar (HS 17, 17%), cocoa (HS 18, 20%), wheat flour and bakery products (HS 19, 14%) and tobacco (HS 24, about 11 %). Interestingly, with all these products the tariff levels have remained nearly unchanged since 2000 and therefore have not been subject to any liberalization.

Apart from these restrictions on certain products, the tariffs on agricultural products both on the European and the Mexican side have dropped significantly under the Free Trade Agreement. From 2000 to 2009, the European Union reduced its average tariffs on agricultural products from 7.1% to 2.44%. In the same period, the Mexican average tariff rate on agricultural products decreased from 30% to about 8%. While this is indeed a significant difference in absolute numbers, the relative reduction of 73% on the part of Mexico, and 66% on the EU side are clearly within the same order of values. The development of tariff levels between Mexico and the EU on the HS-6 digit level is quite similar. In 2009, 96.64% of all HS-6 tariff lines were already fully liberalized (0.67% in 2000), while in Mexican trade relations with third countries only 21% of the HS 6-digit tariff lines were fully liberalized (in 2000 the figure was also 0.67%).

Both sides have completely liberalized duties on industrial products (EU: 0%, Mexico 0.04% in 2009), which means that the exceptions to Article XXIV GATT are almost exclusively on agriculture. That Article XXIV GATT permits exceptions is undisputed. However, as during the formation of EFTA in 1960 there were some concerns because of the limitations to Article XXIV GATT. It is important to emphasize that the actual situation between the EU and Mexico is different. Both Mexico and the EU have made extensive liberalizations in the agricultural sector and only maintained duties on some sensitive sectors. While the wording of Article XXIV GATT still lacks an exact definition, it seems that this reservation of some areas is what was intended during its creation. The EU and Mexico are liberalizing over 90% of their agricultural trade (both by trade volume and HS tariff lines) and there can be therefore no doubt that the Free Trade Agreement is consistent with the multilateral rules of the WTO.

7. Conclusions

Like other preferential agreements, the free trade agreement between Mexico and the European Union is still caught between multilateral liberalization in the WTO and deeper integration via bilateral agreements. Here, the agreement between Mexico and the European Union is of particular interest, as it was one of the first transcontinental free trade agreements, granting the EU preferential access to a NAFTA country, and its deadline for full implementation has now expired.

The discussion about whether preferential agreements are consistent with the multilateral rules of the GATT is almost as old as the GATT itself and had reached its first peak with the discussions on European integration in the late fifties and early sixties. Since then the exact scope and limits of the relevant Art. XXIV GATT have remained uncertain, as they have not been defined until now. Particularly the criterion that a free trade agreement or a customs union must eliminate tariffs on "substantially all the trade" in order to be consistent with the GATT has not been defined either by the text of Art. XXIV GATT or by jurisprudence of the WTO Dispute Settlement Body or by the current State practice.

It is also unclear whether this criteria applies to trade volume as a whole or if it applies to the majority of certain trade sectors and product groups, e.g. under the HS-6 digit tariff system.

An issue which is controversially discussed is whether the agricultural sector may be partly or wholly exempted from trade liberalization under a free trade agreement, as for example in the creation of EFTA in 1960. In this sense, Australia has expressed some criticism on the agricultural regime between Mexico and the European Union during the evaluation of the free trade agreement in the WTO. While both the EU and Mexico have provided some information on agricultural trade to the Committee on Regional Trade Agreements, the data provided to the WTO was so ambiguous that a clarification of whether the trade regime was consistent with the multilateral rules could not be reached on that basis.

The impact of the FTA becomes clear when one compares the trade data between the EU and Mexico to their trade with third countries. From 2000 to 2010 the EU tariff rate for Mexican goods decreased from 1% to 0.1%, while it remained almost the same for trade with third countries. While the average Mexican import duties for European products were higher (15% to 2% from 2000 to 2009), it is interesting to note that the relative degree of liberalization is about the same. Both Mexico and the European Union have established lesser degrees of liberalization in the agricultural sector, but even under the strict Australian criteria to use the 6-digit HS tariff lines, both Mexico and the EU achieve over 90% of liberalization on agricultural products (EU: 98% of the HS-6 tariff codes, Mexico: 97%).

In general, all trade data between the EU and Mexico show a significant liberalization of over 90%, so that we can – regardless of the ambiguity in the WTO – conclude that the free trade agreement between the EU and Mexico clearly meets the multilateral rules of Art. XXIV GATT. It must therefore be seen as a supplement to the WTO that intensifies the economic relations between Mexico and the European Union.

References

Baldwin, R. E. (1997). The Causes of Regionalism. The World Economy, 865-888.

Baldwin, R. E., & Venables, A. J. (1995). Regional Economic Integration. In G. M. Grossman & K. Rogoff (Eds.), Handbook of International Economics. Volume 3 (Vol. 3, pp. 1597-1644). Amsterdam et al: Elsevier.

Berrisch, G. (2003). Das allgemeine Zoll- und Handelsabkommen (GATT 1994). In H. J. Prieß & G. Berrisch (Eds.), WTO-Handbuch (pp. 71-168). München.

Bhagwati, J. e. a. H. (1999). Trading blocs: alternative approaches to analyzing preferential trade agreements. Massachusetts.

Bhagwati, J., & Panagariya, A. (1999). Preferential Trading Areas and Multilateralism – Strangers, Friends or Foes? In J. Bhagwati, P. Krishna & A. Panagariya (Eds.), Trading blocs: alternative approaches to analyzing preferential trade agreements (pp. 33-100). Massachusetts.

Crawford, J. A. (2007). New Transparency Mechanism for Regional Trade Agreements, A. SYBIL, 11, 133.

de Melo, J., & Panagariya, A. H. (1993). New Dimensions in Regional Integration. Cambridge.

GATT 1947. (29.11.1957). Treaty Establishing the European Economic Community. Report submitted by the Committee on the Rome Treaty to the CONTRACTING PARTIES on 29 November 1957. L/778.

GATT 1947. (4.6.1960). Report of the Working Party on the European Free Trade Association. L/1235.

Haight, F. A. (1972). Customs Unions and Free-Trade Areas under GATT. Journal of World Trade, 391-404.

Hipold, P. (1993). Regionale Integrationszonen und GATT. Die Neuerungen der Uruguay-Runde. Recht der internationalen Wirtschaft(8), 657-670.

Hipold, P. (2003). Regional Integration According to Article XXIV GATT – Between Law and Politics. In A. von Bogdandy & R. Wolfrum (Eds.), Max Planck Yearbook of United Nations Law (pp. 219-260). Leiden et al.

Kemp, M. C., & Wan, H. Y. (1999a). An Elementary Proposition Concerning the Formation of Customs Unions. In J. Bhagwati, P. Krishna & A. Panagariya (Eds.), Trading blocs: alternative approaches to analyzing preferential trade agreements (pp. 203-206). Cambridge: MIT Press.

Kemp, M. C., & Wan, H. Y. (1999b). The Comparison of Second-Best Equilibria: The Case of Customs Unions. In J. Bhagwati, P. Krishna & A. Panagariya (Eds.), Trading blocs: alternative approaches to analyzing preferential trade agreements (pp. 207-213). Cambridge: MIT Press.

Krueger, A. O. (1999). Are Preferential Trading Arrangements Trade-Liberalizing or Protectionist? Journal of Economic Perspectives, 13(4), 105-124.

Lamy, P. (2002). Stepping Stones or Stumbling Blocks? the EU's Approach Towards the Problem of Multilateralism vs Regionalism in Trade Policy. The World Economy, 1399-1413.

Marceau, G., & Reimann, C. (2001). When and How Is a Regional Trade Agreement Compatible with the WTO? Legal Issues of Economic Integration, 297-336.

Mathis, J. H. (2000). The Community's External Regional Policy in the WTO. In P. van Dijck & G. Faber (Eds.), The External Economic Dimension of the European Union (pp. 127-150). Den Haag et al.

Panagariya, A. (1999). The regionalism debate: an overview. The World Economy, 477-511.

Roselieb, G. (1961). Die rechtliche Stellung der europäischen Wirtschaftszusammenschlüsse (Montan-Union, EWG, EFTA) zum GATT. Österreichische Zeitschrift für Öffentliches Recht, XI, 27-69.

Tevini, A. G. (2011). Article XXIV. In R. Wolfrum, P.-T. Stoll & H. P. Hestermeyer (Eds.), WTO – Trade in Goods (pp. 616-661). Leiden et al.: Martinus Nijhoff.

Then de Lammerskötter, R. (2004). WTO und Regional Trade Agreements (RTAs). Artikel XXIV und die enabling clause im Lichte eines idealen Regulierungssystems. Hamburg: Lit Verlag.

Venables, A. J. (2003). Winners and Losers from Regional Integration Agreements. The Economic Journal, 113(October), 747-761.

Viner, J. (1950). The customs union issue. New York: The Carnegie Endowment for International Peace.

WTO. (1996). Organization, Comittee on Regional Trade Agreements, Decision of 6 February 1996. WT/L/127.

WTO. (1998a). Communication from Australia. WT/REG/W/22.

WTO. (1998b). Communication from Australia, Addendum. WT/REG/W/22/Add.1.

WTO. (1998c). Committee on Regional Trade Agreements, Sixteenth Session, Note on the Meetings of 16-18 and 20 February 1998. WT/REG/M/16.

WTO. (1998d). Committee on Regional Trade Agreements, Seventeenth Session, Note on the Meetings of 4-5 and 7-8 May 1998. WT/REG/M/17.

WTO. (1999a). Turkey – Restrictions on Imports of Textile and Clothing Products, Report of the Panel. WT/DS34/R.

WTO. (1999b). Turkey – Restrictions on Imports of Textile and Clothing Products, Report of the Appellate Body. WT/DS34/AB/R.

WTO. (2001). Thirtieth Session, Examination of the Free Trade Agreement between the European Communities and Mexico, Note on the Meeting of 26 September 2001. WT/REG109/M/1.

WTO. (2006a). Transparency Mechanism for Regional Trade Agreements. WT/L/671.

WTO. (2006b). Free Trade Agreement between the European Communities and Mexico, Communication from the Parties. WT/REG109/6.

WTO. (2011). *Regional trade agreements information system (RTA-IS)*. Retrieved from http://rtais.wto.org/UI/PublicMaintainRTAHome.aspx.

Investment Protection Standards in the Mexico – European Union Bilateral Investment Treaties: Fair and Equitable Treatment and Full Protection and Security

Gabriel Cavazos Villanueva & Magda Carolina Sánchez Navarro[†]

1. Introduction

The purpose of this article is to analyze the Mexican experience with respect to the negotiation and implementation of the Bilateral Investment Treaties (BITs) concluded with countries of the European Union (EU). The analysis is focused on two of the most controversial standards in international investment law. On one hand, the obligation to provide "fair and equitable treatment" (FET) is part of the protection due to foreign direct investment (FDI) by host countries. In this context, this obligation refers to the "standard of treatment" often stated in most BITs and the investment chapters of some of the free trade agreements (FTA's) concluded by Mexico. On the other hand, the obligation to provide "full protection and security" (FPS) is in many treaties linked with FET as part of the minimum standard of treatment.

The level of protection given to an investment in a foreign territory is a significant element to consider for international investors. The most common international practices for the protection of foreign investments are the execution of a BIT or the inclusion of an investment chapter in FTAs. The former type of international agreement is implemented between two States for the reciprocal protection of the investments made by investors of the other contracting Party in their territory.

Consequently, each BIT is different. Nonetheless, international law and the practice of international investment arbitration have identified a number of basic elements that a BIT must contain, e.g., the scope of application of the agreement, namely, what is considered as an investment as well as the definition of an investor.

In addition, BITs generally contain several basic substantive standards. Among these we can find absolute standards, such as the obligation to grant FET and FPS to all foreign investments made in the host state, and relative standards,

---

EGAP Gobierno y Política Pública, Tecnológico de Monterrey.

† Corporate Affairs, Industrias Alen.

such as Most Favored Nation (MFN) and National Treatment (NT). (UNCTAD, 2007, page 28.) [1]

The execution of BITs and the inclusion of these protection standards may be one of the reasons foreign investment from European Union (EU) Countries in Mexico has grown in the past years. (Alexander, 2008, page 829). [2] Thus, even while FDI in Mexico experienced a decrease of 50.7% in 2009, the flow of investments from EU countries was still implortant (Secretariat of Economy, 2010) amounting to 24.4% of the total of FDI in Mexico, positioned just after the investments of the United States' investors.

As of January 2012, Mexico had concluded BITs with 15 EU Countries (Secretary of Foreign Affairs, 2010),[3] each of them were negotiated individually, due to the fact that the conclusion of treaties regarding FDI was, at the time, under the exclusive authority of Member States.[4] In this context, each BIT contains minimum but substantial differences. However, a common element is that most of them establish the obligation of the state to grant FET as well as FPS to foreign investments. Nevertheless, some BITs connect these obligations to the minimum standard established by customary international law, while some others link the standards to the principles of international law, and others consider FET and FPS as self-contained standards. Each classification involves different rights and obligations for both the investor and the host state.

In the field of international investment law, compliance with these standards is essential with respect to the relationship between foreign investors and host States, regardless of the classification they are linked to.

The interest on this particular subject and specially the focus on FPS and FET of this article, are due to the fact that they both constitute absolute standards of investment protection included in most BITs between Mexico and EU Countries. Also, as causes of action, FET and FPS are common allegations which tribunals must construe in almost every case, but that still remain undefined. For example, FET is probably the most nebulous and vague of the standards of treatment, and

1 An absolute standard of treatment, also called non-contingent, means that the treatment given to investments in a situation will not reference the standards that are applicable to other investments or entities; when referring to a relative standard, the treatment to be granted to an investment will reference the treatment accorded to another investment.

2 Other factors to consider are the country's gross domestic product, population, levels of domestic investment, level of political risk, stability, availability of human capital, and degree of market liberalization as well as a company's predictions for immediate profit also play critical roles in affecting an investor's decision to choose a particular country.

3 The Belgium/Luxembourg Union, Germany, France, Sweden, Spain, The Slovak Republic, United Kingdom, The Czech Republic, Austria, Denmark, Finland, Greece, Italy, the Netherlands and Portugal.

4 See Section 1 of this paper for an explanation of the changes under the Lisbon Treaty.

its content "... has become a focal point of discussion, particularly as claimants have placed emphasis on this standard of treatment in NAFTA (NAFTA, 1992) litigation." (Sornarajah, 2004), Accordingly, even while the context of this article is the Mexico-EU BITs, the analysis made of FET and FPS may serve as a guideline to understand said standards even outside EU BITs.

Consequently, this article seeks to explain the normative content of the FET and FPS standards included in the BITs that Mexico has executed with EU countries, by identifying the obligation of a host state with respect to foreign investments in the context of these standards. In other words: What is the consequence of linking an obligation to international law principles as opposed to the minimum standard of customary international law? Which conducts of a host country are permitted and which are forbidden? And, what is the consequence of the fact that a standard for the protection of investments is considered as an autonomous concept?

To provide possible answers to these questions, this article is divided into four sections: In the first section, the process of negotiation of Mexico-EU BITs is explained. This section also addresses the recent modifications made to the Treaty of the European Community (The Lisbon Treaty, 2008)[5], particularly the new authority of the EU to conclude BITs, as opposed to the authority for each Member state.

Section 2 sets a general notion of FET and its contractual nature. As a first approach to the understanding of the concept, two standpoints are analyzed: the additive and restrictive interpretations. The fundamental elements and relevant interpretations to the standard made by arbitral tribunals are also examined. Also, this section analyzes FET in accordance with each of the classifications given to the standard by the BITs concluded between Mexico and EU Countries, i.e., in accordance to international law principles, as well as in accordance to customary international law, and as a self-contained standard, providing examples of interpretations by tribunals in various cases. A special emphasis is given in this section to the *Tecmed* (TECMED v. The United Mexican States, 2003) case, which up to now is the only dispute adjudicated by an arbitral tribunal under a BIT concluded between Mexico and a EU country. Finally, this section deals with the relationship between FET and other standards of investment protection.

---

5 The Treaty of Lisbon amended the EU's two fundamental treaties, the Treaty on European Union and the Treaty establishing the European Community. The latter is renamed as the Treaty on the Functioning of the European Union. See Treaty of Lisbon amending the Treaty on European Union and the Treaty establishing the European Community, signed at Lisbon, 13 December 2007 *Official Journal C 306 of 17 December 2007.*

Section 3 deals with the meaning and content of FPS, and also with the interpretations given to the standard, in accordance with the references made in the Mexico-EU BITs.

Finally, the last section contains the conclusions of this article.

2. The new EU investment policy

2.1 General Framework of the new policy

Before the entry into force of the Treaty of Lisbon (The Lisbon Treaty, 2008) on December 2009, the EU as a whole was not entitled to negotiate investment treaties or investment chapters in FTAs as a single entity; therefore, each Member State had to negotiate and conclude BITs.[6] Accordingly, Mexico signed 15 BITs with 16 EU Member States between 1996 and 2009.

Some commentators highlight the importance of BITs as the main way to secure FDI (Delegation of the European Union to Russia, 2010). In this context, it is interesting to note that Mexico has concluded BITs with 12 of the top 13 European countries investing in Mexico[7]. As of 2012, all the agreements remain valid and only the Mexico-Spain BIT ("Mexico-Spain BIT", 2010) has been renegotiated in 2008.

Article 188C of the Treaty of Lisbon states, *inter alia*, the following: "... The common commercial policy shall be based on uniform principles, particularly with regard to changes in tariff rates, the conclusion of tariff and trade agreements relating to trade in goods and services, and the commercial aspects of intellectual property, foreign direct investment, the achievement of uniformity in measures of liberalization, export policy and measures to protect trade such as those to be taken in the event of dumping or subsidies.

The common commercial policy shall be conducted in the context of the principles and objectives of the Union's external action..." (The Lisbon Treaty, 2008)[8], pursuant to this, the European Commission has launched a comprehensive European international investment policy. In this context, a *Proposal for a Regulation of the European Parliament and of the Council establishing transitional arrangements for BITs between EU Member States and third countries*

6 Prior to the entry into force of the Treaty of Lisbon, Article 133 did not establish foreign direct investment as a part of the common commercial policy of the EU, also the ECJ, in its Opinion 1/94, judged that Member States remained competent for many topics embraced by GATS and TRIPS.

7 Secretariat of Economy, the only of these 13 countries with witch Mexico has not signed a BIT is Ireland.

8 See *supra* note 5.

(European Commission, 2010)[9] was issued on July 7, 2010. The Proposal establishes a transitional framework towards the harmonization of an EU investment policy and arguably a possible development of an EU Model BIT (European Commission, 2010).

Nonetheless, the European Commission has expressed concerns in this respect, stating that:

> "one-size-fits-all model for investment agreements with 3rd [sic] countries would necessarily be neither feasible nor desirable. The Union will have to take into account each specific negotiating context. The interests of our stakeholders as well as the level of development of our partners should guide inter alia the standards the Union sets in a specific investment negotiation. In the same way, the nature of the existing agreements of Member States with any given third country need to be taken into account. While BITs recently concluded by Member States have largely a similar structure and content, there are some variations. These might equally determine the objectives to be pursued in a specific negotiating context." (European Commission, 2010)[10]

Despite the above referred caveat, the new European policy seeks to integrate investment liberalization and investment protection. From now on, investment negotiations with Non-EU countries will enlarge and protect the competitive space currently available to all EU investors, making sure that the best levels of protection negotiated by some Member States are extended to all (European Commission, 2010). Furthermore, by negotiating as a block, the EU will have a better leverage than individual Member States, and increased investment flows will lead to increased trade flows (European Commission, 2010).

Also, the above referred Proposal is aimed at "providing for an explicit guarantee of legal certainty as regards the conditions under which investors operate" (European Commission, 2010). It also establishes the conditions as well as a procedural framework for the negotiation and conclusion by EU Member States of BITs. It is important to note, that the Proposal authorizes the continuation in force of all international agreements relating to investment concluded between EU Member States and third countries.

Overall, the Proposal seeks, *inter alia,* to:

1. Authorize the continued existence of all investment agreements currently in force between Member States and third countries;
2. Establish a framework and conditions to empower Member States to enter into negotiations with a third country with a view to modifying an existing BIT; and

---

9 Proposal for a Regulation of the European Parliament and of the Council establishing transitional arrangements for BITs between EU Member States and third countries,

10 Communication from the Commission to the Council, the European Parliament, the European Economic and Social Committee and the Committee of the Regions.

3. Allow Member States to negotiate and conclude, under certain conditions set out by the Proposal, a new BIT with a third country. This includes a requirement to submit to the European Commission a notification in which the Member State expresses its intention to negotiate an agreement. In this context, the Commission shall conduct a review of the conformity of the proposed agreement with the law of the EU and other relevant policies (European Commission, 2010).

Even though the European Commission has not established a centralized *ad hoc* body that conducts negotiations of BITs on behalf of the EU, the power of the Member States to conclude BITs is now limited to the scrutiny of the Commission, as provided by the new policy. Given that the Union is exclusively competent for FDI, and that an EU investment policy will be gradually developed, the procedure established by the proposal must be regarded as an exceptional transitional measure.

Additionally, México has reiterated its intent to renegotiate the investment chapter within the EU-Mexico FTA, and incorporate the protections granted to foreign investment by the BITs concluded between Mexico and UE Member States; therefore, Mexico anticipates that the Union's new exclusive competence on FDI will allow for the negotiation and conclusion of a single investment chapter (Comisión parlamentaria mixta México-UE, 2009).

2.2 Evolution of investment regulation in the EU

Prior to the entry into force of the Treaty of Lisbon, Article 43 of the Treaty Establishing the European Community (EC Treaty) recognized the freedom of establishment within the EU. This meant that an EU citizen was entitled to establish and pursue self-sustained profitable activities under the same conditions laid down by the law of the host state for its own nationals. In addition, under article 48 of the EC Treaty, companies incorporated pursuant to the law of a Member State and having their registered office, central administration or principal place of business within the EU, as well as companies from third countries incorporated in accordance to the law of an EU Member State, had the same rights as a natural person national of a member state (Hjälmroth y Westerberg).

Nonetheless, the EU Treaty granted substantive protections beyond the prohibition of discrimination. The Treaty also required for the removal of any unjustified barriers to establishment. In this context, the use of discriminatory measures could only be justified when they arose from the exercise of official authority (as permitted by article 45) and as a matter of public policy, public security and public health (article 46).

The conditions for the use of non discriminatory measures have been analyzed by the European Court of Justice (ECJ). In the case of *Dieter Kraus v. Land Baden-Württemberg* in which the ECJ established that a measure that hinders the freedom of establishment must fulfill the following: a) it must be applied in a non-discriminatory manner; it must be justified by imperative requirements in the general interest; it must be suitable for securing the attainment of the objective which it pursues and must not go beyond what is necessary in order to attain it (principle of proportionality) (Kraus v. Baden- Württemberg, 1993)

As has been stated, and pursuant to the Treaty of Lisbon, FDI has been included as a part of the EU's common commercial policy. However, some issues such as the scope of the EU's common commercial policy over FDI remain unclear. According to some commentators, article 188C (formerly article 133) of Treaty of Lisbon could be given a wide interpretation, meaning that the EU would have exclusive competence over both the pre and post-establishment phase in the conclusion of a BIT, as opposed to a narrow interpretation, which would limit the EU's competence to post-establishment issues, namely, a similar approach as to the one established by the EC Treaty in Articles 56 and 57 (Hjälmroth y Westerberg).

In this line of argument, a wide interpretation, meaning that the EU competence covers both the pre-establishment phase and the post-establishment phase of investment, would enable the EU to negotiate investment protection for all Member States, and arguably, that could also imply that many EU Member States' BITs could eventually be replaced by EU BITs containing homogeneous substantive protections (Hjälmroth y Westerberg). This ′wide interpretation′ position was adopted by the Commission in the above referred Communication.[11]

The Commission rationalizes its view of article 188C based on an analysis of the economic impact of investment provisions in regional trade agreements concluded in the framework of the OECD[12] which states that "research has confirmed that substantive investment provisions in broad trade agreements impact trade and FDI flows more profoundly, also, the combination of substantive investment rules and provisions liberalizing other parts of the economy jointly impact trade and investment more significantly" (OECD, 2006). Additionally, the Commission states that investment negotiations with third countries should

11 See *supra* note 10, 2(b) Towards a common international investment policy. "A comprehensive common international investment policy needs to better address investor needs from the planning to the profit stage or from the pre- to the post-admission stage. Thus, our trade policy will seek to integrate investment liberalization and investment protection." This communication was issued simultaneously to the Proposal. Both are considered to be the first steps in the development of a European International Investment Policy.

12 Organisation for Economic Co-operation and Development.

be substantially based on the more than 1100 BITs currently in force for EU Member States, because this "will enable the EU to enlarge, better define and protect the competitive space that is available to all EU investors". (European Commission, 2010)

It is important to mention, the Treaty of Lisbon includes a restriction to the scope of Article 188C, which is that the competence of the EU regarding FDI will not be extended to other areas, such as taxation or labor laws, unless it is explicitly established, this is, the EU's exclusive competence on FDI will not affect the division of competence in other areas. (Hjälmroth y Westerberg)

2.3 BITs Concluded by EU Member States prior to the entry into force of the Treaty of Lisbon

Before the entry into force of the Treaty of Lisbon not all Member States had concluded BITs and not all the agreements that were concluded included similar levels of investment protection. This lack of consistency has lead to an uneven playing field for EU companies investing in third countries. Also, some of the existent BITs refer to the treatment of investors "post-entry" or "post-admission" only. In this context, they did not provide for specific binding commitments regarding the conditions of entry, neither to EU nor vice versa. (European Commission, 2010)

In general, most existing BITs contain the following provisions: a) Non-discrimination of foreign investors, through the standards of national treatment and most favored nation treatment; b) minimum standard of treatment, such as FET and FPS; c) Free transfer of capital; d) The right to compensation for expropriation; e) A mechanism for the settlement of disputes, via state-state or investor-state.

In the framework of the new EU investment policy a possible objective will be to fill the gaps at EU level covering investment market access and investment liberalization, especially by ensuring the non-discriminatory treatment of EU investors upon entry to a third country. (Hjälmroth y Westerberg, at 3A).

2.4 BIT Arbitration under the proposed regulation

Pursuant to the Proposal (European Commission, 2010), the Commission will control BIT arbitration between Member States and third parties. This regulation states that the "Member State shall … immediately inform the Commission of any request for dispute settlement … as soon as the Member State becomes aware of the request". Also, it requires the Member State to "fully cooperate" with the Commission and "take all necessary measures to ensure an effective defence which may include, where appropriate, that the Commission participates in the procedure". (European Commission, 2010, Article 13[2])

Also, the Proposal establishes that Member States will lose the capacity to initiate (or not initiate) arbitrations under BITs (McDermott Will & Emery, 2010). It establishes that they "shall seek the agreement of the Commission before activating any relevant mechanisms for dispute settlement … and shall, where requested by the Commission, activate such mechanisms". (European Commission, 2010, Article 13[3])

Furthermore, in its Communication, the Commission also states some guidelines towards a comprehensive European International Investment Policy noting, inter alia, that the "current [international dispute resolution] structures are to some extent ill-adapted to the advent of the Union". (European Commission, 2010 at. 3[d])

This Communication also highlights that since the EU cannot be a party to the International Centre for Settlement of Investment Disputes (ICSID) Convention (since it is neither a member state of the World Bank nor a party to the Statue of the International Court of Justice), when approaching investor-state dispute settlement mechanisms the EU should base its perspective on Member States' experiences, always working for transparency in the process, consistency and predictability, as well as the use of quasi-permanent arbitrators and/or appellate mechanisms. (European Commission, 2010 at. 3[d])

Nonetheless, the Communication raises the possibility of the EU (as a single member) of seeking to accede to the ICSID Convention; however, this would require the ICSID Convention to be amended. A similar situation was presented to the World Customs Organization, with whom the European Communities successfully negotiated the amendment of, and subsequent accession to its agreement. (European Commission, 2010 at. 3[d])

Overall, the Commission also acknowledges investor-state as the desired dispute settlement mechanism stating that "investor-state is such an established feature of investment agreements that its absence would in fact discourage investors and make a host economy less attractive than others" (European Commission, 2010 at. 3[d])

2.5 Substantive investment protections under the new investment policy

As has been stated in section 1.3 of this chapter, the EU's investment policy has relied mostly on the principle of non-discrimination (European Commission, 2010 at. 3[c]), and while this is a fundamental element of investment protection, BITs also include other standards of treatment such as FET and FPS. Moreover, BITs also include the protection of contractual rights through umbrella clauses, as well as the conditions in which a State can exercise its right to expropriate.

Therefore, the EU's investment policy should contemplate the need to include precise clauses on investment protection standards. In this respect, the Commission states that:

> "A clear formulation of the balance between the different interests at stake, such as the protection of investors against unlawful expropriation or the right of each Party to regulate in the public interest, needs to be ensured. Likewise, EU clauses ensuring the free transfer of funds of capital and payments by investors should be included, taking also into account the way the EU and its Member States regulate economic activities in and out of the Union, this is, investment agreements should be consistent with other policies, including protection to the environment, conditions for work, health and safety at work, consumer protection and cultural diversity, among others, and guided by the principles and objectives of the Union. (European Commission, 2010 at. 3[c]).

In sum, the new EU investment policy will not substantially modify the current status of the Mexico-EU BITs; however it does introduce a more active control of the EU institutions over the negotiation of future agreement and the operation of the dispute settlement mechanisms, whit the clear objective of future harmonization. In this context, it seems that a clear formulation of the FET and FPS standards needs to be ensured in future investment treaties. Relevant for the purposes of this paper, and as it is explained in the following chapters, these standards are somehow inconsistent in the current language of the various EU BITs with Mexico.

3. Fair and Equitable Treatment in the context of the Mexico-EU BITs.

As has been established in the previous chapter, FET is one of the substantive investment protection standards included in the EU BITs. Because the different BITs have not been negotiated by the EU as a block, the standard has been formulated in different manners in the various treaties concluded with Mexico. In the following sections, this chapter analyzes the general notion of the standard based on the language of relevant provisions of the BITs, and the interpretations given by arbitral tribunals when the standard is used a as a cause of action.

3.1 General notion of FET

FET has evolved throughout the development and evolution of international investment arbitration and currently constitutes a fundamental concept within the investment protection field. Every BIT concluded between Mexico and EU Member States contains a provision relating to FET as well as the level of treatment expected from the host state to foreign investment. Furthermore, considering the growth of investment arbitration in the past years[13] the uncertainty as to the content of FET could impose a considerable burden for the state or an unreachable threshold for investors, hence, the need to provide a normative content of FET.

Two basic standpoints have appeared when trying to interpret FET; an additive interpretation, also called the plain meaning view, by which the standards will be considered as independent, separate from the minimum standard, imposing obligations and granting rights on their own (Kill, 2008), and a restrictive interpretation which argues that absolute standards of treatment merely affirm the minimum standard (Vasciannie, 1990) and do not impose obligations to the state beyond those generally acknowledged under customary international law.

However, the existence of radically opposed views of FET has not help clarify the content of the standard. Moreover, a survey made by UNCTAD of the existing BITs throughout the world identified at least seven (UNCTAD, 2007)[14] different standpoints for the interpretation of the FET standard.

In the context of the Mexico-EU BITs three of these standpoints emerge: FET as a self-contained standard, FET as a standard linked to international law, and FET as a standard linked to customary international law. Due to these inconsistencies throughout BITs, arbitral tribunals have taken upon themselves the task to identify elements that pertain to each classification of FET. The following are some examples of interpretations given to FET in cases involving BITs which did not have a consistent position for the standard.

4.3.1 The interpretation of FET in accordance to international law principles

Currently only the Mexico-Sweden BIT ("Mexico-Sweden BIT") and the Mexico-France BIT ("Mexico-France BIT") connect FET to the principles of international law. One case has been filed before the ICSID pursuant to the latter between an investor from France and Mexico, although an award was rendered on June 18, 2010, as of November 2010 it has not been published. (Gemplus, S.A., SLP, S.A. and Gemplus Industrial, S.A. de C.V. v. United Mexican States)

---

13 This assertion can be made particularly in the case of Mexico, which as of December 2008 had 18 claims filed against it before the ICSID, making it the second most recurred defendant, just after Argentina.

14 Some BITs provide the FET standard without any reference to international law or any further criteria; some establish that the FET clause that sets national treatment or most favored nation treatment as the minimum standard for FET; others provide for a FET obligation that appears in the same clause as the duty to abstain from impairing the investment through unreasonable or discriminatory measures; others consider the FET standard to be linked to the principles of international law; others consider FET as a standard that is linked to international law; some others provide for FET that is contingent on the domestic legislation of the host country; and others establish the FET standard as referring to the minimum customary international law standard.

In the Mexico-France BIT, FET is connected to international law principles, reading as follows:

> "Article 4. Protection and treatment of investments. 1. Each Contracting Party shall undertake to accord in its territory and maritime zone just and equitable treatment, in accordance with the principles of international law, to the investments made by investors of the other Party and to ensure that the exercise of the right so granted is not impeded either de jure or de facto". ("Mexico-France BIT")

One case solved by an ICSID tribunal dealing with the scope of FET in accordance with international law was *CMS v. Argentina* (CMS v. Argentina, 2005). In this case the claimant asserted that Argentina had violated the standard by failing to provide stability and predictability of the investment environment, with particular reference to the *CME* (CME v. The Czech Republic, 2001) case where it was held that "[The Government] breached its obligation of fair and equitable treatment by evisceration of the arrangements in reliance upon [which] the foreign investor was induced to invest." Consequently, the scope of FET had to be defined. In doing so, the tribunal considered the objective of the BIT and held that "a stable legal and business environment is an essential element of fair and equitable treatment" (CMS v. Argentina, 2005, at. para. 274) and also that the standard is "inseparable from stability and predictability". (CMS v. Argentina, 2005, at. para. 276)

In this context, by linking FET to international law principles, the reach for its interpretation is extended, allowing for any norm or provision considered to be a part of the international legal system to constitute a reference point when analyzing FET.

Another case that dealt with the interpretation of FET in accordance to international law was *Metalclad v. Mexico,* (Metalclad v. United Mexican States, 2000) pursuant to NAFTA Article 1105(1) "*each Party shall accord to investments of investors of another Party treatment in accordance with international law, including fair and equitable treatment and full protection and security*". It is important to point out that the award on this case came out before the binding interpretation from the NAFTA Free Trade Commission (Foreign Affairs and International Trade Canada, 2001); therefore FET was interpreted in accordance to the international law principles.

In this case the investment of *Metalclad,* an American investor, was damaged by the host state's interference with the development and operation of a hazardous waste landfill in San Luis Potosí, Mexico. The interference was basically the denial of a municipal construction permit citing environmental impact considerations, which prevented *Metalclad* from continuing its activities. (Metalclad v. United Mexican States, 2000, at. p. 47-51)

The tribunal in *Metalclad* held that transparency is a fundamental notion of FET and stated that this notion includes "all relevant legal requirements for the purpose of initiating, completing and successfully operating investments made, or intended to be made, under the Agreement" (Metalclad v. United Mexican States, 2000, at. para. 76.), therefore when Mexico denied the municipal permit it "failed to ensure a transparent and predictable framework for Metalclad's business planning and investment" (Metalclad v. United Mexican States, 2000, at. para. 99.)

After the award was issued, Mexico challenged it in Vancouver, Canada, the place where the arbitration took place. The British Columbia Supreme Court concluded that the breaches of FET found by the arbitral tribunal, based on lack of transparency, were beyond the scope of the submission to arbitration, since lack of transparency is neither a violation to customary international law nor a violation to NAFTA Chapter 11. (Cavazos, 2007)

In sum, when the treaty makes an explicit reference to international law principles, it allows the adjudicator to consider every rule that pertains to international law. In this respect, even interpretations of legal bodies foreign to a particular jurisdiction, such as the case of the NAFTA FTC (Foreign Affairs and International Trade Canada, 2001) in the context of Mexico-EU BITs, can be argued as applicable since it not only can be considered to reflect the opinion of Mexico as to the content of FET, but also because, as a binding resolution issued by a recognized subject of international law, it is arguably a part of general international law. (Glamis Gold Ltd. v. United States, 2010)

3.1.2 The interpretation of FET as a standard linked to customary international law

Four[15] BITs concluded between Mexico and EU Countries connect FET to customary international law, however, most of the examples of cases where tribunals have had to analyze FET in accordance to customary law have taken place in the context of NAFTA, after the FTC binding interpretation.

An example of this type of provision reads as follows:

> "ARTICLE 3. Minimum Standard of Treatment in Accordance with Customary International Law. 1. Investments of investors of each Contracting Party shall at all times be accorded treatment in accordance with customary international law, including fair and equitable treatment and full protection and security, in the territory of the other Contracting Party". (OCDE, 2004)

15 The Mexico-Spain BIT, The Mexico-Slovak BIT, The Mexico-Czech Republic BIT and the Mexico-United Kingdom BIT.

A case dealing with FET linked to customary law was *Waste Management v. Mexico* (Waste Management, Inc. v. Mexico, 2004). This claim arises from a concession for the provision of waste disposal services in Acapulco, Guerrero, granted to Acaverde, a Mexican company created in 1994, and a wholly owned subsidiary of Waste Management Inc. The concession agreement provided that the city would not grant to any other company or person any right or concession inconsistent with the exclusive rights of the concessionaire. In addition to providing collection services, Acaverde would build and operate a permanent solid waste landfill for the city, which would allow for the closure of two existing temporary sites, the city was responsible for providing a site for this new landfill, and pending the construction of the permanent landfill Acaverde would be given, free of charge, access to one of the existing sites (Waste Management, Inc. v. Mexico, 2004, at pp.40-55). The city also received a line of credit from Banobras, a Mexican bank in order to pay for Acaverde's services. However, before Acaverde began its activities under the agreement, the city issued a regulation for the Rendering of the Public Cleaning Service Concession, which established exclusivity of waste collection services, prohibited dumping of rubbish in the area and provided for enforcement by way of fines. Waste Management's claim was based among others, on a breach of NAFTA articles 1105, the minimum standard of treatment, and 1110 the prohibition to expropriation. The claimant argues that the city failed to comply with the payments and granted permits to third parties that violated the terms of the concession agreement. (Waste Management, Inc. v. Mexico, 2004, at para. 109).

The tribunal analyzed FET in accordance to the FTC interpretation, this is, in accordance to the minimum standard of customary international law, and held the following:

> "The minimum standard of treatment of fair and equitable treatment is infringed by conduct attributable to the State and harmful to the claimant if the conduct is arbitrary, grossly unfair, unjust or idiosyncratic, is discriminatory and exposes the claimant to sectional or racial prejudice, or involves a lack of due process leading to an outcome which offends judicial propriety – as might be the case with a manifest failure of natural justice in judicial proceedings or a complete lack of transparency and candour in an administrative process. In applying this standard it is relevant that the treatment is in breach of representations made by the host State which were reasonably relied on by the claimant." (Waste Management, Inc. v. Mexico, 2004, at. para. 98.).

This definition establishes two preconditions for a conduct to constitute a violation to FET, first that the conduct is undoubtedly attributable to the state, and second that said conduct translates into an actual damage to foreign investment. Also, the tribunal holds that a conduct violates FET when is arbitrary, grossly unfair, unjust or idiosyncratic, this elements encompass a wide variety of actions.

In other words, each one can be extended beyond its wording, for example, the concept of idiosyncrasy contains the prohibition to violate an international agreement alleging domestic law, and the concept of an arbitrary, grossly unfair, unjust conduct contains elements of not only absolute, but relative standards of treatment that can constitute a violation of FET.

Consequently, when a BIT links FET to customary law it limits the references for its interpretation to those rules that have actually reached this rank. This would, at first, seem to benefit a state since it would only be obligated to abide by the recognized rules of customary international law, which entail very specific and sometimes difficult requirements for their existence. However, some interpretations by arbitral tribunals appear to indicate the contrary. Concepts such as arbitrariness (which has been defined by the ICJ as a "willful disregard of due process of law, an act which shocks, or at least surprises, a sense of judicial propriety") *(United States of America v. Italy, 1989)* and unfairness have been used as elements to analyze a conduct and determine whether it violates FET or not, giving a certain advantage to the investor since these concepts can very well be broaden and encompass many elements that can cause a tribunal to consider that the state has breached its obligations under the BIT.

3.1.3 The interpretation of FET as a self-contained standard

Several[16] BITs concluded between Mexico and EU Member States consider FET as a self-contained standard, to this date there has not been a dispute relating to these BITs.

An example of this type of provision can be found in the Mexico-Portugal BIT in the following terms:

> "ARTICLE 2. Promotion and Protection of Investments. 1. Each Contracting Party shall promote and encourage, as far as possible, within its territory investments made by investors of the other Contracting Party and shall admit such investments into its territory in accordance with its laws and regulations. It shall in any case accord such investments fair and equitable treatment". ("Mexico-Portugal BIT")

FET was analyzed as a self contained standard by the arbitral tribunal in the *EDF v. Romania* case, which interpreted FET in accordance to the UK-Romania BIT. ("UK-Romania BIT", 1995)[17] In the analysis of their interpretational standpoint

16 The Mexico-Germany BIT, the Mexico-Belgium/Luxembourg Union BIT, the Mexico-Austria BIT, the Mexico-Denmark BIT, the Mexico-Finland BIT, the Mexico-Greece BIT, the Mexico-Italy BIT, the Mexico-Netherlands BIT, and the Mexico-Portugal BIT.

17 "Article 2. Promotion and Protection of Investment (2) Investments of nationals or companies of each Contracting Party shall at all times be accorded fair and equitable treatment and shall enjoy full protection and security in the territory of the other Contracting Party."

the tribunal noted: "there is no definition in the BIT of "fair and equitable treatment" (FET), nor is there a general consensus on the meaning of this phrase by ICSID tribunals" (Edf Limited v. Romania, 2009), hence, FET had to be considered as a self-contained standard. In their resolution the tribunal also acknowledged the existence of some fundamental elements of FET, such as transparency, stability and the protection of the investor's legitimate expectations, good faith, freedom from coercion and harassment, and compliance with contractual obligations, as well as the generally accepted view that the standard is independent of legality or illegality under domestic law (Edf Limited v. Romania, 2009, at para. 104).

Finally, the Tribunal held that the conduct of Romania with regard to *EDF's* investments violated its obligation under the BIT to provide FET, not to impair the maintenance, use or enjoyment of the investment by unreasonable or discriminatory measures, to observe its contractual agreements, and to compensate investors for expropriation.

A similar case dealing with the interpretation of FET as a self-contained standard was *Saluka v. Czech Republic* (Saluka v. Czech Republic, 2006) resolved pursuant to the Czech Republic-Netherlands BIT. ("Czech Republic-Netherlands BIT", 1975) In this case the claimant argued that FET was a specific and autonomous standard and it should be interpreted broadly. To support this view, *Saluka* relied upon the decision on the *Pope & Talbot* (Pope & Talbot Inc. v. The Government of Canada, 2002) case where the tribunal held that even when the treaty provision containing the standard makes no particular reference, the protection afforded by it cannot be considered as existing only against conduct that is "egregiously unfair", but to guarantee "the kind of hospitable climate that would insulate them from political risks or incidents of unfair treatment" (Pope & Talbot Inc. v. The Government of Canada, 2002). The claimant also argued that the BIT provision does not refer to any high threshold of unreasonableness or flagrancy of the conduct constituting a breach, and it must be considered broadly enough to provide real and effective protection, which would encourage investors to participate in the economy of the host state (Oxford University Press, 2006).

On the other hand, the respondent argued that FET is only a part of the minimum standard and its content must be defined in accordance to customary international law. The respondent relies on the *Genin* (Credit Limited, Inc. and A.S. Baltoil v. The Republic of Estonia, 2001) award, where the tribunal found that FET was a minimum standard and held that "acts that would violate this minimum standard would include acts showing a willful neglect of duty, an insufficiency of action falling far below international standards, or even subjective bad faith" (Credit Limited, Inc. and A.S. Baltoil v. The Republic of Estonia, 2001, at para. 367).

Both positions were analyzed. Finally, the tribunal concluded that since customary rules are immediately binding upon states, the conduct of the state would have to reflect a higher degree of incompatibility with the BIT to constitute a violation. The existence of a BIT that includes FET cannot be considered as a reflection of customary law, and the tribunal would be overreaching its power if it decided to interpret FET in accordance to customary international law. Therefore, in the present case, a low degree of incompatibility from the State's conduct with the BIT could constitute a violation to the standard (Saluka v. Czech Republic, 2006, p.p. 285-295).

In its award, the *Saluka* tribunal also stated that the *Genin* tribunal did acknowledge FET as a minimum standard but not as "the" minimum standard, therefore, FET must be interpreted autonomously and in accordance to the Vienna Convention. The tribunal also acknowledges the existence of essential elements of the standard and in that regard states that the legitimate expectations of the investor constitute a dominant element of FET (Saluka v. Czech Republic, 2006, at. para. 302), and held that a foreign investor under the BIT was entitled to expect the other party to act in a way that is not manifestly inconsistent, non-transparent, unreasonable or discriminatory.

In sum, when the FET standard is analyzed as an autonomous provision it allows for the tribunal itself to unveil its content, within the boundaries established by the Vienna Convention for the interpretation of treaties. This, even while seemingly dangerous due to its high of discretionary power, allows for a wider view of the external circumstances surrounding the claim, in other words, the consideration of the context of the investment and the possible reasons for the state's conduct, all this, while remaining aware and vigilant of the elements of FET already acknowledged to be contained by the standard.

As has been stated, as of November 2010 the only dispute involving a BIT between Mexico and a EU country, from which an award has been issued, is *Tecmed*, a case discussed in the following section.

3.1.4 Tecmed[18]

Técnicas Medioambientales Tecmed, S.A. v. The United Mexican States (Tecmed S.A. v. The United Mexican States, 2003) is the first investment dispute that arises out of a BIT against Mexico from which an arbitral tribunal renders an award.

This dispute was presented before the ICSID through an application requesting arbitration filed on January 28, 2000 by Técnicas Medioambientales Tecmed, S.A. against acts of the government of the United Mexican States. The Agreement on the Reciprocal Promotion and Protection of the Investment signed by

18 (Cavazos, 2007, pp. 168-174)

the Kingdom of Spain and the United Mexican States (Mexico-Spain BIT, 1996) constitutes the legal framework to the case, as it had already entered into force.

Tecmed is a commercial company organized under Spanish law, domiciled in Madrid, Spain which owns 99 % of Técnicas Medioambientales de México, S.A. that in turn holds 99 % of the shares of Cytrar, S.A. de C.V., both companies incorporated under Mexican law.

The investment that gives rise to this dispute was made through Cytrar, which kept the rights and obligations that Tecmed obtained in a public auction called by Promotora Inmobiliaria del Ayuntamiento de Hermosillo, a decentralized agency of the Municipality of Hermosillo, the capital of the State of Sonora, Mexico. The purpose of the auction was the sale of real property, buildings and facilities and other assets relating to a landfill of hazardous industrial waste located in Las Víboras, a community within the jurisdiction of the Municipality of Hermosillo. After the auction, Cytrar requested the Hazardous Materials, Waste and Activities Division of the National Ecology Institute[19], a Mexican Federal agency within the Ministry of the Environment, Natural Resources and Fisheries (SEMARNAP)[20], to issue at its name the operating license of the landfill, which at the moment, was in favor of an entity called Confinamiento Controlado Parque Industrial de Hermosillo O.P.D. This authorization entailed a permanent permit of operation. INE responded to Cytrar's request by issuing the authorization at its name, but also by changing its temporality, from a permanent to a temporary permit.

On November 25, 1998 the INE rejected the application for renewal of the authorization to operate the landfill made by Cytrar in order to replace the previous permit that expired on November 19, 1998. This action, according to the claimant, is the '... essential breach, which has caused the damage for which compensation is requested in this arbitration' (Tecmed S.A. v. The United Mexican States, 2003, at para. 57). In this context, it is important to mention that even though Tecmed refers to other actions and measures of the respondent in the briefs it submitted to the tribunal, the only act it is properly challenging is the refusal to renew the license to operate Cytrar's landfill.

Regarding the merits of the dispute, there are three causes of action alleged by the claimant: the first one is the argument of expropriation; the second is the violation to the FET standard, and the third one refers to FPS and other guarantees under the BIT. The issue on expropriation is worthy of a brief analysis, even though its discussion is beyond the scope of this paper.

19 Hereinafter referred as INE.

20 Currently the Ministry of the Environment and Natural Resources (SEMARNAT) due to the change in the Public Federal Administration Law on November 30, 2000.

With respect to the expropriation argument, the claimant affirmed that the fact of not renewing the permit to operate the landfill 'deprived Cytrar of its rights to use and enjoy the real and personal property forming the Landfill in accordance with its sole purpose, the Resolution put a end to the operation of the Landfill as an ongoing business exclusively engaged in the landfill hazardous waste, an activity that is only feasible under a permit, the renewal of which was denied (Tecmed S.A. v. The United Mexican States, 2003, at para. 96). As a response, the Mexican government referred to the discretionary powers of INE with respect to the granting and denying of permits, an action solely governed by domestic and not by international law. The respondent also relied on the legitimate action made by INE in compliance with State policy, and on the fact that the legislative framework remained unaltered.

In contrast, the claimant challenged the legitimacy of the refusal; by invoking arbitrary conduct due to the incoherence between the reasons stated and the proportion of the resolution.

The tribunal found the allegations made by the claimant as meritorious. It concluded that the resolution of the Mexican agency can be deemed as tantamount to an expropriation under section 5(1) of the Mexico – Spain BIT. The main reasons for this conclusion, as explained by the arbitral tribunal, are: a) the deprivation of the investor rights to obtain benefits arising from the investment made on the foreign country; b) the destruction of the economic and commercial value of the investment; and c) the impossibility to use the investment for another purpose because of the accumulation of hazardous waste and the new regulations applicable.

In addition, the tribunal made an interesting analysis on the reasonableness and proportionality of the measure. The tribunal analyzed the motives of the resolution in which concurred two opposite points of view: the claimant referred to political circumstances and to an environment of social pressure against the investment. In contrast, the respondent referred to an incident (the Alco Pacífico) in the transportation and managing of hazardous wastes, attributed to the claimant. With respect to the socio-political circumstances, the tribunal found that the pressures were not the most important factor to consider for the permit and, therefore, the agency's resolution was disproportionate with respect to the alleged cause.

In addition, the tribunal asserted that the Alco Pacífico situation was not a strong reason to deny the permit considering that PROFEPA (the Mexican agency in charge of the enforcement of environmental law) had already found certain violations, imposing a fine to Cytrar. This was certainly a minor penalty, because the agency concluded that the environment, the ecological balance and the health of the population were not compromised or at risk. In this context, the tribunal also finds a disproportion between the resolution and its alleged causes. In sum, the tribunal found that the Resolution and its effects amount to an expropriation in violation of Article 5 of the Mexico – Spain BIT (Tecmed S.A. v. The United Mexican States, 2003, at para. 151).

Regarding the alleged violation of the standard on FPS and other guarantees under the relevant BIT, the claimant based its arguments on the presumption that Mexican authorities encouraged the social pressure against the investors and consequently, they acted in an unreasonable and discriminatory manner. The tribunal on this claim considered that there were not sufficient evidence to get to that conclusion, and 'that the guarantee of full protection and security is not absolute and does not impose strict liability upon the State that grants it (Tecmed S.A. v. The United Mexican States, 2003, at para. 177). The tribunal also found that the refusal was not discriminatory and that was issued in accordance with the Mexican legal framework.

The most important analysis for the purposes of this paper is the one on FET. However, it is interesting to note that some normative elements considered for the analysis of expropriation and FPS, can also serve as a basis for a FET analysis. That is the case of the arguments on reasonableness and proportionality as well as the acts of the host-state in a discriminatory manner.

An interesting element in *Tecmed* is that the tribunal establishes a conceptualization of the FET standard as an expression and part of *bona fide* (good faith), taken as a principle recognized by international law (Tecmed S.A. v. The United Mexican States, 2003, at para. 153). The tribunal emphasizes that it is not necessary to act in bad faith (considered as the opposite of the previous) in order to breach this principle, as was stated in the *Mondev* case (Mondev v. United States, 2006). Consequently, after giving a statement on the conceptualization of this principle, the tribunal establishes a connection between the good faith principle with the concept of 'basic expectations'[21] by literally stating:

> "The Arbitral Tribunal considers that this provision of the Agreement, in light of the good faith principle established by international law, requires the Contracting Parties to provide to international investments treatment that does not affect the basic expectations that were taken into account by the foreign investor to make the investment. The foreign investor expects the host State to act in a consistent manner, free from ambiguity and totally transparently in its relations to the foreign investor, so it may know beforehand any and all the rules and regulations that will govern its investments, as well as the goals of the relevant policies and administrative practices or directives, to be able to plan its investment and comply with such regulations." (Mondev v. United States, 2006, at para. 154)

It is interesting to note that the arbitral tribunal, in one short paragraph, highlights and links at least three fundamental elements to define the normative content of

21 Also referred as 'fair expectations' and in other cases as 'legitimate expectations'.

the FET standard: good faith, legitimate (or basic) expectations, and transparency. With respect to the legitimate or basic expectations of the investor, the tribunal further explains some host State actions that can be included in the concept: (1) when the host State acts in a consistent manner, 'without arbitrarily revoking any preexisting decision or permits issued by the State that were relied upon by the investor to assume its commitments as well as to plan and launch its commercial and business activities (Mondev v. United States, 2006, at para. 154). (2) As has been stated, when the host state acts free from ambiguity and totally transparent in its relation with the foreign investment. (3) When the host State uses the legal instruments in conformity with its assigned function, '… the fair expectations of the Claimant were that the Mexican laws applicable to such investment, as well as the supervision, control prevention and punitive powers granted to the authorities in charge of managing such system, would be used for the purpose of assuring compliance with environmental protection, human health and ecological balance goals underlying such laws (Mondev v. United States, 2006, at para. 157).

The eloquent analysis of the standard given by the tribunal provides some other interesting elements. The arbitral tribunal attempts to provide an autonomous interpretation of the FET standard, although the bulk of the discussion is centered in the "good faith" principle, linked with those of basic expectations and transparency: 'The Arbitral Tribunal *understands that the scope of the undertaking of fair and equitable treatment* under Article 4(1) of the Agreement described above is that *resulting from an autonomous interpretation*, taking into account the text of Article 4(1) of the Agreement according to its ordinary meaning (Article 31 (1) of the Vienna Convention), or from international law and the good faith principle, on the basis of which the scope of the obligation assumed under the Agreement and the actions related to compliance therewith are to be assessed (Mondev v. United States, 2006, at para. 155).[22] Nevertheless, it can also be said that, for the construction of the FET standard in this case the tribunal used various methods, such as the literal interpretation: 'taking into account the text of Article 4(1) of the Agreement according to its ordinary meaning (Mondev v. United States, 2006, at para. 155), and the teleological interpretation: 'This is the goal of such undertaking in the light of the Agreement's preambular paragraphs which expresses the will and intention of the members States … (Mondev v. United States, 2006, at para. 156)

An important fact regarding the violation of the FET standard, according to the claimant, is the commitment of Cytrar to relocate the facility to a place free of socio-political pressure (Mondev v. United States, 2006, at para. 44). This

22 Emphasis added.

relocation was supposed to happen as soon as the authorities and Cytrar find the right place for the exchange of operations, where there was not an opposition by the citizens or a perceived potential damage to the environment. This fact was taken into account by the tribunal, which considered it was a reasonably expectation of Cytrar, based on the good faith principle, that the permit would continue operating in its original facilities until the relocation date. In addition, the tribunal points out that the authorities' statements to Cytrar about the landfill's relocation lacked of transparency (Mondev v. United States, 2006, at para. 44). INE did not unequivocally and clearly specify the deadlines, terms and conditions that would apply to the relocation …' (Mondev v. United States, 2006, at para. 44).

An additional form of treatment that it is considered in this case as inconsistent with the FET standard is the pressure that can be made through various forms of coercion. From the evidence presented in the case, the tribunal concludes that the resolution had, *inter alia*, the objective of forcing Cytrar to relocate the facility. 'Under such circumstances, such pressure involves forms of coercion that may be considered inconsistent with fair and equitable treatment to be given to international investment …' (Mondev v. United States, 2006, at para. 163) This conclusion is somehow similar to the arguments of "politicization" presented in *Azurix* (Azurix Corp. v. The Argentine Republic, 2006).

In sum, the decision on this case was adverse to the Mexican Government's interests because the tribunal found that the behavior of the respondent lead to a violation of the Mexico – Spain BIT, specifically of the provisions of Article 4(1). The arbitral tribunal found that INE's behavior '… conflicts with what a reasonable and unbiased observer would consider fair and equitable, and that amounts to a violation of Article 4(1) of the Agreement (Tecmed S.A. v. The United Mexican States, 2003, at para. 166) and 'the Respondent's behavior constitutes sufficient basis for the Claimant's claim founded on such violation to be admissible, given the time at which the damage occurred and the time when the damage and the violation of the Agreement …' (Tecmed S.A. v. The United Mexican States, 2003, at 174)

According to the tribunal award, Mexico has to pay Tecmed the amount of US$ 5,533,017,12, plus a compound interest on such amount to an annual rate of 6%. The cost on legal expenses and counsel's fee was decided to be bear by each party.

Tecmed is still the leading case for Mexico regarding its participation in the BITs framework. In contrast to NAFTA cases after *Metalclad, Tecmed* highlights transparency as a fundamental element of the normative content of the FET standard. It makes a clear definition of the FET standard in the context of the principle of good faith. However, the lack of good faith is not a necessary component of the standard. It links these elements with a principle of basic expectations, which has been also important for NAFTA cases such as *Thunderbird* (Thunderbird v. The United Mexican States, 2006).

3.2 The relationship between FET and other standards of investment protection.

Some tribunals have suggested that FET is no more than an overarching principle that embraces the other standards granted to foreign investors in treaties (Petrobart v. The Kyrgyz Republic, 2005), and at the same time there is evidence that the FET standard also interacts with other standards of protection (Reinish, 2008), one of the most important is the FPS standard. Some tribunals have equated the FET and FPS standards; however, others emphasize the separateness of the two (Azurix Corp. v. The Argentine Republic, 2006, at. para. 407-408).

Some[23] BITs specifically link FET to the Most Favored Nation Standard (MFN), one example of this is the Mexico-Portugal BIT. This type of clause merges into one single provision the FET standard, an absolute standard of protection, with NT or MFN, which are considered relative standards of treatment.

MFN treatment standard means that investments or investors of one contracting party are entitled to treatment by the other contracting party that is no less favorable than the treatment the latter grants to investments or investors of any other third country.

One example of a case dealing with an MFN claim liked to FET was the case of *Maffezini v. Spain* (Maffezini v. The Kingdom of Spain, 2002) based on the Argentina-Spain BIT. The treaty provided that investors had to exhaust all domestic judicial remedies before submitting an arbitral claim. *Maffezini* argued that he could bypass this precondition by invoking the MFN clause. Here, the MFN clause was intended to give access to less stringent procedural provisions established in the Chile-Spain BIT, which does not have the same precondition. The tribunal agreed, and held that, the MFN clause of the Argentina-Spain BIT, could give access to the investor to the procedural benefits of the Chile-Spain BIT (Cavazos, 2007, p 144).

Another example was the case of *Pantechniki S.A. Contractors & Engineers v. The Republic of Albania* (Pantechniki S.A v. The Republic of Albania, 2009), based on the Albania-Greece BIT ("Albania-Greece BIT", 1991) which contained a MFN and a NT clause. In this case the treaty did not explicitly promise investors FET, however, the Claimant still asserted an entitlement to such treatment under two arguments; first, that the treaty as an instrument of international

23 In the context of México-EU BITs only the Mexico-Portugal links FET directly to MFN, however other examples are the Chile-Portugal BIT and the Chile-Brazil BIT.

law encompasses such standard, and second, that article 3 of the BIT promised MFN treatment, thus they were entitled to FET.

However, the tribunal did not make a full analysis since the claimant agreed that he could not prove that more favorable treatment existed, either towards nationals or other foreign investors, therefore, it was not possible to assert FET from the MFN or NT clauses.

A third case dealing with the application of a MFN clause to assert FET was the case of *Renta 4 v. Russia* (Renta 4 v. Russian F, 2007) in accordance with the Spain-Russia BIT. Said instrument contained MFN clause connected to FET in the following terms:

> "Article 5. Treatment of Investments. 1. Each Party shall guarantee fair and equitable treatment within its territory for the investments made by investors of the other contracting Party. 2. The treatment referred to in paragraph 1 above shall be no less favorable that that accorded by either Party in respect to investments made by investors of any third State …"

In this case the claimant argued that, since the Spain-Russia BIT limited the range of causes of action to base a claim on, the tribunal should assert jurisdiction by extending the benefits of the Russia-Denmark BIT that contained a more liberal arbitration clause. Russia objected to this argument, by stating that the claimant failed to include in its request for arbitration its desire for an expanded jurisdiction through MFN, thus, forfeiting this possibility. Moreover, it asserts that the Tribunal must regard the expansion of jurisdiction as inadmissible because otherwise this would prejudice the respondent's right to "challenge unfounded assertions of jurisdiction" (Renta 4 v. Russian F, 2007, at 70).

The Tribunal dismissed the respondent's arguments, stating that the claimant was entitled to request an extension of jurisdiction through a MFN clause. However, the question was whether the benefits of a MFN clause refer to substantial or procedural issues. In this respect, the tribunal refers to the dichotomy of primary/secondary rules,[24] namely, considering issues referring the treatment of the investment as primary or substantive rules, apart from procedural or secondary rules.

In this case, the tribunal acknowledges that MFN covers only matters of FET, since the same article states this limitation. And, since FET is a substantive standard of treatment, Russia argues that access to arbitration is not an inherent part of FET, given that this would constitute a procedural right.

---

24 The classification of primary/secondary rules does not have a normative origin. However, it has been the classification by which the International Law Commission determined its field of work on State responsibility. *"The law relating to the content and the duration of substantive State obligations is as determined by the primary rules. The law of State responsibility as articulated in the Draft Articles provides the framework – those rules, denominated "secondary", which indicate the consequences of a breach of an applicable primary obligation. (James Crawford, The International Law Commission's Articles on State Responsibility 16 (2002.)"*

In this respect, the tribunal believes that the possibility of access to international arbitration does not *per se* mean a higher degree of FET. It concludes that "the specific MFN promise contained in Article 5(2) of the Spanish BIT cannot be read to enlarge the competence of the present Tribunal ... the terms of the Spanish BIT restrict MFN treatment t the realm of FET as understood in international law. This relates to normative standards and does not extend to either (i) the availability of international as opposed to national for a or (ii) "more" rather than "less" arbitration..." (Renta 4 v. Russian F, 2007, at. 119).

The following chapter provides an analysis of the FPS standard and the relevant references made by the Mexico-EU BITs with respect to this standard.

4. Full Protection and Security

FPS is considered to provide a general obligation to the host state to exercise due diligence in the protection of foreign investment, as opposed to strict liability, which would make the state liable even for damage to the investment caused by third parties (Dolzer and Stevens, 1995, p. 61).

The opinions of tribunals are still divided, while some consider FPS as an element of FET and almost equivalent to it, others do acknowledge the separation and independence of these two standards (Azurix Corp. v. The Argentine Republic, 2006, at. 407-408). In the case of the Mexico-EU BITs, a clear majority separates the two as independent concepts. Among those, only one exception appears, this is the Mexico-Sweden BIT ("Mexico-Sweden BIT ") which does not make any reference to FPS but does, in its Article 2 subsection 3, connect the obligation to grant FET to the "relevant international standards of international law".

One example of FPS not being considered as a separate standard from FET was the *PSEG v. Turkey* (PSEG v. Turkey 2007) case, which originated in 1994 after PSEG applied for and was granted by the government of Turkey an authorization to conduct a feasibility study into the building of a coal–fired power plant, only to later revoke it under pressure from the World Bank and the IMF to make its energy sector more competitive by abandoning the BOT model. However, by this time, PSEG had spent a considerable sum of money, on an initial feasibility study, follow-up studies, as well as negotiations with several government agencies.

PSEG was an American company with a wholly owned Turkish subsidiary. The claimants invoked the protections granted by the USA- Republic of Turkey BIT (Treaty between USA and Turkey, 1990).

The claimant argued that a violation of FET, in accordance with Article II(3) had occurred. Said Article states that, "investments shall at all times be accorded fair and equitable treatment . . . in a manner consistent with international law".

PSEG also referred to several cases in order to assert violations to its legitimate expectations (*MTD S.A v. Republic of Chile, 2004)*, arbitrary conduct by the respondent (Cavazos, 2007, pp. 168 – 174) and lack of transparency (Metalclad v. United Mexican States, 2000). With respect to PFS, two separate claims were submitted, first that FPS includes the adverse effects of the amendments of the law or administrative actions on the investment, and second that the breach of FET automatically entails the absence of FPS.

The tribunal however, even while acknowledging a breach of FET, did not consider that FPS constituted a separate standard capable of producing separate liability to the state. In its resolution the tribunal stated that it did "not find that there has been any question of physical safety and security, nor has any been alleged. Neither does the Tribunal find that there is an exceptional situation that could qualify under this standard as a separate heading of liability. The anomalies that have been found are all included under the standard of fair and equitable treatment. This heading of liability is accordingly dismissed" (PSEG v. Turkey 2007, at para. 259).

The drafting of the Mexico-Sweden BIT seems to indicate that the parties agree with the *PSEG v. Turkey* tribunal, and consider that a specific reference to the protection of investments in the host states is not necessary, since the obligation to protect such investments is already contained in the FET standard, as well as in the other relevant standards of international law.

However, it is impossible to assume that the two standards, which appear separately in a BIT, have the same content and purpose. FET consists mainly of obligations to the state to abstain from a course of action, however, by promising FPS the state assumes the obligation to actively create a framework for investments that grants factual and legal security also against third persons (Schreuer, 2008), this is, FET constitutes a *negative* (Narveson, 2001)[25] right to the investor, since the fundamental purpose of the standard is to command the state to abstain from any wrongdoing to foreign investment, while FPS constitutes a *positive* right, this is, the mere restraint from the state from harming an investment does not assure compliance, the state must actively prevent damage to that investment.

As for the content of the standard, ICSID Tribunals have found breaches to the FPS obligation whenever the host state has not taken reasonably expected measures to prevent damages to foreign investments (Asian Agricultural Products Limited v. Sri Lanka, 1990), although aimed mainly at physical property damages, it can also entail other protections. For example, in the case of *Goetz v. Burundi* (Goetz v. Republic of Burundi, 1999) the Tribunal held that the withdrawal of a

25 A negative right entitles its recipient to non-interference, while a positive right entitles its recipient to active protection from the state.

government authorization, vital to the operation of the investor could amount to a violation to the FPS owed to the investor. Another example was the *Azurix* case, where the Tribunal considered that the FPS obligation "it is not only a matter of physical security; the stability afforded by a secure environment is as important from an investor's point of view" (Azurix Corp. v. The Argentine Republic, 2006, at. 408.).

In sum, while FPS is not often referred to as a single standing provision, and almost always connected to FET or subsumed by the prohibition to expropriate, this standard can entail separate and additional obligations and an active and continuous effort from the state to prevent damage to foreign investment.

4.1 FPS linked to Customary International Law

Only the Mexico-UK BIT connects FPS to the minimum standard of customary law. Like FET, when FPS as linked to customary law, its content should only be constituted by and interpreted in accordance to those norms and practices widely accepted as law by the general international community.

Also, when FPS is granted, as required by customary international law, it has been considered to contemplate the protection of the investment against private as well as public action, that is, it requires that the host state should exercise reasonable care to protect investment against injury also by private parties (UNCTAD, 2007).

This idea enhances the scope of FPS and can make the state liable for damages indirectly caused by it, such as the failure of the state to control private parties that have harmed foreign investment.

4.2 FPS as a self-contained standard

Most[26] of the BITs between Mexico and EU Countries consider FPS as a self-contained standard; one example is the Mexico-Germany BIT, which states the following:

> "Article 2. Promotion, Admission and Protection of Investments. (2). Each Contracting State shall grant to the investments made by nationals or companies of the other Contracting State under its laws and regulations, full protection and security."

When the FPS standard is considered as an autonomous provision its range of protection will be broaden to include not only express obligations but reasonably

26 The Mexico-Germany, The Mexico-Austria, The Mexico-Denmark, The Mexico-Spain, The Mexico-Slovak, The Mexico-Finland, The Mexico-France, The Mexico-Greece, The Mexico-Italy, The Mexico-Netherlands, The Mexico-Portugal, The Mexico-United Kingdom, The Mexico-Czech Republic, The Mexico-Sweden and the The Mexico-Belgium/Luxembourg Union.

expected actions or inactions that a State must take in protection of that investment. Also, just like the FET standard, an autonomous interpretation of FPS includes the consideration of the object of the treaty as well as the circumstances surrounding the investment. Therefore, both FET and FPS have been considered as contextual standards, which entails that the realities of an individual country will determine the expectations of FPS, FET, and other substantive obligations. This means that the requirements of international investment law will thus be based on a sliding scale: more developed countries with greater capacity to protect investments will be held to a higher standard. Conversely, a developing country less capable of providing protection will have its behavior judged against a standard based on its own development (Alexander, 2008, page 829).[27] The consideration of the factual background in our opinion serves two purposes, first, not to require impossible and unreachable standards from developing countries, and second to require from those countries who are able to provide it, more specific and regulated investment protection policies. This, consequently, creates a sense of balance in the investment arbitration system. This has a special effect on the content and obligations arising from the FPS standard, since a politically and economically stable country will be more able to prevent damage to an investment than a developing country. In other words, due to the fact that FPS entails a preventive measure a developed country will be able to foresee a possible damage and consequently take the necessary measures to prevent or correct it.

5. Conclusions

This paper has attempted to analyze the operation of the Mexico – EU BITs in light of two of the most controversial standards included in those treaties: FET and FPS. On one hand, it is interesting to note that the investment policy in the framework of the EU is evolving since the coming into force of the Treaty of Lisbon. Consequently, it is foreseeable to expect a more harmonized conception of the relevant standards is foreseeable, although it seems that the establishment of an EU model BIT is not an immediate objective of the new policy.

A fundamental element of the analysis has been the *jurisprudence* created by the decisions of the various arbitral tribunals. It is clear that in the case of International Investment Law, the normative content of the different standards is "forged primarily by the rulings of arbitral tribunals, which are called to determine what international standards of justice require of states in times of a rapidly evolving global economy. One central feature of a system of investor – state

27 See *supra* note 2.

dispute settlement is that arbitral decisions themselves create expectations of investors and states in how principles of investment law will be applied, including [FET]." (Glamis Gold Ltd. v. United States, 2010).

Notwithstanding the fact that most of the BITs between Mexico and the EU refer to the FET as a self-contained standard, the most recent re-negotiation to one of these treaties, the Mexico – Spain, included a definition of FET as a standard linked to customary international law. In this context, it is going to be interesting to analyze an eventual award in *Abengoa* (Abengoa v. United Mexican States, 2009), a pending case under the new Mexico – Spain BIT. As has been discussed in this paper, in *Tecmed*, the elements of lack of transparency, analyzed jointly with the principle of good faith and legitimate expectations, are considered by the arbitral tribunal as fundamental elements of the normative content of the FET standard. Actually, because of this case was decided in accordance with the provisions of the former Mexico – Spain BIT, the tribunal at the outset attempted to interpret the FET as an independent standard. In sum, the tribunal had no problem in interpreting the FET standard as including a requirement of transparency and it did not need to "import" the concept from somewhere else.

An important fact regarding the violation of the FET standard in *Tecmed* was the commitment of Cytrar to relocate the facility to a place free of socio-political pressure (Tecmed S.A. v. The United Mexican States, 2003, at para. 44). This relocation was supposed to happen as soon as the authorities and Cytrar find the right place for the exchange of operations, where there was not an opposition by the citizens or a perceived potential damage to the environment. The tribunal considered it was a reasonable expectation of Cytrar, based on the good faith principle, that the permit would continue operating in its original facilities until the relocation date. Also, the tribunal pointed out that the authorities' statements to Cytrar about the landfill's relocation lacked of transparency (Tecmed S.A. v. The United Mexican States, 2003, at para. 44). From what we know from the available information (Investment Treaty News, 2010), *Abengoa* is somehow similar to *Tecmed* because is related to the location of a waste disposal facility. For these reasons, the interpretation of the standards under a new BIT that defines FET as part of Customary International Law, is going to be crucial.

Both FET and FPS are relevant examples of possible problems in the interpretation of the different Mexico – EU investment treaties. It is foreseeable that controversies between Mexico and European investors could increase in the future, as the economic interaction grows. Therefore, a consistent interpretation of both standards will become even more important.

With respect to FET and FPS, we believe that even while a particular standard may be considered as autonomous, it is still part of the general international law system and can in some cases constitute also a reflection of a customary norm.

Therefore, its content does not need to be bound by a specific reference, which should not only serve as a starting point for its interpretation, but also as a unifying stage. In other words, regardless to its reference, FET and FPS constitute provisions consistently intended for the protection of foreign investment against arbitrary and unfair measures by the host state, therefore its content will vary, depending on the context of the investment, but its main purpose will always remain the same. In the application of both standards, tribunals should have always in mind the necessity of a balance: legitimate domestic public policies, and legitimate interests of investors (Cavazos, 2007, at 193.).

References

Alexander, E. (2008). Taking account of reality: Adopting contextual standards for developing countries in international investment law. *Virginia Journal International Law.*

Cavazos Villanueva, G. (2007), *The fair and equitable treatment standard in international investment law: the Mexican experience.*

Delegation of the European Union to Russia (2010, July 07), *New EU Investment package set to boost trade and underpin investor rights.* [On Line], Retrieved from http://ec.europa.eu/delegations/russia/press_corner/all_news/news/2010/20100707_01_en.htm.

Dolzer and Stevens (1995), *Bilateral Investment Treaties*, International Centre for Settlement of Investment Disputes.

European Commission (2010, July 7), *Proposal for a Regulation of the European Parliament and of the Council establishing transitional arrangements for BITs between EU Member States and third countries* [On Line], Retrieved from http://trade.ec.europa.eu/doclib/docs/2010/july/tradoc_146308.pdf

European Commission (2010, July 7), *Q&A: Commission launches comprehensive European international investment policy* [On Line], Retrieved from http://trade.ec.europa.eu/doclib/press/index.cfm?id=590.

European Commission (2010 July 7), *Communication from the Commission to the Council, the European Parliament, the European Economic and Social Committee and the Committee of the Regions* [On Line], Retrieved from http://trade.ec.europa.eu/doclib/docs/2010/july/tradoc_146307.pdf.

Foreign Affairs and International Trade Canada (2001, August 1), *NAFTA FTC Interpretation,* [On Line], Retrieved from http://www.international.gc.ca/trade-agreements-accords-commerciaux/disp-diff/NAFTA-Interpr.aspx?lang=en.

Hjälmroth C. and Westerberg S., *The contribution of trade to a new EU growth strategy, ideas for a more open European economy. Part 1. A common investment policy for the EU,*[On Line], Retrieved from http://www.kommers.se/upload/Analysarkiv/In%20English/Analyses/LS%20Investments.pdf

Investment Treaty News (2010, January 12), *Spanish firms launch ICSID dispute against Mexico over stalled toxic waste disposal project.* [On Line], Last visited: November 2010, Retrieved from http://www.iisd.org/itn/2010/01/12/spanish-firms-launch-icsid-dispute-against-mexico-over-stalled-toxic-waste-disposal-project/

IX Reunión de la Comisión parlamentaria mixta México-UE (2009, December 10,11) [On Line], México, Last visited November 2010, Retrieved from http://www.senado.gob.mx/hoy/mixta/pdfs/doc_interes2.pdf.

Kill, T. (2008, March), *Don't Cross the Streams: Past and Present Overstatement of Customary International Law in Connection with Conventional Fair and Equitable Treatment Obligations*, Michigan Law Review, 106, No.5 Mich. L. Rev. 853.

Mc Dermott Will & Emery (2010, August 17), *Transitional Arrangements for Bilateral Investment Treaties between EU Member States and Third Countries after the Lisbon Treaty,* [On Line], Retrieved from http://www.mwe.com/ index.cfm/fuseaction/publications.nldetail/object_id/b5a975c0-6dbc-45f7-9db6-4e1ee0a22ea1.cfm

Naverson, J. (2001) *The Libertarian Idea*, Peterborough, Ontario: Broadview.

North American Free Trade Agreement (1992, December 27), 107 Stat. 2057, 32 I.L.M. 605.

OECD (2006 August 11), *Analysis of the economic impact of investment provision in regional trade agreements*, OECD Trade Policy Working Paper No.

OCDE. (2004, September). *Fair and equitable treatment standard in international investment law*. Retrieved from http://www.oecd.org/dataoecd/22/53/33776498.pdf

Oxford University Press (2006) [On Line], Last visited: November 2010, Retrieved from http://www.investmentclaims.com/ViewPdf/ic/Awards/law-iic-210-2006.pdf

Reinish, A. (2008), *Standards of Investment Protection*, Oxford University Press.

Schreuer, C. (2008, March 7), *Fair and Equitable treatment*, Zurich.

Secretariat of Foreign Affairs, *International Trades celebrated by México,* [On Line] Last visited: November 2010, Retrieved from http://www.sre.gob.mx/tratados/.

Secretariat of Economy, the only of these 13 countries with witch Mexico has not signed a BIT is Ireland.

Secretariat of Economy, *General Direction of Foreign Investment,* [On Line] Last visited: on March 2010, Retrieved from http://www.economia.gob.mx/pics/pages/1175_base/dicE09.pdf.

Stephan W. Schill. Glamis Gold Ltd. v. United States. Award 2010, 104 Am. J. Int'l. Law.

Sornarajah, M. (2004), *The International Law on Foreign Investment*, Cambridge, Cambridge University Press.

Synthesis of the relationship between méxico-spain (2010, March 02). Retrieved from http://www.promexico.gob.mx/work/models/promexico/Resource/102/1/images/Espana.pdf

UNCTAD (2007), *Bilateral Investment Treaties 1995-2006: Trends in investment rulemaking*. United Nations, New York and Geneva, Retrieved from http://www.unctad.org/en/docs/iteiia20065_en.pdf.

Vasciannie, S. (1990), *The fair and equitable treatment standard in international investment law and practice*, 70 BYIL 99.

Cases

Abengoa, S.A. y COFIDES, S.A. v. United Mexican States (ICSID case no. ARB(AF)/09/2)

Antoine Goetz and others v. Republic of Burundi, ICSID case no. ARB/95/3, Resolution of February 10th, 1999.

Asian Agricultural Products Limited v. Republic of Sri Lanka, ICSID case no. ARB/87/3, Award June 27, 1990.

Azurix Corp. v. The Argentine Republic ICSID case no. ARB/01/12, Award July 14th, 2006.

CME Czech Republic B.V, v. The *Czech Republic* (2001), UNCITRAL Rules [On line], Last visited: March 2010, Retrieved from: http://ita.law.uvic.ca/documents/CME-2001PartialAward.pdf

CMS Gas Transmission Company v. The Argentine Republic, ICSID case no. ARB/01/8, Award May 12, 2005.

Dieter Kraus v. Land Baden-Wuerttemberg (1993). Referenced in The contribution of trade to a new EU growth strategy, case no. C-19/92

Edf Limited v. Romania, ICSID case no. ARB/05/13, Award October 8, 2009

Elettronica Sicula S.P.A. (ELSI) (United States of America v. Italy). Judgment of July 20, 1989.

Emilio Agustín Maffezini v. The Kingdom of Spain. ICSID case no. ARB/97/7 Decision on Jurisdiction (25 January 2000), 5 ICSID Reports 396 (2002).

Gemplus, S.A., SLP, S.A. and Gemplus Industrial, S.A. de C.V. v. United Mexican States ICSID case no. ARB(AF)/04/3.

Genin, Eastern Credit Limited, Inc. and A.S. Baltoil v. The Republic of Estonia, ICSID Case No. ARB/99/2 award June 25, 2001.

International Thunderbird Gaming Corporation v. The United Mexican States, UNCITRAL Arbitration Rules, Award of January 26, 2006.

Metalclad v. United Mexican States, ICSID case no. ARB(AF)/97/1, award of August 30, 2000.

Mondev v. United States, ICSID case no. ARB(AF)/99/2, Award of October 11, 2002.

MTD Equity Sdn. Bhd. & MTD Chile S.A. v. Republic of Chile, ICSID case no. ARB/01/7, Award of May 25, 2004.

Pantechniki S.A. Contractors & Engineers v. The Republic of Albania, ICSID case no. ARB/07/21, Award, July 30, 2009. [On Line]. Last visited: November 2010. Retrieved from: http://icsid.worldbank.org/ICSID/FrontServlet?requestType=CasesRH&actionVal=showDoc&docId=DC1133_En&caseId=C113.

Petrobart v. The Kyrgyz Republic, Stockholm Chamber of Commerce, Award March 29, 2005.

Pope & Talbot Inc. v. The Government of Canada, (2002).

PSEG v. Turkey, ICSID case no. ARB/02/5, Award of January 19, 2007.

Renta 4 S.V.S.A et al. v. Russian Federation, SCC case no. 24/2007, 1991 (Spain/Russia BIT).

Saluka v. Czech Republic, Partial Award, PCA-UNCITRAL Arbitration Rules; IIC 210 March 17, 2006.

Tecnicas Medioambientales Tecmed S.A. v. The United Mexican States ICSID case ARB (AF)/00/2, award of May 29, 2003.

Waste Management, Inc. v. Mexico, ICSID case no. ARB (AF)/00/3, (NAFTA), Final Award April 30, 2004.

Treaties

Agreement between the Government of the Kingdom of Sweden and The Government of The United Mexican States concerning the promotion and reciprocal protection of investments. [On line], Last visited: November 2010, Retrieved from http://www.unctad.org/sections/dite/iia/docs/bits/mexico_ sweden.pdf. (Mexico-Sweden BIT).

Agreement between the Government of the Republic of France and the Government of the United Mexican states on the reciprocal promotion and protection of investments. [On line], Last visited November 2010, Retrieved from http://www.unctad.org/sections/dite/iia/docs/bits/mexico_france.pdf (Mexico-France BIT).

Agreement between the Portuguese Republic and the United Mexican States on the reciprocal promotion and protection of investments, [On Line], Last visited:

November 2010, Retrieved from http://www.unctad.org/sections/dite/iia/docs/bits/mexico_portugal.pdf (Mexico-Portuguese BIT).

Agreement between the Government of the United Kingdom of Great Britain and Northern Ireland and the Government of Romania (1995, July 13), *For the promotion and reciprocal protection of investments* [On Line], London, Last visited: November 2010, Retrieved from http://www.unctad.org/sections/dite/iia/docs/bits/uk_romania1996.pdf (UK-Northern Ireland, BIT).

Agreement on encouragement and reciprocal protection of investments between the Kingdom of the Netherlands and the Czech and Slovak Federal Republic (1975, August 1*),* [On Line]. Helsinki, Finland. Last visited: November 2010, Retrieved from http://www.unctad.org/sections/dite/iia/docs/bits/czech_netherlands.pdf (Netherlands-Czech-Slovak BIT).

Agreement on the Reciprocal Promotion and Protection of the Investment signed by the Kingdom of Spain and the United Mexican States (1996, December 18). (Mexico-Spain BIT).

Agreement between the government of the Hellenic Republic and the Government of the Republic of Albania for the encouragement and reciprocal protection of investments. [On Line]. Last visited: November 2010, Retrieved from http://www.unctad.org/sections/dite/iia/docs/bits/greece_albania.pdf (Hellenic-Albania BIT).

Treaty of Lisbon (2007, December 17), Official Journal C 306 [On Line], Retrieved from http://europa.eu/lisbon_treaty/full_text/index_en.htm.

Treaty between the United States of America and the Republic of Turkey concerning the reciprocal encouragement and protection of investments (1990, May 18). [On Line], Last visited: March 2010, Retrieved from http://www.unctad.org/sections/dite/iia/docs/bits/us_turkey.pdf. (USA-Turkey BIT).

Reputations and Supportive Behavior of Spanish and U.S. Firms in Mexico

William Newburry , M Abrahim Soleimani[†] *& Armando Borda*[‡]

1. Introduction

Mexico's inward foreign inward investment increased dramatically over the last two decades, in part due to the 2000 Mexican – European Free Trade Association (EFTA) Trade Agreement and the 1994 North American Free Trade Agreement (NAFTA). Foreign MNCs entering Mexico face liabilities related to their foreignness and challenges in gaining legitimacy in Mexico. This chapter studies the role corporate reputation plays in this context. Analyzing perceptions of 43,962 Mexicans regarding the reputations of 18 companies from Mexico, Spain, and the United States over a three-year period, we find that foreign firms, and more specifically US firms, have lower reputations in Mexico. In addition, results suggest that reputation is more influential in predicting supportive behaviors of Mexican citizens (through product purchase, investment or workplace attraction) for Spanish and US firms than for domestic firms.

Corporate reputation refers to the overall knowledge and esteem about a corporation held by the public (Fombrun, 1996). Reputation has been demonstrated to be associated with both important firm outcomes (Dowling, 2006), and individual supportive behaviors (Caruana, Cohen, & Krentler, 2006; Newburry, 2010). Although significant literature exists regarding liabilities facing foreign firms in developed world contexts (Hymer, 1976; Mezias, 2002; Newburry, Gardberg & Belkin, 2006), little empirical work examines whether reputations systematically differ between foreign and domestic firms in emerging markets such as Mexico. Furthermore, while scholars have studied the positive effects of a good reputation on different firm stakeholders (Graham & Bansal, 2007; Greening & Turban, 2000; Larsen, 2002), research in this area is limited in an international context (Newburry, 2010). To address these issues, this chapter studies the effects of foreignness, country-of-origin and degree of internationalization on individual-level reputation assessments of Spanish and U.S. firms in Mexico, as compared to their domestic Mexican counterparts. In doing so, we gain comparative insights into the two main countries investing in Mexico as a result of the

Department of Management & International Business, Florida International University.
† Department of Management, Eastern Washington University.
‡ Department of Marketing, ESAN University.

2000 Mexican – European Free Trade Association (EFTA) Trade Agreement and the 1994 North American Free Trade Agreement (NAFTA). Subsequently, homogeneity of the Mexican society will be investigated in terms of examining how gender and socio-economic status differences influence reputation evaluations of foreign versus domestic firms. Finally, we will examine the instrumentality of corporate reputation and country-of-origin effects on stated supportive behaviors of individuals in Mexico.

The chapter is organized as follows. First, we develop hypotheses predicting reputation assessments in the context of Mexico, followed by hypotheses predicting a respondent's stated propensity to pursue supportive behaviors towards a firm. Next, we discuss our research methods and the measurement of study variables. We then present our results, followed by a discussion and conclusion section.

2. Hypotheses

Corporate reputation is a collective perception of a firm's stakeholders which is formed based on a firm's past and current performance (Fombrun, 1996). From a strategic perspective, corporate reputation can be source of sustainable competitive advantage if it is a value creating, rare, inimitable, and non-substitutable intangible asset (Barney, 1991). Companies with more favorable reputations not only are more attractive to customers and investors, but also attract more qualified job applicants (Graham & Bansal, 2007; Greening & Turban, 2000; Larsen, 2002). From an organizational theory perspective, a favorable corporate reputation reflects that a company is legitimate (Deephouse & Carter, 2005; DiMaggio & Powell, 1983), a critical resource for the survival and success of firms (Pfeffer & Salancik, 1978). In addition to conveying legitimacy of a firm in a society, corporate reputation states the relative standing of a firm to other counterparts. In other words, a favorable corporate reputation not only reflects that a firm is a legitimate actor, but also signals that its performance is higher than its counterparts.

Analyzing corporate reputation in Mexico is important for several reasons. On the one hand, Logsdon, Thomas and Van Buren (2006) argued that Mexicans do not trust in either their government or their institutions. Moreover, they suggested that a large part of Mexico's political history has been associated with corruption, relatively weak regulatory systems and serious institutional gaps at various government levels. Weaknesses in government have been related specifically to the regulation of businesses. On the other hand, Lenartowicz and Johnson (2002) found that Latin American countries considered the most important values in society to be honesty and responsibility. Despite recently developed societal attention to firm behavior in Mexico (Muller & Kolk, 2010), these contradictory arguments suggest that both domestic and foreign companies face the risk of being considered illegitimate actors in the market place, compromising not only their profitability expectations but also their long run survival chances.

2.1 Foreign Headquarters

Companies expanding to a new country incur costs of doing business abroad which put them at a disadvantage relative to local competitors in that country (Hymer, 1976; Kindleberger, 1969). Liabilities of foreignness (LOF) include "all additional costs a firm operating in a market overseas incurs that a local firm would not incur" (Zaheer, 1995, p. 343). Eden and Miller (2004) considered LOF as social costs of doing business abroad and defined three LOF sources: unfamiliarity hazards, discrimination hazards and relational hazards. Organizational legitimacy contributes to these three sources of LOF. MNCs entering a new country are generally at a disadvantage in gaining legitimacy relative to local organizations. Moreover, MNCs entering developing countries have been advised to adopt strategies to gain local legitimacy (Gifford & Kestler, 2008) and social embeddedness (London & Hart, 2004).

To understand the limitations that foreign firms face in gaining legitimacy in Mexico, it is important to explore the evolution of Mexico's policies regarding FDI. Latin American countries have in general changed their policies from inward looking import substitution environments (up until the mid 1980s) to outward looking export and FDI enhancing economies (Brenes, 2000; Brenes & Dominguez, 1997). Mexico has not been an exception. According to Waldkirch (2008), Mexico has been aggressively trying to attract FDI since 1989, initially by relaxing restrictions on foreign investment and then by signing international trade agreements. Nowadays, Mexico has signed more international trade agreements than any other Latin American country (EIU, 2009) and its trade regime is considered one of the most open in the world (US Department of State, 2010). Nevertheless, this opening can still be considered a fairly new process.

Ghemawat (2001) argued that culture, administrative, geographic and economic distances may affect the perceptions of opportunities in foreign markets. While Mexico has worked aggressively in opening its barriers to trade and FDI, other sources of distance affect the liability of foreignness faced by MNCs. For instance, Galbrait, DeNoble and Estavillo (1990) concluded that high legal and cultural differences between Mexico and the US should be taken into account when analyzing potential location decisions of Mexican and U.S. small electronic firms. More recently, Continental tire, a German company that acquired Euzkadi in 1998, decided to leave the country in 2001,"blaming the impossibility of doing business under the nation's current labor laws" (Gower & Randewich, 2002, p. 37).

While these examples indicate difficulties in dealing with the host country environment, they also have implications regarding the legitimacy of foreign firms. First, it seems that there is no consensus regarding the beneficial effects of foreign investment in Mexico, especially in the case of Maquiladoras. According to Waldkirch (2008), FDI targeting unskilled labor intensive industries (such as the Maquiladora industry) may have less technological impact, and as a consequence, less effect on productivity. In fact, he found that the effect of FDI on average compensation per worker is negligible. Moreover, he argued that his findings suggested that the owners of capital, not labor, profit from productivity improvements. Second, Noya (2004) suggested that Latin countries have a long tradition of nationalism and populism, favoring the perceptions of domestic firms over foreign firms. Dussel (2000) argued that the industrialization of the Mexican manufacturing industry not only was built on a history of nationalism and populism, but also was enhanced by forty years of import substitution industrialization. Further, Alloza and Noya (2004) mentioned the erosion of national identity as one of the negative aspects associated with FDI in Latin American countries. Finally, there is a perception in Latin countries (including Mexico) regarding the lack of commitment of foreign companies towards host country problems (Noya, 2004). Indeed, Dussel (2000) mentioned that since liberalization policies were adopted in Mexico, societal outcomes such as income distribution, access to education and health and wage levels have been negatively affected. The sectors that generated more employment showed the lowest productivity (Dussel, 2000). These findings suggest that while certain segments can take advantage of the opportunities brought by the opening of the Mexican economy, most sectors remain isolated to such processes and are unable not only to leverage opportunities, but also to respond to challenges raised. Therefore, we suggest the following hypothesis:

Hypothesis 1: Local firms have higher reputations than foreign firms in Mexico.

Another aspect of foreignness influencing corporate reputation is country-of-origin (COO) (Li & Wyler, 1994; Gardberg, 2006). COO is a perception about a country, which affects a person's evaluations of products, services, brands, or companies from that country (Lampert & Jaffe, 1996), as well as a signal which represents a combination of characteristics and attributes of a firm (Li & Wyler, 1994), and therefore works as a simplifier in individual assessments of firms. COO becomes more important in shaping corporate reputation when foreign firms enter a host country and there is information asymmetry between people in the host country and the entering MNCs, a situation more likely to be present in developing and emerging markets such as Mexico. Limited information and bounded rationality in a host country leads legitimization processes to stereotypical judgments about MNCs based on their industry and COO (Kostova & Zaheer, 1999).

The reputation of MNCs from the US and Spain in Mexico merits particular scrutiny. Liberalization and privatization of key sectors, particularly since 1994, as well as close geographic proximity to the US and historical relations with Spain, make Mexico an interesting FDI destination for both Spanish (Casanova, 2005) and US MNCs. In addition, historical connections and language similarities of Spain and Mexico and the growing Hispanic population in the US (the largest minority group at 14.8% of the US population; US Census Bureau, 2009) highlight the importance of examining these two groups. Furthermore, Spanish and US MNCs differ significantly both in financial and social practices, which shape reputation. Specifically, European and US firms have different approaches in conveying their social responsibility images (Maignan & Ralston, 2002), in corporate donations (Bennett, 1998), and in the way they formulate and implement codes of ethics (Langlois & Schlegelmilch, 1990).

Spain has significantly influenced the development of Latin American countries, both through its colonial history in the region (Skidmore & Smith, 2005) and its more recent role as the largest European investor (Casanova, 2005). In addition to liberalization and privatization since the 1990s in Latin America, and specifically in Mexico, Spanish investment is largely driven by historical and cultural ties (Galan, Gonzalez-Benito, & Zuniga-Vincente, 2007). In other words, historical and cultural ties between Spaniards and Mexicans influence Mexican evaluations of Spanish MNC reputations.

The foreign involvement of Spanish firms is a fairly recent phenomenon. According to Guillen and Garcia Canal (2007), in the mid 1980s, few Spanish firms operated abroad and their total investment was just US$4,500 million. In 1986, Spain entered the European Union and Spanish firms started the process of internationalization in the early 1990s. Nowadays, Spain is the 11th largest investor worldwide with an FDI stock of US$381,000 million in 2007. A total of 743 Spanish firms started operations in Latin American countries between 1986 and 2007, and Mexico represents their second largest recipient in the region (Garcia Canal, Guillen, Sanchez Lorda & Valdes Llaneza, 2008).

Noya (2004) suggested that the perception of Spain as a source of foreign investment in Latin American countries and especially in Mexico was not favorable during the 1980s, and that the perception of this investment did not change much during the 1990s and early 2000s. First, by analyzing the results of several surveys conducted by the Centro Español de Estudios de America Latina (CEDEAL), Noya argued that Spain was considered a country with weak technological and economic power (before the expansion of Spanish firms to Latin

America). Second, based on the results of Latinobarometro (2003), investment from Spain was not perceived positively during the 1990s either. As suggested by Noya (2004), Mexicans tend to evaluate negatively both the impact of the investment of Spanish MNCs and the image of Spain in general. Indeed, by 2003 just three out of ten people surveyed in Latin American countries associated FDI from Spain as beneficial (Guillen, 2005). Third, Casilda-Bejar (2002) argued that Latin American countries tend to consider the brand Spain as distant, arrogant, and unfriendly. Fourth, Spain has an "enduring image problem" (Guillen, 2005, p. 169). According to Guillen (2005), Spain has associated values of poor quality image and, more generally, of weak country reputation. Alloza (2009) also found evidence suggesting that Spanish firms are often viewed negatively in Latin America and elsewhere. Therefore, we suggest:

Hypothesis 2: Mexican firms have a higher reputation than Spanish firms in Mexico.

According to the Economic Commission for Latin America and the Caribbean (Eclac, 2008), the US is the largest investor in Mexico. More than 18,000 US companies have operations and almost one million US citizens live in Mexico (US Department of State, 2010). In 1994, Mexico became part of NAFTA and started a long process of commercial integration with the US and Canada. The expectation was that NAFTA would become a North American Union (McCoy, 2008).

However, the relationship between the US and Mexico has been deteriorating (McCoy, 2008). Several issues may influence the perceptions of Mexicans regarding the US. First, there are problems associated with immigration. McCoy and Fensom (2007, p. 19) mentioned that "US immigration policy is a major irritant" in bilateral relations between the two countries. According to Bustamante (1997), while the perception of Mexico regarding undocumented migration is described as an economic phenomenon by which Mexicans fill jobs that US citizens are unwilling to take, the US perception is that the majority of these undocumented people are either criminals associated with drug dealership or persons who want to subsist on assistance programs. Second, the US is associated with problems of security and drug dealership across the common Mexico-US border. This situation exacerbates the problem of immigration mentioned before. Finally, even though free trade agreements such as NAFTA may have more positive effects in terms of FDI flows and importance to smaller countries involved in the agreements (Cuevas et al., 2005), it may be perceived that the US dominates the rules of the relationship in its favor. For instance, the US Supreme Court removed in 2004 the last legal barrier for Mexican trucks to cross the US border (EIU, 2009). However, in March 2009, the US government decided to refuse to allow Mexican truckers to deliver cargo within its border (McCoy & McLendon, 2009). In response, Mexico retaliated by imposing tariffs on several

US products. These factors may affect the perceptions of Mexicans regarding the US and US MNCs. Therefore we suggest:

Hypothesis 3: Mexican firms have higher reputations than US firms in Mexico.

2.2 *Degree of Internationalization*

Internationalization is the process by which organizations become more international in their transactions (Newburry, Gardberg, & Belkin, 2006). There is a rich body of research on both benefits and costs of internationalization (e.g., Contractor, Kundu & Hsu, 2003; Hennart, 2007). However, there is no consensus as to whether a higher degree of internationalization (DOI) would lead to better financial performance, and therefore, many scholars predict an s-shaped multinationality-performance relationship (Contractor et al., 2003; Lu & Beamish, 2004; Thomas & Eden, 2004).

With respect to the effect of DOI on reputation assessments of firms in Mexico, we suggest that this will be driven by the strong capabilities and resources that internationalization provides MNCs relative to domestic firms, combined with strong signaling power associated with the ability to compete in foreign markets (e.g., Newburry, Belkin & Ansari, 2008). MNCs with a higher degree of international expansion have more knowledge and international experience. They have access to managerial and technological resources not available to local firms as well as the capability to transfer their knowledge and resources from one market to another (Prahalad & Hart, 2002). Particularly in emerging markets such as Mexico, access to capabilities associated with these resources could provide more international firms with strong competitive advantages over their purely domestic counterparts, leading to both greater performance and stronger reputation assessments (Barney, 1991). Being able to compete in an international arena may have particularly strong signaling power for individuals in developing countries (Namazie & Frame, 2007; Newburry, Belkin & Ansari, 2008). As such, perceptions regarding the internationalization of a firm may reinforce reputation perceptions. Accordingly, we suggest:

Hypothesis 4: Firms with a greater degree of internationalization have higher reputations in Mexico.

2.3 *Individual-Level Demographic Influences*

Latin American countries can be characterized as nations with persistent inequalities among different demographic groups (Elvira & Davila, 2005). Considering the power distance index, or the extent to which the less powerful accept that power is distributed unevenly, Mexico is one of the countries with the largest differences among groups not only within the region, but also worldwide (Hofstede, 2001). These differences in power suggest that in Mexico, different demographic groups may have different perceptions of organizations. In this section, we analyze how gender and socio-economic status influence the opinions of constituents about the reputation of Mexican, Spanish and US firms in Mexico.

According to Skidmore and Smith (2005), the concept of "Machismo" has been traditionally attached to Latin American countries, limiting opportunities for women to advance within business and society. The global gender gap report (WEF, 2009) provides evidence supporting this argument in the case of Mexico. According to this report, Mexico is one of the Latin American countries with more gender disparities in access to resources and opportunities (WEF, 2009). In fact, Mexico ranked 98 out of 134 countries worldwide and surpassed only Guatemala within the region. The largest gender disparities found in Mexico are related to labor force participation (ranks 113), wage equality for similar work (ranks 115) and estimated earned income (ranks 106). Women in Mexico may perceive themselves as lacking the capacity to access and control relevant economic resources when compared to men, and therefore, look for alternatives.

Within this type of environment, foreign firms may signal better opportunities for woman. Since most of the FDI received in Mexico comes from developed markets (especially the US and Spain) where the treatment of women may be more favorable than in Mexico, the HR practices of foreign firms may reflect more equalitarian treatment of both genders. HR practices vary across countries (Robinson, 1995) and certain elements of home country policies tend to remain in foreign subsidiaries (Hayden & Edwards, 2001). Moreover, foreign firms are more likely to operate according to international standards regarding women (e.g., Newburry, Belkin & Ansari, 2008), again suggesting better treatment of women. This treatment can represent more opportunities for woman in the market place and positively impact their perceptions of foreign firms. Thus, foreign firms may provide woman access to resources that they currently do not have the capacity to obtain and/or control in the domestic environment. By contrast, while being foreign will also impact the reputation evaluations of men, the difference between their assessments of foreign and domestic firms is likely to be less. Therefore, we suggest:

> Hypothesis 5: Gender moderates the relation between foreignness and reputation, such that the slope of the foreignness-reputation relationship is more positive (or less negative) for females than for males.

However, not all companies from foreign developed markets have similar HR treatments or the same perceptions about woman in the workplace. On the one hand, according to the global gender gap report (WEF, 2009), Spain has its largest gender disparities in the same dimensions as the ones highlighted for Mexico:

labor force participation (ranks 79), wage equality for similar work (ranks 120) and estimated earned income (ranks 82). Moreover, there are perceived larger wage differences for similar work in Spain than in Mexico itself. In contrast, the US consistently shows smaller gender gap differences in these dimensions compared to both Spain and Mexico. Furthermore, US firms operating abroad are required to follow US discrimination legislation to the extent that they do not violate host country laws (Newburry et al., 2006). Given these differences, opportunities for women in Mexico may vary depending upon the home country of the foreign firm, and we expect a relatively more positive signaling of US MNCs vis-a-vis Spanish MNCs for women in Mexico as compared to men. Therefore:

> Hypothesis 6: Gender moderates the relation between foreign HQ and reputation such that the slope of the US HQ-reputation relationship is more positive (or less negative) for females than for males, while the Spanish HQ- reputation relationship is also more positive for females, but to a lesser degree.

Socio economical status captures to some extent the level of both income and education in a particular society. Despite its efforts, Mexico still showed inequalities in both dimensions. While the Gini coefficient, a coefficient that assesses the level of income inequality in the nation, suggests a moderate level of income disparity (Mexican Gini coefficient is 0.461), information obtained from an executive opinion survey (WEF, 2007, 2008) suggested that large differences in access to quality education exist in Mexico. These differences may lead to different expectations and skills among different socioeconomic groups.

The presence of foreign firms has been associated with increased wages in host countries (Caves, 1996). However, these wage benefits tend to be concentrated at upper management levels. Since highly educated individuals are normally clustered in the upper levels of society, people of lower socioeconomic status may not perceive the direct economic benefits associated with foreign investment. Further, Waldkirch (2008) found that in Mexico, the effect of FDI in unskilled industries on average compensation per worker could be considered negligible. Since people at lower socioeconomic levels may perceive themselves with lower abilities and capacities to obtain higher positions in foreign firms, they may possess negative perceptions towards foreign firms, or at least differentiate less between foreign and domestic firms than their higher status counterparts. Moreover, Newburry et al. (2006) argued that foreignness could be considered a liability, but also an asset. People from higher economic status groups may be more capable of recognizing the positive effects associated with foreign investment. Therefore:

> Hypothesis 7: Socio economic status moderates the relation between foreignness and reputation such that the slope of the foreignness-reputation relationship is more positive (or less negative) for higher status individuals.

Mexico is a Spanish speaking country that was a former colony of Spain. According to Ghemawat (2001), these characteristics tend to close the cultural and administrative distances between the two countries. On the contrary, language differences may expand the cultural distance between the US and Mexico. The effect of language differences may be more pronounced in people of lower socioeconomic status due to lesser educational opportunities. People of this status may face barriers not only to interact with US firms, but also to obtain highly qualified jobs. People from lower socioeconomic status not only may recognize Spanish firms as being closer to Mexican firms, but also may perceive that they have the required capacity to obtain managerial positions in such companies. People from higher economic status groups may not face such limitations in interacting with either Spanish or US firms. Moreover, given the commercial ties between the US and Mexico and the levels of foreign investment of the US in Mexico, US firms represent a major source of opportunity for people from the higher economic status. Therefore:

> Hypothesis 8: Socio economic status moderates the relation between foreign HQ and reputation such that the slope of the US HQ-reputation relationship is more positive (or less negative) for higher status individuals, and the Spanish HQ-reputation relationship is also more positive for this same group, although to a lesser extent.

2.4 Supportive Behavior

In addition to investigating the determinants of corporate reputation, we examine the consequences of corporate reputation on its stakeholders. Previous authors have suggested that three critical markets to firm success in emerging economies are labor, capital, and product markets (Khanna & Palepu, 1997; Chacar, Newburry & Vissa, 2010; Newburry, 2010). Therefore, we study the effects of corporate reputation on three firm stakeholders: potential investors, customers and employees.

One of the characteristics of a stock market is the asymmetry of information between investors and companies. Investors try to overcome this lack of information by receiving and interpreting signals sent by companies. Corporate reputation is a valuable information signal, which differentiates companies from each other. Comparing companies with the same level of financial performance, investors consider companies with higher reputation to be less risky (Srivastava, McInnish, Wood, & Capraro, 1997). In addition, Larsen (2002) found that investors are willing to pay a higher price for a more reputed company with the same level of risk and return as a less reputed company. From a psychological perspective, Hanson and Stuart (2001, p. 141) noted that "shareholders may be interested in profit but they will also share the shame and declining profits associated with a deteriorating corporate reputation which is now increasingly the subject of media and public scrutiny".

In conditions of information asymmetry, customers interpret corporate reputation as a signal regarding the quality of a product/service (Carmeli & Tisher, 2005) as well as a company's responsibility towards its customers (Brammer & Millington, 2005). Furthermore, Graham and Bansal (2007) found that customers are willing to pay more for products from firms with better corporate reputations.

Finally, human capital is one of the firm's determining resources in gaining competitive advantage (Barney, 1991). More and more companies are realizing the importance of human capital, and consequently, the competition for high-quality job applicants becomes more serious. According to social identity theory, an employee's self image is shaped by their employer's identity, image, and reputation (Ashforth & Mael, 1989). Therefore, potential employees take into consideration their future self-image if they work for the employer. As a result, companies with higher reputation are more attractive to job applicants (Greening & Turban, 2000). On the other hand, corporate reputation is a signal to job applicants, allowing them to differentiate between potential employers in a condition of incomplete information. Corporate reputation along with social performance, workplace quality, and commitments and goals help potential employees better evaluate working conditions (Greening & Turban, 2000). In sum, we suggest that a favorable corporate reputation is a source of competitive advantage, which attracts investors, customers, and potential employees, and consequently, can help companies to outperform their competitors in capital, product, and labor markets. Accordingly, we hypothesize:

> Hypothesis 9: Firm reputation is positively related to the stated propensity of the public in Mexico to pursue firm supportive behaviors.

As previously mentioned, foreign firms compete at a disadvantage relative to indigenous firms (Hymer, 1976; Kindleberger, 1969). Foreign firms incur additional costs that domestic counterparts will not need to assume (Zaheer, 1995). These LOF may be due to the lack of experience and information in the host country, discrimination of relevant actors in the market place, and the escalation of organizational costs (Eden & Miller, 2004). Corporate reputation may reduce at least two of the main three sources leading to LOF. Corporate reputation signals legitimacy in the marketplace, minimizing the effects of lack of experience. Further, being considered a legitimate actor reduces the risk of being discriminated against by local customers and suppliers. In fact, Newburry, Gardberg and Belkin (2006) argued that foreignness could at times also be considered as a source of advantage for some foreign firms. This may be particularly the case in emerging markets such as Mexico. While domestic competitors may take for granted their position in the market place, foreign firms may leverage their brand name and reputation to overcome LOF. Stated another way, reputation matters more for foreign firms than domestic firms since foreign firms are more likely less known and embedded in the local community, so that the reputation signal provides more information benefit to the individual firm evaluator. Therefore, we argue:

> Hypothesis 10: Corporate reputation moderates the relation between country of origin and supportive behavior, such that the reputation-supportive behavior relationship will be stronger for foreign firms than their domestic counterparts.

3. Methodology

3.1 Sample

We utilize a sample of 43,962 individual perceptions by Mexican citizens of 18 companies headquartered in Spain, the United States and Mexico studied by the Reputation Institute in association with The Foro de Reputacion Corporativa. Data were collected between January 2007 and October 2009. The Reputation Institute administered an online survey to measure perceptions of individuals regarding different aspects of corporate reputation as well as their supportive behaviors. Respondents who have at least minimal familiarity with a focal company were selected from a pool of respondents based upon their abilities to answer three out of four questions about the focal company (Asher, 2004). Respondents were also targeted to represent the general Mexican population based on gender and age. Questions were answered in Spanish from a questionnaire, which was translated and back translated from English by professionals fluent in both languages (Harzing, 2005).

3.2 Dependent Variables

We used the Reputation Institute's measure of *corporate reputation* (Reputation Institute, 2007) to capture individual Mexican's assessment of reputation of Mexican, Spanish, and US firms operating in Mexico. Respondents answered the following four statements about a company on a 7-point scale, where "1" indicates "I strongly disagree" and "7" indicates "I strongly agree." LISREL analyses confirmed the unidimensionality, convergent validity, and fit of the scale items (Alpha=.932; Factor analysis eigenvalue=3.33, explaining 83.12% of variance).

The items contained in this measure are:

1. [Company] has a good overall reputation.
2. [Company] is a company I have a good feeling about.
3. [Company] is a company that I trust.
4. [Company] is a company that I admire and respect.

Supportive behavior of individuals was measured based on their support in three critical markets of a firm in emerging economies: product, financial, and labor markets (Khanna & Palepu, 1997). The following three items were asked and responses were on a 7-point scale from "1" (I strongly disagree) to "7" (I strongly agree). Analyses confirmed the unidimensionality, convergent validity and fit of the scale items (Alpha=.893; Factor analysis eigenvalue=3.53, explaining 70.62 percent of variance).

The items contained in this measure are:

1. I would purchase the products/services of [Company].
2. I would invest in [Company].
3. I would work at [Company].

3.3 Independent Variables

Firm level data were collected primarily from company annual reports, and supplemented when needed with data from the Economatica, Mergent and other sources. *Foreign HQ* (H1) is a dichotomous variable coded as "1" if the company's headquarters is in Spain or the US and "0" if the company's headquarters is in Mexico. Furthermore, to test country-of-origin effects (H2-H3), dichotomous variables were created for *Spanish HQ firms*, and *US headquartered firms*, with a value of "1" if the company's headquarters is in the specified country and "0" otherwise. Degree of internationalization (DOI) (H4) is measured through both objective and subjective measures. DOI is objectively measured by calculating the ratio of a firm's foreign sales to total sales (Contractor et al., 2003) and subjectively, based upon perceptions of *International Scope*, by asking the respondent's opinion about the following statement on a "1" (Does not describe well) to "7" (Describes very well) Likert-type scale: "[Company] has an international scope."

Gender (H5-H6) is a dichotomous variable where "1" indicates females and "0" indicates males. *Socioeconomic status* (H7-H8) is measured by household income and education. Household income is a categorical variable based upon five levels ranging from less than $2400 (pesos) (coded as "1") to greater than $83,000 (pesos) (coded as "5"). Education is also categorical, coded "1" if less than a basic education (e.g. elementary school) ranging to "7" if completed graduate school.

3.4 Control Variables

We controlled for other firm and individual-level effects. *Firm Size* is captured through a firm's sales and *Firm Performance* by a firm's return on assets (ROA). Muniz, Ramirez, Murgan, and Castillo (2009) found differences in the level of positive newspaper coverage of Spanish firms investing in Mexico. Accordingly, categorizing firms into manufacturing and service firms broadly controls for industry effects. The variable *Manufacturing* is coded "1" for firms in manufacturing industries and "0" for firms in service sectors. At the individual level, *Familiarity* with a company was measured using the item, "I am familiar with [Company]", with responses ranging from 1 (Not at all familiar) to 4 (Very familiar). As respondents needed to meet a familiarity threshold to be included in the sample, responses for this variable were highly biased towards the top end of the scale. *Respondent Age* is categorical, ranging from "1" if under 18 to "10" if over 60. Respondents under 18 were eliminated from the sample. Finally, *Social Class* is categorical based on 4 categories.

3.5 Analysis

We use the hierarchical linear modeling program HLM 6 (Raudenbush, Bryk, Cheong, Congdon, & du Toit, 2004) to analyze the two-level effects of our nested data: individual within company. Thus, we are able to control for the effect of firm-level data on its nested individual-level data, and simultaneously take into account the interdependence of individual-level data in firm-level data, which ordinary least squares (OLS) regression is not capable of. Prior research examined related concepts in multi-level settings (e.g., Martin, Cullen, Johnson & Parboteeah, 2007; Bailey & Spicer, 2007).

4. Results

Table 1 presents the results of our analyses in seven models. The first four models test the effect of a firm's international characteristics (foreignness, country-of-origin, and degree of internationalization) on perceptions of the general public about its reputation as well as the effects of those characteristics in influencing perceptions of different demographic groups regarding the firm (H1 to H8). The last three models test the effect of firm reputation and its interaction with foreignness in predicting general public support for a firm. All models are significant at the $p<.001$ level. While not presented due to space limitations, correlations were run between all study variables, and collinearity diagnostics were computed for all models, with no significant issues found.

Table 1: Corporate Reputation and Supportive Behavior Regression Analyses[1]

	Corporate Reputation				Supportive Behavior		
Variables	**Model 1 - Foreign HQ - DOI**	**Model 2 Country of Origin**	**Model 3 Foreignness Interaction**	**Model 4 COO Interaction**	**Model 5 Reputation Foreign HQ**	**Model 6 Reputation COO**	**Model 7 Reputation Interaction**
Intercept	2.64(.07)***	2.58(.07)***	2.59(.07)***	2.59(.07)***	.88(.65)***	.82(.06)***	3.88(.10)***
Level 1 – Individual							
International Scope (H4)	.48(.01)***	.48(.01)***	.48(.01)***	.48(.01)***	.21(.01)***	.21(.01)***	.22(.01)***
Gender	.06(.02)**	.06(.02)**	.00(.03)	.00(.03)	.05(.01)***	.05(.01)***	.04(.01)***
Gender*For. HQ (H5)			.14(.04)***				
Gender*SP HQ (H6)				.11(.05)*			
Gender*US HQ (H6)				.18(.04)***			
Education	-.06(.01)***	-.06(.01)***	-.04(.01)***	-.04(.01)***	-.04(.00)***	-.04(.00)***	-.04(.00)***
Education*For. HQ (H7)			-.03(.02)+				
Education*SP HQ (H8)				-.03(.02)			
Education*US HQ (H8)				-.04(.02)+			
Household Income	-.01(.00)**	-.01(.00)**	-.00(.00)	-.00(.00)	-.02(.01)***	-.02(.00)***	-.02(.00)***
H.Inocme*For. HQ (H7)			-.02(.02)				
H.Inocme*SP HQ (H8)				-.03(.03)			
H.Inocme*US HQ (H8)				.00(.02)			
Corp. Reputation (H9)					.60(.01)***	.60(.01)***	.60(.01)***
Corp. Reputation* SP HQ (H10)							.04(.01)***
Corp. Reputation* USA HQ (H10)							.06(.01)***
Control – Age	.00(.00)	.00(.00)	.00(.00)	.00(.00)	-.00(.00)*	-.00(.00)+	-.00(.00)*
Control – Social Class	.03(.01)**	.03(.01)**	.03(.01)**	.03(.01)**	.03(.01)***	.03(.01)***	.03(.01)***
Control – Familiarity	.00(.00)+	.00(.00)*	.00(.00)*	.00(.00)*	-.00(.00)	-.00(.01)	-.00(.00)

1 ***p<0.001; **p<0.01; *p<0.05; +p<0.10; Regressions present standardized beta coefficients (standard errors in parentheses).

	Corporate Reputation				Supportive Behavior		
Variables	**Model 1 - Foreign HQ - DOI**	**Model 2 Country of Origin**	**Model 3 Foreignness Interaction**	**Model 4 COO Interaction**	**Model 5 Reputation Foreign HQ**	**Model 6 Reputation COO**	**Model 7 Reputation Interaction**
Level 2 – Company							
Foreign HQ (H1)	-.15(.07)*				-.02(.05)		
Spanish HQ (H2)		-.05(.08)	-.12(.08)	-.11(.08)		.05(.06)	-.02(.10)
U.S. HQ (H3)		-.29(.09)***	-.36(.09)***	-.37(.09)***		-.14(.07)+	-.41(.12)***
For. Sales/Total Sales (H4)	-.07(.09)	-.13(.08)	-.13(.08)	-.13(.08)	-.14(.07)*	-.19(.07)**	-.22(.12)+
Control – Manufacturing	.39(.06)***	.47(.07)***	.46(.07)***	.46(.07)***	.02(.04)	.08(.05)	.50(.08)***
Control – Sales	.00(.00)***	.00(.00)***	.00(.00)***	.00(.00)***	-.00(.00)	.00(.00)	.00(.00)***
Control – ROA	-.45(.43)	.16(.47)	.16(.48)	.16(.48)	.62(.36)+	1.11(.42)**	2.48(.67)***
X^2 Levels 1 and 2	383.77***	350.89***	352.29***	350.69***	240.34***	207.34***	515.72***
Deviance	95800.39	95801.42	93915.19	93929.48	87095.27	87095.80	8712301
N – Level 1	43962	43962	43962	43962	43962	43962	43962
N – Level 2[2]	46	46	46	46	46	46	46

2 Level 2 N represents company study years less company years with missing data.

4.1 Corporate reputation

Model 1 compares the reputations of domestic (Mexican) companies with foreign companies (H1). H1 predicted that in Mexico, domestic companies are better reputed than foreign companies. Model 1 provides significant support for H1 ($p<.05$). Model 2 extends Model 1 and tests the country-of-origin (COO) effect on reputation. H2 and H3 predicted that in Mexicans' opinions, Spanish and US firms have lower reputations than Mexican firms. Although the results show that Spanish firms have lower reputations than their Mexican counterparts, the difference was not significant. However, results strongly support H3 that US firms have lower reputations than Mexican firms ($p<.001$). The effect of degree of internationalization of a firm on its reputation is predicted in H4. Two measures were used to test this hypothesis: an objective measure and a subjective measure. The objective measure used was the firm's ratio of foreign sales to total sales (Contractor et al., 2003). The subjective measure was based upon respondents' perceptions of firms' international scope. The results in Models 1 to 4 consistently show that while the subjective measure was highly significant ($p<.001$) in the predicted positive direction, the objective measure was not significant. Thus, H4 is only supported for our subjective measure.

H5 suggested that females have relatively more favorable opinions about foreign firms than males. Model 3 tested this hypothesis and found a highly significant ($p<.001$) positive result, supporting H5. H6 broke down the previous hypothesis to examine moderating effects of Spanish and US firms compared to their Mexican counterparts. Model 4 tested H6 and shows significant ($p<.05$) and highly significant ($p<.001$) support for Spanish and US firms, respectively. H7 predicted that individual perceptions regarding the reputations of foreign firms compared to domestic firms is a function of their socioeconomic status. We used household income and education to measure socioeconomic status. Model 3 reports marginal significance for education ($p<.10$), although in the direction opposite our hypothesis. We did not find support for income. Thus, the H7 was not supported. H8 extends H7 to test the effects of socioeconomic status on reputation assessments of Spanish and US firms, compared to Mexican firms. Model 4 provides marginal support ($p<.10$) for an education interaction, such that the slope of the US firm-reputation relationship was marginally more positive for higher educated Mexicans. Model 4 did not demonstrate support for a moderating effect of household income on either country-of-origin-reputation relationship.

5. Supportive behavior

Model 5, 6, and 7 tested the effects of corporate reputation along with foreignness and COO on the general public's stated propensity to pursue supportive behaviors towards a firm. H9 proposed that the general public supports firms with higher reputations. Model 5 tested this hypothesis and demonstrates strong support ($p<.001$) for this relationship. Finally, Model 7 tested H10, which predicted that the reputation-supportive behavior relationship would be moderated by country of origin such that the reputation would be more positive for Spanish and US firms. The results reported in Model 7 for both Spain and the US are highly significant ($p<.001$) in the expected direction.

6. Discussion

Overall our results suggest that foreign firms, and more specifically US firms, have lower reputations than domestic firms in Mexico. By contrast, firms with stronger perceived internationalization have higher reputations. Additionally, our findings show that reputation impacts the stated propensity of individuals to pursue behaviors that support a firm. Moreover, reputation is more influential in predicting supportive behaviors that benefit Spanish and US firms than Mexican firms. These findings bring support to the argument that corporate reputation may not only reduce the effect of liabilities of foreignness (LOF) faced by non-domestic firms, but also may become a source of competitive advantage for foreign firms in host countries.

Our first hypothesis predicted that domestic firms have higher reputations than foreign firms in Mexico. Our findings support the arguments of LOF and lack of legitimacy faced by foreign multinationals in host countries. Eden and Miller (2004) argued that one of the sources of LOF is related to discrimination hazards where local stakeholders treat foreign and domestic firms differently. In countries such as Mexico with long traditions of populism and nationalism (Dussel, 2000; Noya, 2004), discrimination hazards may undermine the reputations of foreign firms.

Further, our second and third hypotheses evaluated the influence of country of origin on corporate reputation in Mexico. While our results for both Spain and the US are in the expected negative directions, they reach significance only in the case of US firms. These results suggest a different appreciation of Spanish and US firms. On the one side, Spain and Mexico share several attributes that may reduce the overall distance between these two countries and the negative perceptions associated with foreign firms from Spain. For instance, both countries use the same language and share the same religion. These characteristics reduce considerably the cultural distance between these two countries. Moreover, considering the administrative distance between the two countries, we can highlight two aspects: First, Mexico was a former colony of Spain for almost three hundred years. Second, Mexico was the first Latin American country to sign a partnership agreement with the EU in the 1997 agreement that entered into force in 2000. These two aspects diminish the relative administrative distance between Spain and Mexico. Finally, regarding economic distance, Mexicans consider Spain a relatively similar country to Mexico (Noya, 2004). Overall, these commonalities in different dimensions may reduce the costs and risks of Spanish firms in doing business in Mexico and can help them to overcome some of the LOF faced by foreign firms.

On the other hand, US firms may leverage only the administrative distance between the two countries, which is reduced via NAFTA. Other sources of distance continue to play a significant role. For instance, given the problems associated with the common border between the US and Mexico explained before, geographic distance still constitutes a significant barrier between these two countries. Further, cultural and economic differences enhance the overall distance between Mexico and the US. Therefore, the large distance between the US and Mexico may affect the capacity of US firms to deal with LOF in Mexico, and therefore account for the lower perceived reputations of US firms.

Our fourth hypothesis argued that firms with higher levels of internationalization have higher reputations. Since Sullivan (1994) argued that internationalization is a multidimensional construct, we used foreign sales/total sales and the scope of international operations (as perceived by the respondent) to grasp the construct. Since the concept of corporate reputation is strongly linked to personal perceptions, the perceived international scope of operations is probably a better measure for this study. This is also evident in its high degree of statistical significance. One of the main benefits associated with higher internationalization is that multinationals may face different environments and gain international experience through this direct interaction. The higher the international experience, the more capacity these MNCs have to deal with LOF in new host markets. According to Johansson and Vahlne (1977), relevant learning can be gained only by direct international interaction in host countries. The scope of international operations may capture this dimension better than the ratio of foreign sales/total sales.

Our fifth and sixth hypotheses evaluate the influence of gender on corporate reputation. Our findings support the argument that females look for alternatives in foreign firms to gain access to resources and opportunities that they currently may not have access to domestically. Further, the results suggest that females may perceive better opportunities in US firms than Spanish multinationals.

Our seventh and eighth hypotheses analyzed the impact of socioeconomic status on corporate reputation. Neither of these hypotheses was supported. As mentioned, we used two proxies to capture socioeconomic status: education and income. According to Logsdon, Thomas and Van Buren (2006), the Mexican corporate sector is lead by family-owned diversified business groups. Newburry and Gardberg (2010) suggested that in emerging markets, people from higher economic status tend to leverage their existing network ties within important domestic firms, a setting in which their previous ties tend to be more relevant. On the other side, Mexicans from lower economic status may find foreign firms attractive because currently they may have not access to those relevant domestic networks. Given the concentration of activities in Mexico within relatively large family-owned business groups, it seems a plausible preference for Mexicans with higher education to prefer domestic firms at a greater rate than people with lower education. Nonetheless, our lack of results for these hypotheses suggests further study is needed.

Further, contrary to our expectations, we found that highly educated individuals tend to associate higher reputation with Spanish firms rather than with US firms. According to Noya (2004), Spanish multinationals tend to concentrate their activities in relatively few sectors such as banking, telecommunications and energy. Further, the involvement of Spanish multinationals in Latin America can be associated with the process of privatization in the early 1990s. However, US multinationals are more dispersed in terms of both time periods and industries covered. Mexican conglomerate business groups may compete with US firms more often and in more sectors than with Spanish firms. Hence, Mexicans from higher economic status may perceive US multinationals as a menace not only to the companies in which they work but also to their own position in society. On the contrary, Mexicans from lower economic status may perceive US multinationals as a unique employment opportunity. For instance, the investment in unskilled labor intensive industries may represent one of the few employment opportunities available to uneducated people.

Hypothesis 9 suggests that firms with higher reputation will receive more support from the general public. Our results provide strong evidence that corporate reputation matters. The results supported the idea of corporate reputation as a source of competitive advantage. This fact is further evaluated in our last hypothesis. Hypothesis 10 argues that the reputation-supportive behavior relationship examined in hypothesis 9 will be stronger for foreign firms than domestic firms in Mexico. While not explicitly hypothesized, we evaluated the direct impact of country of origin on supportive behavior (Model 6). The direct results associated with country of origin failed to reach significance in the case of Spanish multinationals and reached only marginally significance in the case of US firms. According to these findings, US firms receive less support from the general public in Mexico. However, once corporate reputation is considered, the slope of the reputation-supportive behavior relationship was stronger for both Spanish and US multinationals. While country of origin only has a weak direct effect on supportive behavior, the moderating effect of corporate reputation becomes essential for foreign firms to obtain support from the general public. These results provide evidence supporting the argument that corporate reputation may not only reduce the effects of LOF faced by foreign firms, but may also be a source of competitive advantage in host countries.

7. Conclusions

Mexico witnessed a dramatic increase in inward investment by MNCs in the 1990s due to the 1994 NAFTA and the 2000 Mexican – EFTA Trade Agreement. De facto to MNC presence in the Mexican market is the escalating importance of foreignness liabilities (LOF) to MNCs. Corporate reputation as an intangible asset can be an advantage to lower LOF. Therefore, this chapter tried to investigate the effects of international characteristics of firms on their reputations among Mexican citizens. Furthermore, this chapter compared foreign firms with domestic firms and finally studied the possible outcomes of reputation for an MNC.

Our analysis showed that foreign HQ companies on average have lower reputations than domestic companies. This is consistent with LOF (Zaheer, 1995) arguments. However, reputation perceptions vary in Mexican society among different groups. Females have more favorable opinions about foreign companies and people with higher household income and higher education perceive domestic firms as more reputed companies. Degree of internationalization (DOI) is another international characteristic of MNCs, which affects the general public's perceptions. The analysis showed that general public perceptions favor companies perceived as more international in scope. However, the accounting measure of DOI was not supported, signaling that MNCs need to better communicate with their stakeholders. Furthermore, Spanish and US firms were compared with their Mexican counterparts to investigate the effect of COO on their reputations. Spanish and US companies create interesting contrasts. On the one hand, Spanish companies are representatives of their European neighborhood and a more stakeholder-oriented approach, while US firms represent more profit and shareholder-oriented ideology. On the other hand, Spanish companies have historical and cultural ties and language similarities to Mexico, while US firms have geographic proximity. The analysis found that US companies are perceived to have lower reputations than domestic companies. A similar negative effect, although not a statistically significant one, was found for Spain. Moreover, being female significantly affected the US and Spanish firm-reputation relationship, such that females were relatively more attracted to foreign firms from both these countries than their male counterparts.

To complete the picture, we studied the influence of reputation on people's decisions to support a company. In general, our findings support previous works that people are more likely to support companies with higher reputations (Newburry, 2010; Graham & Bansal, 2007; Greening & Turban, 2000; Larsen, 2002). Furthermore, we found that reputation matters relatively more for Spanish and US firms than their Mexican counterparts in gaining behavioral support from the general public in Mexico.

References

Alloza, A. (2009). La reputation de España en el mundo. Madrid, Spain: Instituto de Análisis de Intangibles.

Alloza, A., & Noya, J. (2004). Capital disonante: la imagen de las inversiones españolas en América Latina, Real Instituto Elcano de Estudios Internacionales y Estratégicos Documentos de trabajo, 6,1-23.

Ashforth, B., & Mael, F. (1989). Social identity theory and the organization. *Academy of Management Review, 14,* 20-39.

Bailey, W., & Spicer, A. (2007). When does national identity matter? Convergence and divergence in international business ethics. *Academy of Management Journal, 50,* 1462-1480.

Barney, J. (1991). Firm resources and sustained competitive advantage. *Journal of Management, 17(1),* 99.

Bennett, R. (1998). Corporate philanthropy in France, Germany and the UK international comparisons of commercial orientation towards company giving in European nations. *International Marketing Review, 15(6),* 458-475.

Brammer, S. & Millington, A. (2005). Corporate reputation and philanthropy: An empirical analysis, Journal of Business Ethics, *61(1)*, 29-44.

Brenes, E. (2000). Strategies for globalizing Latin American business. *Journal of Business Research, 50,* 3-7.

Brenes, E., Dominguez, L. (1997). Strategic choices in the new international enterprise in Latin America. *Journal of Business Research, 38,* 1-2.

Bustamante, J. (1997). Mexico-United States labor migration flows. *International Migration Review, 31(4),* 1112-1121.

Carmeli, A. & Tishler, A. (2005). Perceived organizational reputation and organizational performance: An empirical investigation of industrial enterprises. *Corporate Reputation Review, 8(1),* 13-30.

Caruana, A., Cohen, C., & Krentler, KA. (2006). Corporate reputation and shareholders' intentions: An attitudinal perspective. *Brand Management, 13(6),* 429-440.

Casanova, L. (2005). Latin America: Economic and business context. In M.M. Elvira, & A. Davila (Eds.). *Managing human resources in Latin America* (pp 25-56). London/New York: Routledge.

Casilda-Bejar, R. (2002). *La década dorada: Economía e inversiones Españolas en América Latina 1990-2000*. Alcala, Spain: Universidad de Alcala servicio de publicaciones.

Caves, R.E. (1996). *Multinational enterprise and economic analysis (2nd ed).* Cambridge, England: Cambridge University Press.

Chacar, A., Newburry, W. & Vissa, B. (2010). Bringing Institutions into Performance Persistence Research: Exploring the Impact of the Product, Financial and Labor Market Institutions, *Journal of International Business Studies,* forthcoming.

Contractor, F.J., Kundu, S.K., & Hsu, C. (2003). A three-stage theory of international expansion: The link between multinationality and performance in the service sector. *Journal of International Business Studies*, *34(1),* 5.

Cuevas, A., Messmacher, M., Werner, A. (2005). Foreign direct investment in Mexico since the approval of Nafta. *The World Bank economic review, 19(3),* 473-488.

Deephouse, D., & Carter, S. (2005). An Examination of Differences between Organizational Legitimacy and Organizational Reputation. *Journal of Management Studies*, *42(2),* 329-360.

DiMaggio, P., & Powell, W. (1983). The iron cage revisited: Institutional isomorphism and collective rationality on organization fields. *American Sociological Review*, *48,* 147-160.

Dowling, G. (2006). How good corporate reputations create corporate value. *Corporate Reputation Review, 9(2),* 134-143.

Dussel, E. (2000). *Polarizing Mexico: The impact of liberalization strategy.* Boulder, CO: Lynne Rienner Publishers.

Eclac, (2008). Foreign direct investment in Latin America and the Caribbean. Retrieved July 28, 2009, from http://www.cepal.org/publicaciones/xml/4/36094/LCG2406if.pdf.

Economist Intelligent Unit (2009). Country Commerce Profile: Mexico. Retrieved October 8, 2009, from http://www.eiu.com/index.asp?autologin=bulk&rf=0.

Eden, L., & Miller, S. (2004). Distance matters: Liability of foreignness, institutional distance and ownership strategy. In: M.A. Hitt & J.L.C. Cheng (Eds.), *The Evolving Theory of the Multinational Firm. Advances in International Management*, Vol. 16. Amsterdam: Elsevier, 187-221.

Elvira, M.M. & Davila, A. (2005). Emergent directions – HRM in Latin America. In M.M. Elvira & A. Davila (Eds.), *Managing human resources in Latin America* (pp. 235-252). London/New York: Routledge.

Fombrun, C.J. (1996). *Reputation: Realizing value from the corporate image.* Boston, MA: Harvard Business School Press.

Galan, J.I., Gonzalez-Benito, J. & Zuniga-Vincente, J.A. (2007). Factors determining the location decisions of Spanish MNEs: An analysis based on the investment development path. Journal of International Business Studies, 38, 975-997.

Galbraith, C.; DeNoble, A. & Estavillo, P. (1990). Location criteria and perceptions of regional business climate: A study of Mexican and U.S. small electronics firms. Journal of Small Business Management; 28 (4), 34-47.

Garcia Canal, E., Guillen, M., Sanchez Lorda, P., & Valdes Llaneza, A. (2008). La expansión de las empresas españolas hacia América Latina: Un balance. Revista de globalización, competitividad y gobernabilidad, 2(2), 18-45.

Gardberg, N. (2006). Reputatie, reputation, réputation, reputazione, ruf: A cross-cultural qualitative analysis of construct and instrument Equivalence. Corporate Reputation Review, 9(1), 39-61.

Gardberg, N.A., & Schepers, D.H. (2008). Do stakeholders detect corporate social performance signals? Academy of Management 2008 Annual Proceedings.

Ghemawat, P. (2001). Distance still matters: The hard reality of global expansion. Harvard Business Review, 79(8), 137-147.

Gifford, B. & Kestler, A. (2008). Toward a theory of local legitimacy by MNEs in developing nations: Newmont mining and health sustainable development in Peru. Journal of International Management, 14, 340-352

Gower, M. & Randewich, N. (2002). Mexico's 50 most prestigious foreign companies. Business Mexico, 12(7), 32-43.

Graham, M., & Bansal, P. (2007). Consumer's Willingness to Pay for Corp Reputation: The Context of Airline Companies. *Corporate Reputation Review, 10(3),* 189-200.

Greening, D., & Turban, D. (2000) Corporate social performance as a competitive advantage in attracting a quality Workforce. *Business and Society, 39(3),* 254-280.

Guillen, M. & Garcia Canal, E. (2007). La expansión internacional De la empresa española: Una nueva base de datos sistemática. *La internacionalización de la empresa española, 839,* 23-34.

Guillen, M. (2005). *The rise of Spanish Multinationals. European business in the global economy*. New York, NY: Cambridge University Press.

Hanson, D. & Stuart, H. (2001). Failing the reputation management test: The case of BHP, the big Australian, *Corporate Reputation Review, 4,* 128-143.

Harzing, A. (2005). Does the use of English-language questionnaires in cross-national research obscure national differences? *International Journal of Cross Cultural Management, 5(2),* 213-24.

Hayden, A., & Edwards, T. (2001). The erosion of the country of origin effect: a case study of a Swedish multinational company. *Industrial Relations, 56(1),* 116-140.

Hennart, J. (2007). The theoretical rationale for a multinationality-performance relationship. *Management International Review, 3(3),* 423-452.

Hofstede, G. (2001). *Culture's Consequences.* Beverly Hills, CA: Sage.

Hymer, S.H. (1976). *The international operations of national firms: A study of direct investment.* Cambridge, MA: MIT Press.

Johanson, J., & Vahlne, J.E. (1977). The internationalization process of the firm: A model of knowledge development and increasing foreign market commitment. *Journal of International Business Studies, 8(1),* 23-32.

Khanna, T., & Palepu, K.G. (1997). Why focused strategies may be wrong in emerging markets. *Harvard Business Review, 75(4),* 41-51.

Kindleberger, C. (1969). *American business abroad.* New Haven, CT: University Press.

Kostova, T., & Zaheer, S. (1999). Organizational legitimacy under conditions of complexity: The case of the multinational enterprise. *Academy of Management Review, 24(1),* 64.

Lampert, S., & Jaffe, E. (1996). Country of origin effects on international market entry. *Journal of Global Marketing, 10(2),* 27-52.

Langlois, C.C., & Schlegelmilch, B.B. (1990). Do corporate codes of ethics reflect national character? Evidence from Europe and the United States. *Journal of International Business Studies, 21(4),* 519-539.

Larsen, D. (2002). Determining the relationship between investor relations and reputation. *6th International Conference on Corporate Reputation, Identity and Competitiveness*, Boston, MA.

Lenartowicz, T. & Johnson, J. (2002). Comparing managerial values in twelve Latin American countries: An exploratory study. *Management International Review, 42(3),* 279-307.

Li, W., & Wyer, R.S., Jr. (1994). The role of country of origin in product evaluations: Informational and standard-of-comparison effects. *Journal of Consumer Psychology, 3(2):* 187-212.

Logsdon, J.M., Thomas, D., & Van Buren, H. (2006). Corporate Social Responsibility in Large Mexican Firms. *The Journal of Corporate Citizenship, 21,* 51-60.

London, T. & Hart, S. (2004). Reinventing strategies for emerging markets: Beyond the transnational model. *Journal of International Business Studies, 35,* 350-370.

Lu, J.W., & Beamish, P.W. (2004). International diversification and firm performance: The S-curve hypothesis. *Academy of Management Journal, 47(4),* 598.

Maignan, I., & Ralston, D.A. (2002). Corporate social responsibility in Europe and the U.S.: Insights from businesses' self-presentations. *Journal of International Business Studies*, *33,* 497-514.

Martin, K., Cullen, J., Johnson, J., & Parboteeah, K. (2007). Deciding to bribe: A cross-level analysis of firm and home country influences on bribery activity. *Academy of Management Journal*, *50,* 1401-1422.

McCoy, T. (2008). Latin American business environment report. Retrievd December 15, 2009, from www.latam.ufl.edu/labe/Content/LABER08.pdf.

McCoy, T., & Fensom, M. (2007). Latin American business environment report. Retrieved January 5, 2010, from http://www.latam.ufl.edu/LABE/Content/LABER2007.pdf.

McCoy, T., & McLendon, T. (2009). Latin American business environment report. Retrieved January 5, 2010, http://www.latam.ufl.edu/LABE/Content/2009LABER.pdf.

Mezias, J.M. (2002). Identifying liabilities of foreignness and strategies to minimize their effects: The case of labor lawsuit judgments in the United States, *Strategic Management Journal*, *23(3),* 229-244.

Mexico. In Background note: Mexico. Retrieved October 28, 2009, http://www.state.gov r/pa/ei/bgn/35749.htm

Muller, A., & Kolk, A. (2010). Extrinsic and intrinsic drivers of corporate social performance: Evidence from foreign and domestic firms in Mexico. *Journal of Management Studies*, *47(1),* 1-26.

Muniz, C., Ramirez, J., Murgan, A. & Castillo, J.M. (2009). Framing investment in Mexico: An exploratory content análisis of the news frames of the main Spanish companies in the Mexican press. *European Journal of International Management*, *3(2),* 216-231.

Namazie, P. & Frame, P. (2007). Developments in human resource management in Iran', *International Journal of Human Resource Management*, *18(1)*, 159-171.

Newburry, W. (2010). Reputation and supportive behavior: Moderating impacts of foreignness, industry and local exposure. *Corporate Reputation* Review, *12(4),* 388-405.

Newburry, W., Belkin L., & Ansari, P. (2008). Perceived career opportunities from globalization: Influences of globalization capabilities and attitudes towards women in Iran and the U.S.' *Journal of International Business Studies, 39,* 814-832.

Newburry, W., Gardberg, N.A., & Belkin, L.Y. (2006). Organizational attractiveness is in the eye of the beholder: The interaction of demographic characteristics with foreignness. *Journal of International Business Studies, 37,* 666-686.

Newburry, W., Gardberg, N.A. & Sanchez, J. (2010). Marginalization and attraction to foreign and international firms. Working paper.

Noya, J. (2004). La imagen de España y sus inversiones en América Latina. *Universia Business Review 3(3),* 46-61.

Pfeffer, J., & Salancik, G.R. (1978). *The external control of organizations. A resource dependence perspective*, Herper Row, NY.

Prahalad, C.K., & Hart, S.L. (2002). The fortune at the bottom of the pyramid. *Strategy+Business, 26(First Quarter),* 2-14.

Raudenbush, S., Bryk, A., Cheong, Y.F., Congdon, R., & du Toit, M. (2004). *HLM6: Hierarchical linear and nonlinear modeling*. Lincolnwood, IL: Scientific Software.

Reputation Institute. (2007). Global RepTrak™ Pulse 2007: Summary of Results. New York, NY: Reputation Institute.

Robinson, P. (1995). Structural interdependence and practice conformity: An empirical examination of American MNEs and their subsidiaries in Japan. *Academy of Management Best Paper Proceedings*, 192-196.

Skidmore, T.E. & Smith, P.H. (2005). *Modern Latin America* (6th ed.). New York/Oxford: Oxford University Press.

Srivastava, R. K., McInnish, T. H., Wood, R. A., & Capraro, A.J. (1997). The value of corporate reputation: Evidence from the equity markets. *Corporate Reputation Review, 1,* 62-68.

Sullivan, D. (1994). Measuring the Degree of Internationalization of a Firm. *Journal of International Business Studies, 25(2),* 325-342.

Thomas, D.E. & Eden, L. (2004). What is the shape of the multinationality–performance relationship? *Multinational Business Review, 12(1),* 89–101.

United States Census Bureau. (2009) *Hispanics in the United States*. Retrieved June 12, 2009, http://www.census.gov/population/www/socdemo/hispanic/hispanic.html.

US Department of State (2010). *U.S. Relations With Mexico.* Retrieved January 10 2010, http://www.state.gov/r/pa/ei/bgn/35749.htm.

Waldkirch, A. (2008). *The Effects of Foreign Direct Investment in Mexico since NAFTA.* Department of Economics, Colby College, USA.

World Economic Forum (2007). *The global competitiveness report.* Retrieved November 10, 2009, http://gcr07.weforum.org.

World Economic Forum (2008). *The global competitiveness report.* Retrieved January 10, 2010, http://gcr07.weforum.org.

World Economic Forum (2009). *The Global Gender Gap Report.* Retrieved December 8, 2009, http://www.weforum.org/en/Communities/Women%20 Leaders%20and%20Gender%20Parity/GenderGapNetwork/index.htm.

Zaheer, S. (1995). Overcoming the liability of foreignness. *Academy of Management Journal*, 38(2): 341.

Regulatory Changes of the Financial Industry in the E.U.

Roberto Joaquín Santillán Salgado *

1. Introduction

The national regulatory bodies of the financial industry consist of government sponsored supervisors plus a collection of legally binding rules and principles of behavior. The violation of those regulations may result in penalties that go from simple pecuniary fines for minor violations, to the loss of franchises in the case of institutions, or penitentiary reclusion in the case of individuals guilty of major offenses. The loss of a franchise may happen in a variety of forms, which sometimes disguise the true nature of the measure. For example, government authorities not responding to bail-out calls from institutions that have gone too far astray and have fallen into financial distress, or even tacit or explicit expropriation in extreme cases.

Since the Great Depression of the 1930s, when many financial intermediaries' franchises were lost, such extreme episodes occurred only sporadically, and were more likely to happen during severe recessions or periods of systemic stress[1]. However, during the recent 2007-2009 financial crisis, they became frequent again. Several implicit "temporary" franchise expropriations, including different governments' take-over of institutions (e.g. the cases of the Royal Bank of Scotland in Great Britain[2], the Bank of America and Citibank[3] in the U.S., Fortis

* EGADE Business School, Tecnológico de Monterrey.

1 The "Savings and Loans" crisis, which brought along the bankruptcy of a large number of S&L banking institutions and required extensive government involvement to bail-out and build a new institutional framework to deal with that crisis.

2 In October 13, 2008, Royal Bank of Scotland announced that the British Government would take a stake of up to 58% in the Group. The aim was to "make available new tier 1 capital to UK banks and building societies to strengthen their resources permitting them to restructure their finances, while maintaining their support for the real economy, through the recapitalization scheme which has been made available to eligible institutions. HM Treasury (2008-10-13). *Treasury statement on financial support to the banking industry*. Press release.

3 In October 2008 the U.S. government was set to buy preferred equity stakes in Goldman Sachs Group Inc., Morgan Stanley, J.P. Morgan Chase & Co., Bank of America Corp. – including the soon-to-be acquired Merrill Lynch – Citigroup Inc., Wells Fargo & Co., Bank of New York Mellon and State Street Corp., and probably thousands of other banks. However, Bank of America, J.P. Morgan, Wells Fargo and Citibank were the largest recipients with 25 billion dollars each. During the first months of 2009, Citibank required additional resources. (Salomon, Paletta, Hilsenrath, & Lucchetti, 2008).

Bank in Belgium, and Hypo Real Estate in Germany), made clear that the polemic doctrine of "too-big-to-fail" was, after all, acceptable under extraordinary circumstances, and that the stability of the system had the highest priority.

But, bailouts have a limit, as evidenced during the extremely turbulent late summer weeks of 2008 when an icon of Wall Street, the 150 years old venerable Lehman Brothers, was subject to a definitive franchise "expropriation". Lehman was forced into bankruptcy[4] and subsequent liquidation when its anguished bailout claims were not responded by the U.S. government (Treasury Department) due to legal impediments and industry efforts, coordinated by the Fed and the Treasury Department, could not find a private sector buyer for the ailing institution.

As a corollary of the enormous economic costs and the dramatic loss of confidence that resulted from the global financial crisis, the idea that an increasingly globalized financial industry desperately needs a revamping of its regulatory frame became highly popular.

Typically, after historical episodes of financial crises, governments have responded with encompassing regulatory reforms, which some time later have been called "exaggerated". That was the case in the United States after the market crash that detonated the 1930s Great Depression[5] (Glass-Steagall legislation), and after the scandals of the Savings and Loans institutions in the late 1980s, or the Enron, Xerox, Tyco and others' fraudulent scandals at the beginning of the 21st century (Oxley-Sarbanes legislation).

Recently, the "Subprime-Mortgages Financial Crisis" of 2007-2009 once again provoked an encompassing financial sector regulatory revamping in major industrialized countries, home of the largest multinational banks, the most affected by the crisis, with likely ripple effects across many other countries and high odds that, for the first time, the financial industry's regulatory framework finally achieves a supra-national status[6].

It is highly unlikely that the new regulation or any other institutional measures will be capable of fully eliminating the risks of new asset bubbles or financial crises occurring in the future, but there are good reasons to believe that well-coordinated regulatory and supervisory measures can significantly reduce the probability of their occurrence, as well as to reduce the depth of their gravity, whenever they happen.

---

4 Lehman filed for Chapter 11 bankruptcy protection on September 15, 2008.

5 The "Glass-Steagall Act", named after its two authors, separated the investment banking activity from the commercial banking in American banks during a little more than half a century.

6 One of the most recent encompassing initiatives to minimize not the probability but the cost of possible future banking crises has been the imposition of a special tax on larger banks, that for their large assets fall in the category of "too big to fail" in order to create a reserve that may be used to bail them out, instead of resorting to the taxpayers' pockets. ("Bank Tax gains momentum", Wall Street Journal, March 29, 2010)

Economic history shows that financial institutions do not actively internalize the costs of risky operational decisions, and that represents one of the major reasons why a good financial regulation is deemed absolutely necessary. A "systemic risk" exists due to the financial system's many extensive and complex links with all other sectors in the economy such that the collapse of one or several large financial institutions can detonate a chain reaction and may impact many others, as well as having more encompassing effects on the domestic and the international financial markets. This sequence of events is also likely to transmit dangerous ripple effects to the rest of the economy.

From the point of view of the individual citizen, regulatory protection is necessary because there is asymmetry of information between the suppliers of financial products and savers. Regulation is necessary to guarantee the flow of information on the financial health of the provider of financial products and services, in particular when "the pay-off to the customer is contingent on the continued health of the seller (e.g., in the market for deposits and insurance)" (Nier, 2009).

Following we present a brief recount of the origins of the 2007-2009 financial crisis and how it affected financial institutions in the United States and Europe. Then we address the antecedents of the European Union's financial regulatory framework before the recent financial crisis, and finally discuss the major regulatory initiatives that focus on the sources of regulatory weakness that were detected during the intense-turbulence period of 2008-2009.

2. The origins of the 2007-2009 financial crisis in the United States

After the 2001 recession the housing market experienced a fast expansion, in a good measure explained by the abundant liquidity and low interest rates engineered by the Fed to facilitate economic recovery. In that macroeconomic environment, careless lending practices combined with inadequate compensation schemes and pushed up residential homes' prices to generate a classical speculative bubble. As is invariably the case, the price bubble finally imploded, resulting in a generalized collapse of real estate prices, as well as severe liquidity problems for the largest financial (and non-financial) companies, immerse in an environment of drastically increased volatility.

This time the bubble-burst was much worse compared to previous inflated asset prices episodes because innovative securitization mechanisms had facilitated the rollover of mortgage loans granted by specialized banks through the issuance of the so-called Asset Backed Securities (ABSs) and Collateralized Debt Obligations (CDOs) to investors. ABSs and CDOs mechanisms allowed a much faster recovery of liquidity by the lenders and exponentially increased their lending capacity.

The relative abundance of credit created the conditions to constantly raise promoters and other sales agents' performance targets, which in turn, accelerated credit analysis and shortened authorization periods. In retrospective, available evidence suggests that participants' incentives were misaligned with the objective of maintaining an ordered mortgage loans' market and that the lack of transparency of the new financial-engineering products misled both, institutional and individual investors, to greatly increase their holdings of apparently profitable and safe securities while, unfortunately, the reality was very different. Credit analysis and parametric tests were easily by-passed in order to achieve credit placement targets and often times mortgage loans were granted to people with "no-income, no-job" (NINJs), apparently under the belief that that the increase in residential prices that had been going on more or less constantly for the last decade would continue forever and that soon they would be able to refinance their property at a lower financial cost thanks to its growing equity value. What happened was that the bubble effectively burst, and low-income debtors holding loans that far exceeded their payment capacity experienced serious difficulties to meet their compromises (Grosse, 2010).

The deterioration of the US subprime mortgage market revealed an unfortunate combination of "lax underwriting standards and adverse trends in employment and income in certain U.S. regions". That explosive combination resulted in rapidly increasing delinquency rates on subprime mortgage loans, soon reaching well beyond the highest recorded historical levels. Simultaneously, prices declined in the U.S. home market and reduced the equity cushion that had supported numerous credit authorizations, increasing the probability of defaults. (IMF, 2009)

As subprime-loans default rates increased and the associated ABSs and CDOs valuations deteriorated, the crisis spread to the rest of the U.S. financial industry, soon contaminating other national financial markets. The cross-national contagion occurred because many subprime mortgage-backed securities had been widely distributed geographically. Increasing uncertainty about the value of mortgage-backed securities resulted in a rapid loss of confidence and a drastic credit-crunch that compromised the liquidity of a large number of financial and non-financial firms worldwide followed suit.

With the fast degradation of their asset portfolios' value, many American banks were affected with drastic reductions of their equity base, in several cases forced to issue new equity under highly unfavorable market conditions. New equity became absolutely necessary not only to meet regulatory requirements, but most importantly, to avoid a stampede of investors. Often times, U. S. and European banks turned to sovereign wealth funds looking for fresh capital injections[7].

During the second quarter of 2008 numerous financial intermediaries were bailed out by the U.S. government through the Treasury and the Federal Reserve, including Freddie Mac and Fannie Mae[8], the U.S. largest mortgage banks, which required an emergency bailout and a government managerial intervention, illustrating the prototypical idea of "too big to fail"[9]. Just a few weeks later that was also the fate of American Insurance General (AIG)[10], the largest insurance company in the world.

Finally, at first hard to believe after so many large financial institutions, victims of the credit crunch, had been bailed-out, Lehman Brothers was left alone, incapable to meet its short-term liquidity compromises, and forced to file for bankruptcy protection. The announcement of Lehman's demise produced one of the most extreme global financial turbulence episodes ever, because it sent financial markets the message that financial firms until then deemed "too-big-to-fail" no longer were excluded from the possibility of bankruptcy and liquidation. In response big and small financial institutions became more wary and cautious of credit ratings, reducing new loan granting to a minimum and contributing to the implosion of the financial markets.

Such defensive measures had important macro-financial repercussions, since a large number of intermediaries without direct access to deposits financing (e.g., investment banks, hedge funds and others) faced such a sudden credit-crunch. Commercial banking entities focused on the quality of their loans portfolio and on the build-up of contingency reserves, which affected their income statement bottom line, and reduced their lending capacity, as well as their willingness to lend, sending additional bad news to the market.

Among the United States intermediaries that were severely affected were the traditional "pure" investment banks, which in the face of a life-threatening illiquid environment and with the willing support of monetary and financial authorities

---

7 During January 2008, funds of Singapore, Kuwait and South Korea extended a total of $21 billion to Citigroup and Merrill Lynch. (Cadieux, 2008)

8 The two largest U.S. based mortgage banks, which in mid-2008 together either held or guaranteed 43% of all outstanding US mortgages, totaling $12.1 trillion, had to be placed under government administration on account of the erosion of their assets. (Bundesanstalt für Finanzdienstleistungsaufsicht 2008)

9 The combined magnitude of Freddie Mac and Fannie Mae's mortgage portfolios was in the order of five trillion dollars plus.

10 AIG, needed an emergency loan of $85 billion from the U.S. Federal Reserve. In return, the Federal Reserve was granted access to large parts of the insurer's assets. (Bundesanstalt für Finanzdienstleistungsaufsicht, 2008)

opted for major restructurings. The Federal Reserve facilitated the acquisition of Merrill Lynch by Bank of America and the two other large traditional investment banking houses, Goldman Sachs and Morgan Stanley, swiftly applied for a commercial bank charter that would give them access to the general public deposits, plus the protection of the Federal Deposit Insurance Corporation and the Federal Reserve support as lender of last resort.

As extreme volatility finally receded and a balance of the damages became clearer, the markets, governments and politicians had in front of their eyes hard evidence of the largest destruction of financial wealth in history. Since that moment onwards many political groups enthusiastically embraced the initiative of revising the financial regulation framework of the United States and, in January 2010, President Obama sent Congress an initiative that aims to recover some of the firewalls that existed before 1999, when the Glass-Steagall Act was abrogated. While the subject of the regulatory changes of the financial services industry in the United States is of great interest, it lies, unfortunately, beyond the limits of this work, and has been briefly discussed because of its relevance to the process that is taking place in Europe, given the close bonds between the U.S. and the E.U. financial industries.

3. The European Union's Financial Regulation Framework: Some Antecedents

The creation of the European Common Market[11] in 1957 represented an institutional platform for the increasing commercial integration of Western European countries. Almost four decades later, very significant volumes of cross-border trade and investment also justified a still more intense integration of the different national financial markets. The constantly increasing volume of daily financial transactions justified a centralized supervision and the support of information flows across borders, ideally coordinated by national supervisory agencies. The institutional framework needed to organize the harmonic coexistence of all member states' economic activities originated new institutions and regulations that, nowadays, define many different aspects of their social, political and economic relations.

According to the legislative process principles in force within the E.U. the greater part of the legislation that applies in the field of financial services is adopted at the European Commission level, with the purpose to ensure that the same rules or, in some case, minimum standards prevail throughout all member

11 The European Common Market was formed by France, West Germany, Luxembourg, Italy, Belgium and Holland.

countries; however, some regulation and supervision areas still remain under the control of the member states[12]. The European Commission can propose new legislative measures, but only after the adoption of the Commission's proposals by the member governments and the European Parliament, they become legally binding legislation.

There are two kinds of legislative acts in the EU, directives and regulations. The former are more common and, once adopted by the member states, they must be implemented at the national level, usually within two years; however, they leave member states a margin of maneuver to adapt the contents of the directive to the specificities of their national environment. In the case of regulations, once adopted, they apply directly in the legal order of the member states, i.e., there is no margin of maneuver to adapt them (European Comission, 2010).

4. The First Bank Directive

The first antecedent of a common financial regulation for all EU member countries[13] was the "First Bank Directive", issued on December 12, 1977, that established the principle that all banks established in a member state had the freedom to start operations in other member states, conditioned only by the scrupulous observance of the host country's legislation and the national authorities' guidelines. Due to the fact that a number of obligatory rules substantially differed from one country to another, notably in relation to minimum capital requirements, the First Directive had a limited impact in terms of promoting the integration of a Single European Financial Market.

Many of the problems contained in the First Directive guidelines were addressed and completely reformulated in the "White Book" of 1985. Among the most remarkable innovations, was the introduction of the explicit intention to constitute a Single Financial Market in Europe. Such an ambitious objective required the gradual elimination of differences across different domestic markets, a complex challenge due to the inexistence of a unified conception of the regulatory frame that would be desired to establish in all member countries, as well as the obvious inherent political implications.

12 Mainly those referred to the sanctions imposed in cases of breach of rules in force.

13 "European Community" is a term that referred to the European Economic Community (EEC), the European Coal and Steel Community (ECSC), and the European Atomic Energy Community (Euratom). The EC is now a separate legal entity within the European Union (EU), which was established under the Maastricht Treaty (1992) and includes intergovernmental cooperation on security and judicial affairs.

The White Book would proof decisive towards the future financial integration of the region. Its follow-up was the adoption of the "Single Act" of December 1989, where the principle that all national legislations were inspired by the same set of concerns (consumers' protection, savers safety, etc.) justified the belief that with a minimal harmonization of rules and principles each member country could trust in its communitarian partners and recognize the measures adopted by them as equivalent to their own. This initiative avoided the need to attempt a replacement of the different national regulations as a pre-condition to advance towards a unified financial market.

5. The Second Bank Directive

In January of 1993, a Second Banking Directive modified and complemented the First Directive in what regards the notion of freedom of establishments and the principle of mutual recognition, by replacing them with the concept of "Single Communitarian License".

The Second Banking Directive included interest rate controls, the regulation of cross-border movements of capital and restrictions on borrowing and reserve requirements that varied from one country to another[14]. Among its main achievements was the definition of the exact meaning of "banking", as there were significant differences in the activities performed by banking institutions in different countries of the E.U., and in line with the so called "Continental" model, mainly present in Germany, and which stood in stark contrast to the "Anglo-Saxon"[15] model. With the Second Banking Directive, the E.U. adopted the "universal banking model"(Contingent Analysis)[16].

The Second Bank Directive also introduced the principle of "home-country control" or "mutual recognition", which means that each bank has to conform to the regulation and legislation of its home country(Murphy, 2000). It also introduced the "Banking Passport", enabling banks that were registered in any E.U. member country to expand their business to all other member countries. This principle of mutual recognition eliminated the bank's need to obtain a local

14 EU Financial Services Market: From the idea of common market to financial services action plan: http://www.eestipank.info/pub/en/dokumendid/publikatsioonid/seeriad/kroon_majandus/_2003_2/_50-58aarma.pdf?objId=314192.

15 The Anglo-Saxon model of financial services separated banking and securities activities, while Germany had a tradition of universal banking, making no distinction between banks and security firms.

16 European Financial Regulation: http://www.riskglossary.com/articles/european_financial_regulation.htm.

banking charter for branches or bank products permitted by the regulations of the bank's home country, and made cross-border banking and branching easier (Federal Reserve Bank of San Francisco, 1996).

The intention of the new legal framework was to formalize the freedom of capital movements, to establish some general rules for the provision of services in the banking sector, and the preservation of stability of the financial system. Furthermore, it also aimed to prevent that financial resources moved through the pipelines of the E.U. banking institutions could be used to finance terrorist activities, and should serve as a significant component of the institutional infrastructure that would support the creation of a single European payments area[17].

The development of the legal framework was guided by three main principles. First, each nation should retain its own banking supervisory and regulatory institutions. Second, a minimal harmonization from a level above the national level should be achieved, i.e., individual countries would maintain their own regulatory and supervisory regimes, but all member nations within the E.U. should provide minimum standards. Third, directives would have to be issued at EU level, which meant that individual nations would have to take legislative action to incorporate the directives' intentions, but the exact content of the legislation was not be dictated to them(Murphy, 2000).

6. The Investment Services Directive

In 1996, the full enforcement of the Investment Services Directive (ISD) represented the completion of the first stage of regulatory changes for the three major financial services (banking, insurance and investment services). "The ISD created a European Passport for non-bank investment firms to carry out in all Member States a wide range of investment business (i.e. order collecting, execution of orders on an agency basis, dealing, portfolio management and underwriting), as well as certain additional services (such as investment advice, advice on mergers and acquisitions, safekeeping and administration of securities and foreign exchange transactions) if mentioned specifically in the authorization" (European Comission, 1996) . Since then, national financial authorities supervise the observance of the country-of-origin's regulations, and host countries' regulators establish and supervise the rules of conduct.

17 The legal framework for a single European Banking Market: http://www.hba.gr/4news/FYROM.pdf.

7. The Capital Adequacy Directive

To minimize the probability that regulatory conflicts could hinder the stability of financial institutions subject to different national capital requirements, in 1993 the EC also decided to implement the Capital Adequacy Directive (CAD) to establish uniform capital requirements for universal banks and security firms.

The European Union countries developed the CAD at the same time that the Basel Committee was working on a model to establish adequate capitalization rules for banks that responded to market risk conditions, but the Basel Accord was complete until 1996. The CAD, however, did not provide internal Value at Risk (VAR) measures, putting European banks at a relative disadvantage with respect to banks outside Europe. It was amended in 1998 to allow for the use of VAR models (CAD 2), and with the update of the Basel Standards, a new Capital Adequacy Directive (CAD 3), which implemented Basel II principles, was developed. That directive had a much wider scope of application. The new Basel Accord renewed and significantly improved the then existing rules: it provided incentives for good risk management practices, increased risk sensitivity of calibration models and reduced opportunities for regulatory arbitrage(HM Treasury, 2003).

8. Financial Services Action Plan

The Financial Services Action Plan (FSAP) was presented by the European Commission in May 1999, with the aim to achieve full integration of the EU banking and capital markets by 2005. The plan was less radical compared to others proposed in the early 1990s, but rather improved on achievements and adjusted the legal framework to fast changing market developments.

Its conception was developed with three strategic goals in mind:

Completing a single wholesale market for financial services
Developing open and secure retail banking and retail insurance markets
Ensuring state-of-the art prudential rules and supervision[18]

The FSAP covered a vast area of financial services activity and comprised 41 separate measures designed to complete the legislative framework for the internal market in what regards financial services, related to wholesale as well as to retail

18 EU Financial Services Market: From the idea of common market to financial services action plan: http://www.eestipank.info/pub/en/dokumendid/publikatsioonid/seeriad/kroon_majandus/_2003_2/_50-58aarma.pdf?objId=314192.

markets. The measures that were introduced by this instrument were categorized under a series of general priorities for action.

Moreover, the FSAP contained measures that were either relevant to the prudential supervision of an integrated financial system, or were designed to improve the general conditions for financial efficiency, notably in the areas of corporate governance and taxation[19].

9. The Commission of Wise Men and the Lamfalussy Report

In July of 2000, Baron Alexander Lamfalussy, former President of the European Monetary Institute in Frankfurt[20], and co-founder of the European Central Bank (ECB), was appointed by the council of Finance Ministers of the EU to chair a Commission that would be in charge to propose regulatory measures aimed at developing the E.U. financial services industry (securities, banks and insurance) [21]. The proposals were meant to achieve a more consistent interpretation of the EU legislation, greater convergence among national supervisory practices and improve the technical quality of the financial services legislation. The report of the Commission was delivered on February 2001, and the discussion, as well as the gradual adoption of the Committee's recommendations, known as the "Lamfalussy Process", had the stated purpose to reinforce the European financial regulatory and supervisory framework by working at four levels:

Level 1: Consisting of legislative acts, namely Directives or Regulations, proposed by the Commission following consultation with all interested parties, and adopted under the "co-decision" procedure by the Council and the European Parliament, in accordance with the EC Treaty.

Level 2: The European Securities Committee, the future regulatory committee, would assist the Commission in adopting the relevant implementing measures, and ensure that technical provisions can be kept up to date with market developments.

Level 3: Improving the common and uniform implementation of Level 1 and 2 acts in the member states, a process in which the Committee of European Securities Regulators would have a particular responsibility.

19 Ibid.

20 The European Monetary Institute was the immediate predecessor of the European Central Bank, before the introduction of the euro in 1999.

21 The Lamlaussy Commission became known as the "Committee of Wise Men on the Regulation of the European Securities Markets".

Level 4: The Commission would strengthen the enforcement of Community law. That four-level approach was fully endorsed by the European Council at Stockholm in March 2001. At that time, it was agreed that in those cases where implementing measures in the field of securities markets were acknowledged to be particularly sensitive, the Commission would avoid going against predominant views within the Council.

The Lamfalussy Commission also proposed a set of "best practices" that had the objective to reinforce the EU's supervisory framework, especially during market instability periods.

One of the most tangible institutional results of the Lamfalussy report's recommendations was the creation of two pan-European institutions, the European Securities Committee and the European Securities Regulators' Committee.

The most generalized opinion about the Lamfalussy Process is that it was positive and contributed to the advancement of the financial markets of the region. However, although it's positive aspects are undeniable (flexible regulation, convergence, cooperation, etc.) several improvements were deemed necessary. During the following years the European Commission and the European Parliament consistently worked in developing the organization and mechanisms to facilitate the operation of an increasingly complex interlinked group of national financial markets.

10. Why did the existing regulations fail in 2007-2009?

During the last three decades of the 20th century there was a dramatic increase in the relative size of wholesale financial services, as well as a deepening of their links with other productive sectors of the economy. The more globalized the world economy was, the more complex the functions of global banks, managing their own multinational treasury and helping corporate entities to manage risks that naturally arise from simultaneous global operations and from the continuous fluctuation of exchange rates, interest rates and commodities prices in many countries.

The Bank for International Settlements (BIS) responded to the new environmental conditions by promoting a profound revision of international standards to consolidate practices and reduce systematic risk. That effort was conducted by a Committee, integrated by several nations that after the 1974 liquidation of the Cologne-based Bank Herstatt decided to form a cooperative council to harmonize banking standards and regulations within and between all member states[22].

22 The Basle Committe founding countries were France, Germany, Italy, Japan, the Netherlands, Sweden, Switzerland the United Kingdom, the United States and Luxembourg, also known as the G-10.

The Basle Committee drafted its first version of quantitative and technical benchmarks (the Basel I Accord) aimed to help harmonize banking supervision, regulation and capital adequacy standards, in 1988. The latest version of international prudential regulation, as set forth by the Basel II accords (2004), was drawn up as an improvement over the original Basel Accord. The main points addressed were the need for risk-sensitive capital ratios, increasing risk mitigation practices by addressing both operational and credit risk separately, and lastly, seeking for more supervision and market discipline to reduce regulatory arbitrage. The main objective of Basel II is to standardize international regulations with the purpose that national regulators can base on them for the design of their own laws and regulations (how much capital banks need to put aside to guard against diverse risks that banks face like market risk, operational risk and credit risk, etc.).

Basel II has been accused by some analysts as one of the major culprits of the 2007-2009 financial crisis. In our opinion, such an accusation is flawed since Basle II principles were introduced in the E.U. as late as January 1, 2008, and were to be incorporated in the U.S. legislation until April 1st of 2010[23].

However, it is illustrative to briefly review what several authors have written about this issue. For example, Danielsson et al. (2001) suggested that Basle II derived regulations failed to address risk as an internal or endogenous factor. They argued that Value-at-Risk, Basle II's preferred measure of risk, can destabilize the economy and induce a crisis fueled by itself. They also stressed the heavy reliance of Basle II on credit agencies and their standard way of risk measuring, as measures used in credit risk assessment by banks for individual creditworthiness, as well as the lack of operational risk modeling due to the lack of adequate technologies and comprehensive data bases. Cannata and Quagliariello (2009) suggest that among several other responsibilities attributed to Basle II in connection with the financial crisis, there are such aspects as the fact that the average level of capital required by the new discipline is inadequate; that the new Capital Accord, interacting with fair-value accounting, has caused remarkable losses in the portfolios of intermediaries; that capital requirements based on the Basel II regulations are cyclical and therefore tend to reinforce business cycle fluctuations; that in the Basel II framework, the assessment of credit risk is delegated to non-banking institutions, such as rating agencies, which are potentially subject to conflicts of interest; that the key assumption that banks' internal models for measuring risk exposures are superior than any other has proved wrong; and, finally, that the new framework provides incentives to intermediaries to deconsolidate from their

23 Several voices suggest there are strong reasons to believe that Basle II does need an extensive revision.

balance-sheets some very risky exposures. However, they recognize that in most cases it is not appropriate to link the current financial crisis to Basel II, and that some of the main drivers of the crisis simply cannot be entirely ascribed to the new regulation. Finally, Fees and Hege (2005) suggests that relying on external Credit Rating Agencies is not the best alternative to credit risk measuring, and does not lead to efficient risk management practices nor to optimal capital requirements. If banks control their own portfolios' risk, they can increase its size and make the whole industry safer, by observing high credit quality standards.

11. The integration of the financial markets in Europe, national regulations and the convergence efforts

Since the first signs of the financial crisis appeared during 2007, several national governments announced initiatives to implement extensive bailout measures and recovery plans backed up with tax-payers money. The official language was very similar in all countries; extraordinary measures were required to avoid a systemic collapse that could endanger economic stability. However, it was during the Global Finance summit that took place in London in November of 2008 that the most industrialized and the biggest emerging economies agreed on the implementation of a global financial reform to close loopholes in regulation and supervision.

After the initial meeting, the G20 leaders endorsed a document called "Framework for Strong, Sustainable and Balanced Growth", in which they committed to a timetable to achieve specific objectives and initiated a new consultative mutual assessment to evaluate whether their policies would collectively deliver the desired objectives. The implementation of that effort was delegated to international organizations capable of developing in-depth studies to inform the Leaders on what the policy alternatives were, as well as their pros and cons. They designated the International Monetary Fund (IMF) and the World Bank (WB) to perform multiple analyses, supported with inputs from other international organizations, including the Financial Standards Board, the Organization for Economic Cooperation and Development, the International Labor Organization, the World Trade Organization and the United Nations Conference on Trade and Development. The stated objective was to provide technical and conceptual foundations required to:

Set out national and regional policy frameworks, programs and projections by the end of January 2010;

Conduct the initial phase of a cooperative mutual assessment process, supported by IMF and World Bank analyses, of the collective consistency of national and regional policies;

Develop a basket of policy options to deliver those objectives, for Leaders to consider at their Summit in June 2010; and,

Refine mutual assessments and develop more specific policy recommendations for Leaders at their Summit in November 2010.

While the discussion about the origins and consequences of the recent financial crisis will continue for many years to come, a number of national governments, regulatory agencies and international financial organizations, have already taken the initiative and started the implementation of new regulatory frameworks, as well as more robust supervision mechanisms of the financial industry. There is no doubt about the interest of national authorities to minimize the probability of a repetition of a systemic financial stress episode or, worse yet, another fully fledged financial crisis.

12. The Larosière and Turner Reports

In October 2008, the Chancellor of the U.K. Exchequer and the President of the European Commission, commanded the preparation of in depth analyses of the causes of the financial crisis and recommendations to minimize the likeliness of its recurrence to Lord Turner, head of the Financial Services Authority, and Jacques de Larosière, chairman of the de Larosière group (created for that purpose), respectively.

Jacques de Larosière released his report on February 25, 2009, and Lord Turner on March, 2009. Both reports make an extensive and in-depth analysis of the origins of the financial crisis and coincide in several points, but also have significant differences. Highly sophisticated analyses of the causes of the financial crisis, they reflect the point of view of notable specialists on the more relevant issues to consider towards the implementation of new regulations that better serve the needs of the global financial industry, but particularly that of the U.K. and the E.U. Both shared in many aspects of the diagnosis of the financial crisis, like the fact that it was macroeconomic imbalances which created the conditions for excessive lending practices that eventually provoked a credit bubble in the United States and other developed nations, or that massive growth in the scale and complexity of securitized credits surpassed the ability of financial intermediaries to control their risk exposure.

They also hold supervisory authorities and bank management executives responsible for relying on mathematical models and credit ratings to control their portfolios which, in an environment of extensive deviations from "normality", were likely to have resulted in lax decisions and recommend reviewing Basel II in order to improve several aspects. The main point is to avoid procyclicality measures in Basel II's implementation, in order to reduce the extent to which lending capacity is impaired in an economic downturn. However, what seems to be an original contribution of the reports and a shared concern is the conviction that the members of the E.U. urgently need to have a consistent set of national rules and regulations that eliminate existing inconsistencies.

The de Larosière group report emphatically argues that "an efficient single market should have a harmonized set of core rules. In order to have this set of core rules the E.U. needs to harmonize rules and regulations from country to country. The main problem is that each country has its own regulations and it's impossible to have an efficient market with these characteristics" (Larosière, 2009).

Among the most relevant proposals of the de Larosière report are:

1. A specific and detailed review of Basel II to increase the minimum capital requirements and enforce a better set of rules for off-balance sheet items that reduce procyclicality. For better results in Basel II, according to the de Larosière report, there need to be more strict rules and laws for the internal control of the banks and to guarantee liquidity.
2. The idea that credit rating agencies need a fundamental review of their models to achieve a better interpretation of what is the economic reality of securities issuers, and that with time there needs to be a reduction in the use of ratings.
3. That there should be a standard accounting reporting methodology in order to achieve better transparency in the valuation of assets in illiquid markets, where mark-to-market mechanisms cannot be used.
4. That all financial firms should be subject to a common regulation that explicitly establishes appropriate capital requirements.
5. That the risk management function needs to be independent of financial institutions in order to have effectiveness. Risk monitoring within financial institutions evidently failed during the recent crisis.
6. The need to develop an encompassing EU efficient regulatory framework.
7. That the Deposit Guarantee Schemes (DGS) in the EU need to provide an equal and high level of protection to all bank customers, i.e., to set the same rules in all countries.

The de Larosière group also recommended that the European Central Bank (ECB) should play a major role in the new European supervisory system in two aspects: macro-prudential supervision and micro-prudential supervision. The following diagram, reproduced from the de Larosière report, introduces the European Systemic Risk Council and the European System of Financial Supervision as the instances responsible for both levels of supervision and continuous risk assessment.

The de Larosière report institutional proposal to improve regulation and supervision in the European Union

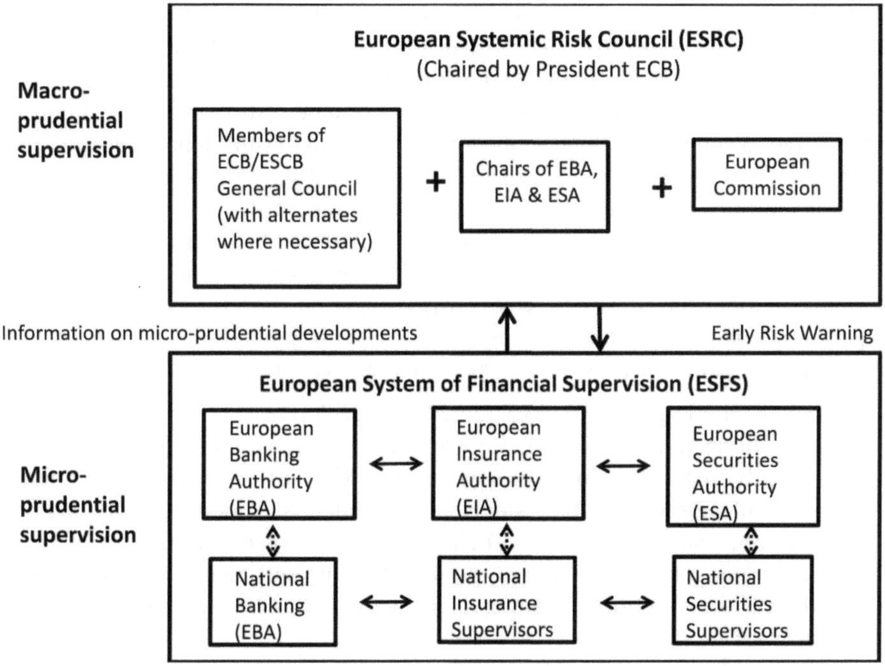

Source: de Larosière, "The High-Level Group on Financial Supervision in the EU". February 2009 pp. 57

The macro prudential supervision component aims to establish the European Systemic Risk Council (ESRC) to replace the current Banking Supervision Committee (BSC). Its task would be to form judgments and make recommendations on macro-prudential policy, issue risk warnings, compare observations on macro-economic and prudential developments and give direction to these issues.

There is a need to assure a proper flow of information between national supervisors and the ECB/ESCB to allow the ESRC to perform its function; as well as an effective early warning mechanism to detect the first signs of weakness at the institutions level. With such early warning system, and depending on the nature of the risks detected, the relevant EU authorities would be alerted to take a proper action.

The micro-prudential supervision proposal suggests the need to establish a European System of Financial Supervisors (ESFS) where existing national supervisors will continue to carry-out-day-to-day supervision and three new Pan-European Authorities will be set up (the European Banking Authority or EBA; the European Insurance Authority, or EIA; and the European Securities Authority, or ESA).

Some of the main tasks of the Authorities are the legally required mediation between national supervisors, adoption of obligatory supervisory standards, adoption of required technical decisions applicable to individual institutions, oversight and coordination of colleges of supervisors, licensing and supervision of specific EU-wide institutions, compulsory cooperation with the ESRC to ensure adequate macro-prudential supervision, and strong coordinating role in crisis situations.

Baron Lamfalusy, who in 2009 advised the Belgian government on the reforming of financial architecture, expressed wide support for the de Larosière report, and contributed to this discussion by expressing that in his personal view, macro-prudential crisis prevention process comprises three stages[24]:

1. The collection of information, signaling developments in banks, financial intermediaries and markets that could give rise to crisis manifestations. The potentially most valuable source for this kind of information is micro-prudential supervision; but, since micro-prudential supervisors are neither trained nor mandated to detect such crisis signals, macro-prudential supervisors – coming from ECB/Eurosystem – shoul be sufficiently closely associated with the "traditional" supervisory activities to be able to identify any such crisis signals.
2. The second stage includes (a) the pooling of the information collected at the level of systemically significant individual banking groups and (b) the analysis of the aggregated figures. The ECB would have to play a key role in setting up and organizing the work of this team. According to the Recommendation 16 of the de Larosière Group: "A new body called the European Systemic Risk Council (ESRC), to be chaired by the ECB President, should be set up under the auspices and with the logistical support of the European Central Bank" Without an effective pooling of information and a scrupulously independent analysis, the European Systemic Risk Council will not be able to do its job (de Larosiere, 2009).
3. The third stage is the functioning of the risk warning system, under the auspices of the ESCR. This is a crucial part of the proposals: what has been missing so far has not only been the lack of information, of the pooling of information and of its analysis, but also the lack of policy reaction.

---

24 IMF-NBB-Bruegel Conference, Policy Panel 2 on 24 March 2009.

13. Lord Turner's Report

Published as "The Turner Review"[25], the Financial Services Authority (FSA, the UK's financial markets supervisor) version of an encompassing effort to diagnose the causes of the recent financial crisis and prevent something similar occurring again seeks to achieve five outcomes for the global banking regulatory and supervisory framework:

i. That the global banking system is better capitalized and more resilient to liquidity shocks throughout the business cycle;
ii. That the regulatory framework in general, and its capital component in particular, are explicitly counter-cyclical;
iii. That the supervisory, crisis management and resolution arrangements for cross-border financial services groups are effective and reflect the interests of host countries as well as those of the home state;
iv. That any material risks to financial stability posed by unregulated activities or firms are identified and controlled to the extent possible; and
v. That macro-prudential and other risks to financial stability are identified at both the international and national levels and effective action is taken to mitigate them.

The Turner report aims to correct what went wrong in the recent crisis. To that end, it suggest there has to be an increase in international cooperation in supervision through closer communication of colleges of supervisors, as well as more intense international cooperation and coordination in crisis management, and a use of host country powers to require strongly capitalized local subsidiaries, and restrictions on intra-group exposures and flows.

The Turner's Review is organized around eight central axes, as follows:

i. Increase quality of bank capital
ii. Increase in trading book capital
iii. Avoiding procyclicality in Basel II
iv. Growth leverage ratio backstop
v. Contain liquidity risks
vi. Credit ratings agencies
vii. Remuneration in Banks
viii. Regulation and supervision of cross border banks.

25 The Turner Review was made public, along with the FSA Discussion Paper 09/2: A regulatory response to the global banking crisis, on March 18, 2009.

Increase the quality of Bank Capital: According to the FSA, it is necessary to evaluate what minimum ratios should be set for common equity, retained earnings and preferred stocks in banks. Due to the analysis made by the FSA, the Total Capital (preferred stock + subordinated debt) must be greater than 8% of the Weighted Risk Assets (WRA) and preferred stock must be at least 4% of the WRA.

Increase in Trading Book Capital: As the crisis broke, the Value at Risk (VAR) measures of risks proved that prices and market liquidity changed more rapidly than regulators had assumed. Therefore, Turner's Review suggests that a change in the trading book capital approach is necessary. Proposals adopted by the Basel Committee, planned for the implementation by the end of 2010, should make a major difference with requirements for VAR calculations, an incremental capital charge to cover default and credit risk mitigation, and increased charges for securitizations.

Avoiding Procyclicality: The Basel II regime is often criticized for having procyclical effects. This idea arises in practice depending on the design of the risk measurement models used by banks in their assessments, and in particular, if risk models are based on "point in time" rather than "through the cycle" estimates of loan losses. Basel II preferred "through the cycle" methodology because it is less procyclical. The problem is that several banks didn't develop effective "through the cycle" estimates before the launch of Basel II because they didn't have sufficient long historic records of past losses.

Gross Leverage Ratio Backstop: Gross leverage ratio refers to total assets to capital. Turner says there are 2 arguments for using a gross leverage ratio as a backstop control measure:

Assets which are thought to be low risk can become highly illiquid and risky when systemic problems emerge, impacting asset sales related to the gross scale of the balance sheet positions.

Calculating capital requirements based on internal models normally results in judgment between bank management and regulators, so a backstop against the impact of regulatory concessions is a good alternative.

Contain Liquidity Risks: Turner's Review suggests there are some important considerations in liquidity risk management, like the fact that during the current crisis, the simultaneous attempt by multiple banks to improve their liquidity position by shortening the tenor of their placements in the interbank market contributed to a collapse of liquidity. Also, that there has been a growth in the set of potential sources of liquidity making it difficult to base good liquidity regulation based on one or few standard ratios.

Credit Rating Agencies: The report suggests that regulation can solve issues relating to the proper governance of rating agencies and the management of conflict of interest. The recommendation in this case it that in the new legislation, European colleges ensure that appropriate structures and procedures are in place to manage conflicts of interest.

There is always a danger that the use of credit rating within the Basel II capital adequacy rules may introduce a new element of procyclicality in future: However, Turner's Review comments that other measures of assessing risk are more procyclical.

Remuneration in Banks: It is likely that remuneration policies, in combination with capital requirements and accounting rules, created incentives for some executives and traders to take excessive risks in the past. The Financial Services Authority (FSA) published a Code where it states a set of principles which are expected to better align remuneration policies with appropriate risk management. Some of the guiding principles included in the Code are:

Firms must ensure that remuneration policies are consistent with effective risk management.

Remuneration committees should reach independent judgments on the implications of remuneration for risk and risk management.

Remuneration should reflect an individual's record of compliance with risk management procedures, rules and appropriate culture, as well as financial measures for performance.

Financial measures used in remuneration policies should entail the adjustment of profit measures to reflect the relative riskiness of different activities.

Regulation and Supervision of cross border banks: The effective supervision of large cross border institutions can be improved by maximizing the flow of information between home and host country supervisors. In order to do this, the Financial Stability Forum defined the objective that all major cross border financial institutions should be covered by a "college of supervisors".

Besides the Larosière and Turner reports, which represent the official position of the European Commision and the Financial Sevices Agency respectively, the subject of new regulatory mechanisms and institutions for the E.U. financial markets has been discussed extensively by academicians, politicians and several multilateral financial institutions (IMF, BIS, OECD, World Bank, etc), and by the ECB, of course. Most of the positions coincide in that banks should expect a far higher level of regulatory intervention and that the transit to a new system is likely to take places sooner than later. However, one of the areas of greater debate is centered on the issue of which regulators should regulate what institutions. The Larosiere report explicitly affirms that the current regulatory financial framework of the

E.U. lacks coherence, the main reason being the excess of discretion granted to national authorities, a problem that was detected since the initial steps of the Single Financial Market, but that has not found a satisfactory solution yet. There is no possible doubt that a single unified economy requires a single financial regulatory framework, but at the same time there are important political obstacles before a thorough reform of the current national regulations finally converges into a single E.U. financial regulation and supervision. Even while the national regulations are not likely to be replaced in their entireness in the short run, all regulated financial services firms, banks and non-banks, must expect a significantly stricter regulatory overview. The enormous cost of the recent financial crisis is a powerful argument to push through the reforms more quickly that would normally be expected. At this stage, the question is no longer whether there will be significant changes in the regulation of the E.U. financial industry, but in which areas will more intervention is most likely to occur and what will be the timing for that.

14. Concluding Remarks

The current financial regulation in the E.U. presents a number of inconsistencies due to national regulatory and supervisory schemes which, analyzed *ex-post-facto*, may help explain why the damages to European financial institutions were so widely generalized. Among several other aspects that require closer scrutiny, obligations reporting standards are very diverse from one country to another, especially for non-listed firms because they have no obligation to make public their financial reports. The existence of diverse accounting practices for pensions causes serious distortions in the calculation of fund in different nations. Also, the utilization of different methodologies to calculate risks faced by financial institutions makes it very difficult to achieve valid comparisons and establish prudential rules. Some E.U. countries have an extended definition of credit institutions while other members have much more limited definitions and such differences between members can lead to laxer supervision and regulatory arbitrage.

The recent financial crisis showed that the very complex and uneven financial system gave room to arbitrage opportunities, inefficiencies, and huge differences in the constraints that institutions face in very similar economic activities. The most striking example is that of the shift in subprime mortgage originations to less regulated institutions or the shift in risk to where accounting is more favorable.

A post-crisis financial framework should focus on simplifying and making the system more uniform as a whole; rules should apply evenly to entities involved in similar functions.

The crisis proved there is an urgent need for better regulation on capital reserve requirements and requirements on liquidity and reserves should be based more on future forecasts of economic cycles. That is particularly important for institutions subject to risk-based capital requirements like banks, so that it may act as a stabilizer in periods of economic crisis.

The re-regulation of the financial industry efforts are already present in most E.U. countries (more so in those severely affected by the crisis) but, there are still important differences in the approach each country is following. Although for several decades there has been a maybe too-slow convergence process in regulation of financial activity among E.U. members, the post-crisis convergence should move faster. However, we believe that even when convergence is a high priority, resulting regulations should still reflect idiosyncratic considerations, given the significant development differences that still exist among E.U. members.

Although significant advances have been achieved, greater cooperation among national authorities in the European Union would promote more efficiency in the provision of financial services, as well as greater stability and capacity to respond to unexpected volatility or other exogenous factors.

References

Cannata, F., & Quagliariello, M. (2009). The role of Basel II in the Subprime Financial Crisis: Guilty or not Guilty? Milan: Center for Applied Research in Finance, Bocconi University, Working Paper 3/09; Electronic copy available at: http://ssrn.com/abstract=1330417.

Contingent Analysis. (s.f.). Contingent Analysis. Obtenido de Risk Glossary: http://www.riskglossary.com/link/european_financial_regulation.htm.

Danielsson, J., Embrechts, P., Goodhart, C., Keating, C., Muennich, F., Renault, O., et al. (2001). An Academic Response to Basle II. London: LSE Financial Markets Group.

European Comission. (1996). European Comission, Single Market Newa.

European Commission, (2010) http://ec.europa.eu/internal_market/top_layer/quick_en.htm, accessed Februrary 15, 2010.

Federal Reserve Bank of San Francisco. (5 de April de 1996). Eonomic Research and Data. Obtenido de http://www.frbsf.org/econrsrch/wklyltr/el9612.html

Feess, E., & Hege, U. (2005). The Basle II Accord: Internal Rating and Bank Differentiation. HEC School of Management and CEPR.

Grosse, R. (2010). The Global Financial Crisis: A Behavioral View. Monterrey, Nuevo León: EGADE-Tec de Monterrey.

HM Treasury. (December de 2003). Obtained from http://www.hm-treasury.gov.uk/media/9D1/61/cad3condoc03.pdf.

International Monetary Fund. (2009). Global Financial Stability Report. International Monetary Fund.
Larosière, J. d. (February, 2009). The High Level Group on Financial Supervision in the EU. Brussels.
Murphy, N. B. (May de 2000). European Union Financial Developments: The Single Market, the Single Currency and Banking. Obtenido de Federal Deposit Insurance Corporation: http://www.fdic.gov/bank/analytical/banking/2000may/2_13n1.pdf.
Nier, E. W. (2009). Financial Stability Frameworks and the Role of Central Banks: Lessons from the Crisis. The Future of Banking Regulation. Frankfurt am Main: International Monetary Fund, WP/09/70.
Salomon, Paletta, Hilsenrath, & Lucchetti. (14 de October de 2008). The Wall Street Journal. Obtained from http://online.wsj.com/article/SB122390023840728367.html.
Santillán-Salgado, R. (2009). The Case of ABN-Amro Acquisition. EGADE-Tec de Monterrey.
The 2007-2009 Financial Crisis:Causes, Impacts and the Need for New Regulation, Richard Ivey School of Business, the University of Western Ontario, Case # 9B08N014 (2008).

An Approach to the CSR of European Companies Operating in Mexico

Florina Guadalupe Arredondo Trapero , Verónica del Carmen Maldonado de Lozada[†] *& Alfonso Benito Fraile*[‡]

1. Introduction

In recent years, very few topics have captured as much interest among corporations such as Corporate Social Responsibility, which is defined by the European Union as the acquired obligation of a business towards its environment. Even though CSR is not a new topic, more companies are supporting CSR initiatives, such as corporative philanthropy, cause marketing, minority support programs, socially responsible employment and manufacturing – all of which are being done with an important financial and marketing focus.

Since its inception, the Free Trade Agreement between the European Union and Mexico (EUMFTA), signed in 2002, has favored the presence of important European multinationals in Mexico. Furthermore, the progress of Corporate Social Responsibility (CSR) acquired a significant impulse among multinational companies. It is assumed that different venues of international companies should have different concretions of their CSR depending on the specific characteristics of the country or environment in which they are established.

ALIARSE (2009) and the Mexican Centre for Philanthropy (2009), two of the most important promoters of CSR in Mexico, define CSR as the conscious and congruent commitment to fulfill entirely with the company's aims, both internal and external, considering the economic, social and environmental expectations of all the participants; denoting respect for people, ethical values, the community and the environment; and finally contributing to the common good (Cajiga, 2009).

2. European and Mexican Conceptions of CSR

The World Economic Forum (2009) has defined CSR as the contribution made by a company to society through its essential activities as a business, its social investment, its philanthropic programs, as well as its involvement in public policy. Likewise, the European Union defines CSR as the voluntary integration made by

, †, ‡ Department of Philosophy and Ethics, Tecnológico de Monterrey.

a company of the social and environmental concerns to its commercial operations, and its relations among all interlocutors as well (Comisión de las Comunidades Europeas, 2001). It is quite clear how the first definition emphasizes in the internal and external work of an organization, while the other calls the attention to the voluntary assumption of the CSR. For this, it is important to analyze what CSR means to European and Mexican business and what is expected from the social, economical and political demands (Brito, 2005).

In the European sphere, Social Responsibility has been incorporated into diverse entrepreneurial practices, but according to Lozano, et al. (2007), CSR is still not an integral part of the business culture. According to his argument, there is still an important path to clarify and to walk through. There are some key questions that are not yet answered about CSR from the European perspective: Is CSR in expansion in the corporate world? Does CSR media visibility correspond to the way it has been assumed? Is CSR about good negotiations or about a cultural change? Has a true adequate consensus been reached about what CSR s and what is expected from it?

According to the Mexican Center of Philanthropy (Centro Mexicano para la Filantropía, 2009), an association that encourages CSR in Mexico, in most cases, social responsibility is implicitly assumed as donations. It is yet not understood why CSR does surpass this point, since it is not about giving money but about sharing talents, capacities, and infrastructure to respond to social challenges. It is also not about defining social responsibility strategies in terms of costs, since it should be viewed as an investment that the company makes for its society. Although the economical dimension is important and necessary, the erratum is to think that donating is an act of generosity and not of responsibility (Ruíz, 2005). The difference can be enormous: an act of generosity can surge from a spontaneous restlessness, but this does not guarantee its permanence. However, corporate social responsibility implies assuming the commitment of attending the inner, outer and environmental part of an organization. As part of its social responsibility, the company assumes a project which includes collaborators, clients, environment and society in general. When a company assumes its social responsibility, it is not only an altruist company but an intelligent one. For example, every company benefits from having a better prepared workforce, from developing their suppliers or from widening their market. But all of the intellectual, material and economic wealth is not generated on its own. Companies should collaborate to create all of this social development through CSR. Social responsibility should not be seen as a trend but as a permanent topic in the entrepreneurial agenda. In this sense, social responsibility is not a practice focused only on the community but rather, focused on internal, external and environmental challenges.

In the Latin American context, the discussion centers on trying to clarify what CSR demands. As formerly established, for some actors CSR is mistaken with philanthropy; it is implied that CSR is giving a fund to support social causes. For other actors, it is a new way of assuming the role of a corporation in society. It has also been discussed if CSR is a voluntary issue or if this issue is demanded from society. If it was a voluntary matter, it would stay in the businessman's decision; if it were a matter of duty, then it would be more of a responsibility than of willingness and as such, could so be demanded by diverse actors.

It seems that in Europe, as well as in Latin America (specifically, in Mexico) CSR is a subject that is not thoroughly completed and is still in process of construction with different levels of progress. In both contexts, a dialogue process and confrontation among the actors is required. A profound and serious dialogue is required to consider agreements, as well as disagreements, about the limits and possibilities of CSR. CSR must be assumed not from a list of indicators that companies take into practice, but as a result of a reflectional, serious debate and process between the involved parties; since in the majority of cases CSR strategies only follow private interest.

According to the reports presented by national and international companies in Mexico, it is visible that they have achieved important contributions; however, the bond that the company establishes with society through CSR projects has not been sufficiently debated. Defining a basic conception about the significance and implications of CSR could help delimit and delineate the progress that surges from it; otherwise, CSR strategies would be made through arbitrary decisions or deviate from what society truly demands.

With respect to the effort done in the social aspects by the Mexican companies and the European companies with investment in Mexico, in the majority of projects, there is not a thorough analysis that justifies why a specific project is undertaken and not another. Nevertheless, the effectiveness of the results, in terms of generated social change, is not evaluated either.

For this reason, it is necessary that the issues that should constitute the Mexican agenda for CSR fulfill the social demands assertively and their implications be debated. There is not one without the other; the debate about CSR without an agenda for the Mexican reality would be futile. Furthermore, an agenda without debate from the different sectors (economical, social, academic and political) would be an empty one.

It is precisely the lack of dialogue between the economical, social, academic and political sectors that has limited enterprises' more efficient articulation of their contribution to society through CSR practices. What is expected is to orient a decisive effort toward the fulfillment of the human rights and in particular, take the Millenium Development Goals (MDG) as reference given their priority in Mexico.

3. The Millenium Development Goals (MDG) as Reference for CSR in Mexico

The Millenium Development Goals could be an important reference to focus CSR practices, as World Economic Forum (2009. p.1) declared:

> "The Forum believes that partnerships with business can accelerate progress towards meeting the UN's Millennium Development Goals. Businesses are not humanitarian organizations, but to a certain extent they should feel and take the responsibility to fight hunger or poverty in general. The response from the private sector can be highly effective when companies apply their core competencies to fighting poverty and hunger".

The United Nations Global Compact (2009), a strategic policy initiative for businesses that are committed to aligning their operations and strategies with ten universally accepted principles in the areas of human rights, labour, environment and anti-corruption, established an important objective to the international community: reducing the percentage of people with daily income of less than one dollar by 2015 to 50%. Besides this objective, it was proposed to lead the efforts of corporate social responsibility towards the achievement of other social objectives, such as: decrease of hunger, lack of nutrition, illnesses, promotion of equality and autonomy between men and women; also, to support and guarantee basic and elemental education, as well as to promote the 21 principles of sustainable development (Corral et al., 2006).

In this summit, it was proposed that in order to head toward achieving the former objectives, the developed countries should help the third world countries in a direct way: by increasing their commercial relationships, through investment support, as well as with debt handling.

For this reason, the MDG's Report may be considered one of the most valuable and notable documents approved by the United Nations in the last years. This document presents an integrated and common vision of the main problems that have an impact on humanity. Besides, it provides with some guidelines of how to resolve them and promotes corporate social responsibility in the business arena. Corporate Social Responsibility is viewed as a culture that benefits both social and enterprise development, creating a virtuous circle of growth. The UN Secretary General, the specialized organisms of the UN system, representatives of the International Monetary Fund, together with the World Bank and OECD, had the objective to create the MDGs. Besides the objectives, they established quantifiable goals and predetermined periods for each objective. In addition, they proposed indicators that showed and allowed to evaluate the progress achieved during the 1990-2015 period.

The organisms that support, evaluate and supervise these objectives agreed in accepting the MDGs and their criteria of compliance. Both the donating countries and the developing countries agreed that through these objectives world progress was being aspired.

Nevertheless, the social agenda in Latin America is far from been covered. These actions have not yet reduced the social problems that are part of the underdeveloped countries. With this goal international agreements have been established to create networks that focus on the solution of underdevelopment problems.

As a result of the MDGs, different networks among the countries were constituted, in order to monitor the Global Compact, an international initiative proposed by the United Nations. The Global Compact is an international alliance of voluntary junction that unites throughout the world more than 4000 enterprises and organizations; it allows the formation of a network among them whose common denominator is the adherence to the mentioned principles.

To ratify the support to the Global Compact, the states that integrate the United Nations signed a commitment, whose expression was reflected in the MDG's Declaration. After seven years the indicators and goals designed to monitor the countries' advance were revised. This revision represented an opportunity to examine the development processes in the regions related to the pact, besides providing information about the elements that limit their scope.

Thanks to this revision the contribution that is being done to achieve the social responsibility commitments (established by the managerial groups to improve social standards) was known and recommendations to align the company's operation towards the MDG's objectives for Latin America were made.

According to the information provided by the Economic Commission for Latin America and the Caribbean (ECLAC, 2005) it has been observed that in Latin America and the Caribbean, even though there are clusters that have assumed their CSR role, the poverty reduction in the 1990-2004 period has not fulfilled what was expected. According to Kliksberg (2004), Latin America is the continent with the most inequality in the world. In other words, the poor development has only increased the social gap.

The decrease in poverty has been inferior to what was expected; the 2015 goal of decreasing extreme poverty to 50% has not been reached. Adding to this information and according to ECLAC (2005) data, 96 million people, in other words, around 18.6% of Latin America total population, are found in an extreme poverty situation, with a major incidence in rural zones (37% vs. 13%).

According to the United Nations Development Program (UNDP, 2008) and the Prince of Wales International Business Leaders Forum taking a future scope, the private sector is a key factor for the developing world, and the developing world is a critical factor for big businesses. In order for big businesses to help the developing world, hence helping their selves, they must invest in a sound business environment, identify and capitalize on new business opportunities and manage direct costs and risks (Global Reporting Initiative, 2004).

By investing in a sound business environment, companies can have access to a healthy and competitive workforce, which contributes to safer and more stable societies, allowing the business to work better. By harnessing new business opportunities, companies can capitalize on unexplored resources that can yield to greater innovation and value creation. Finally, through a CSR orientation to resolve social problems, diseases, conflicts, poor education and poor health could be reduced.

Although businesses are not primarily responsible for the MDG's accomplishments, they do have a vital role in their development. They have to commit to governments, public sectors, academics and the civil society to achieve the MDGs and move in the same direction.

The relationship between CSR and MDGs had been already corroborated by empirical research (Quiroga, 2007). It was statistically demonstrated that the unfulfillment of the MDGs was closely related to the lack of commitment or absence of corporate social responsibility. Also, the United Nations Development Program (UNDP) mentions: CSR activities result as part of the partnership with UNDP and government (UNDP, 2008). Although it is recognized that CSR is a cornerstone in achieving the MDGs, it is necessary to define what type of CSR is referred to in Latin America. The next set of paragraphs will clarify this concept and link it to the social context in a strategic way.

Based on the latter, it is important that Mexico assume with more strength the corporate social responsibility, taking the MDGs as a reference. In this sense, the traditional CSR conception has to be debated.

4. The Stakeholders' Role in Defining CSR Objectives

Having a debate about the significance of CSR implies that it must be recognized that there are actors that are affected in a certain way by the economical activity. These stakeholders may adopt diverse ties with a company: voluntary or involuntary stakeholders, primary or secondary, internal or external (Mitchell et al. 1997).

Classifications may vary according to the different criteria, but what is interesting to note is that in each one of them, the company is conceptualized as an entity that is not alienated from its surroundings. In other words, the company is part of the public debate as well as of the internal demand; the company is questioned, is pressured, and is demanded by the public sector.

Civil society (and its forms of organization like NGOs) demands are supported by transnational initiatives that become a frame of reference for CSR; some examples are Global Compact, OECD directives and the Global Reporting Initiative (GRI) model.

What CSR signifies is no longer a term understood exclusively by the enterprises. As part of the CSR debate, a sole voice must not only be heard but rather, many voices debating and compromising with the social change that can be achieved through CSR. This is how Corporate Social Responsibility has stopped being a tangential subject and is becoming a transversal subject that seeks to articulate the economical, social, academic and political sectors.

In other words, through social responsibility, it is expected that the company generate quality products, fair prices, decent salaries and adequate working conditions; all together with a commitment to the environment and community (Ruiz, 2004). There is a new type of relationship expected between a company and their stakeholders. The Friedman model establishes that social responsibility is limited to respect the law and be profitable, and anything that drifts from these two concepts implies a deviation from the company's interests. From the Friedman perspective, being a socially responsible company is to pay the correct tax. This model has now been questioned.

Considering the new political, economical and social relationship, it is plausible to expect a new way to assume CSR in the Mexican context. It is also expected that society, through its active participation as stakeholders, should be a speaker to guide CSR efforts towards society's demands. Finally, the government through the elaboration of policies must favor CSR's efforts done by the companies, as well as validate the legitimacy of projects done through the companies.

Spanish Companies in Mexico and their CSR

Fundación Carolina (2009) organized one of the most important conferences on the Mexican CSR issue; participants were from the economic, political, social and academic sectors. According to Fundación Carolina (2009), corporate social responsibility is no longer an exclusive issue of the economic sector. Besides the companies, the diverse groups of interest with whom the companies interact are the most important voices that the companies take in consideration with respect to CSR practices. Those types of practices have contributed, among other things, to achieve competitive advantages in the market; although it must also be said, that not all practices have been integrative and sustainable.

However, the current Mexican economic crisis tests the level of commitment to sustain these practices. As a result, two principal situations are arising: 1) companies that have decided to suspend their CSR practices, since they initially only pretended to keep a good image, and 2) companies that have decided to continue with their CSR practices, according to their current situation; measuring their practice effectiveness in terms of cost-benefit, in view of the reduction in available resources.

The current Mexican economic situation is influencing in a way that companies are refocusing their social responsibility practices, toward a corporate and transparent government; less effort is being made in more traditional issues that used to be linked with CSR, like community and environmental matters.

In this sense, the government may contribute in a direct manner to keep an integral focus on CSR practices. One possible way is to design public politics that promote and encourage CSR; also, through public fund granting oriented to social and environmental investments.

In this way, CSR practices may be a way to reduce the crisis' negative effect. An important aspect to take into account is that companies must avoid making short term decisions that may be counterproductive for the social well-being, such as job reduction or lack of promotion to micro companies' initiatives. An example for reducing the negative effects of the crisis are the social micro-credits offered by banking institutions, which support companies that are at the bottom of the pyramid.

Taking into account the current CSR state in Mexico, it is worth studying the effort of European companies, whose investments are in Mexico and whose strategies are said to be the best in responding to the current crisis.

The Third Spanish- Iberoamerican Conference of Corporate Social Responsibility was conducted with the objective of analyzing the responsibility perspectives that companies assume through the crisis. Throughout the conference, the most important Spanish companies with investments in Mexico debated the role of CSR together with other social, academic, political and economical Mexican organisms (Fundación Carolina, 2009).

Companies, such as BBVA Bancomer Mexico, Santander Mexican Group, Iberdrola, Sol Melía, and Telefónica, participated in the CSR practices debate; the Spanish companies' role in the crisis' risks, how to mitigate them, and how to use these practices to counterattack the crisis' effects were some of the topics.

Mexico's current situation has affected the involved parties' responsibilities; particularly, the company must respond to a situation that has caused a deep economical and social impact. The latter assumes an important change of the past tendencies and opens new possibilities that the CSR should take in the future.

From the Spanish companies' perspective, the current crisis has not diminished their CSR practices, since they consider it a competitive advantage in a crisis context. They are convinced that through CSR they will obtain a more sustainable economy that will become profitable and will generate corporate reputation. For this, it is necessary to create public-private alliances and a better informed society that is actively participating in the promotion and functionality of CSR.

In the following section, we summarize a brief description of what the principal Spanish companies in Mexico have presented as part of their CSR and their CSR strategies during the crisis.

5. BBVA

BBVA (2009) has signed its adherence to two main international agreements – the United Nations Global Compact (2009) to propel corporate responsibility and the United Nations program of initiatives for financial institutions for the environment. Additionally, it has made public its intention to respect the United Nations Universal Declaration of Human Rights and the Labors International Organization's basic labor rules. Besides, BBVA participates in the Corporate Responsibility specific initiative in the financial sector: the Ecuador's Principles. This initiative includes a group of rules of the World Bank to propel social and environmental rigorous criteria to fund big investment projects in emergent countries. Regarding social development, BBVA handles a direct support policy towards the community, supporting social initiatives, such as social assistance, education, culture, encouragement of economic, social sciences, environmental and health knowledge, as well as the promotion of social responsibility in other organizations. Regarding the environment, BBVA uses the System of Environmental Procedures that focuses on inciting environmentally responsible behaviors in every activity that it develops and optimizing its environmental impact, in a direct and indirect manner through the activity that the business produces.

Regarding the crisis, Mexico's BBVA states that it has developed a CSR policy focused on financially educating its clients, supporting them with the correct use of credit cards, as well as their savings and credit decisions; these are done as a strategy to counteract the negative effects of the economy. It also mentions that it has offered didactical workshops, through universities and internet that has generated an increase in the use of banking services, attracting new clients.

6. Santander

As part of their CSR strategies, Santander group has developed the UNIVERSIA project that implies the collaboration of universities and Santander group. UNIVERSIA emerges from this collaboration, and it is part of the largest university network worldwide. It has presence in 10 countries and 781 universities. In Mexico,

234 universities and higher education institutions are part of the project. Thanks to the participation of Mexican universities, the project excels at global online education, as well as having access to a library with international learning resources and services that help the university community.

These agreements are intended to extend progressively to the rest of the Mexican universities; this will imply that part of the investments be canalized in projects developed in conjunction with the universities in the academic, financial or technological spheres. To fund these projects, Santander group assigns around 2.7% of its utility to corporate social responsibility programs.

The Mexican Santander Group, in the face of the crisis, declares having potentiated its CSR practices in the education area, such practices include scholarship-credits to avoid scholar or university abandonment in homes where the head of the family has lost his or her job. It has also focused its CSR in enhancing business innovation among youth, linking them with possible partners and financing their projects in order to generate jobs.

7. Gas Natural Unión FENOSA

For Gas Natural Unión FENOSA (2009) the principles of responsible performance with society are defined in the following points: 1) Positive integration in society, especially in countries where the group develops its activity, respecting the culture, environment and law, 2) Generate value through thedevelopment of its own activity and creation of alliances with the local community, 3) Education, cultural wealth promotion and the inclusion of the most needed groups through social investment.

Gas Natural Unión FENOSA declares in its CSR report to be committed to satisfying the energy demands that respond to the development needs, and in conjunction, protect the environment by supplying cleaner energy sources. Based on the latter, it seeks to cooperate with the energy supply in a secure, efficient and sustainable manner. This allows focusing their efforts on the objectives of the Kyoto protocol, as well as those of the Copenhagen summit. Since 2002, Gas Natural Unión FENOSA (2009) has taken as a reference the Global Reporting Initiative (GRI). This type of report seeks to reasonably equilibrate the economic, social and environmental company's performance.

Its 2007 Corporate Responsibility Report attained an A+ grade, which implies following rigorously and transparently GRI recommendations; this includes allowing the actions to be verified by a third party. Gas Natural Unión FENOSA recognizes that the voluntary work in Mexico focuses in tending to problems, such as: children living in poverty, disabled people, sick people or adults in risk of social exclusion, as well as help to those affected by natural disasters.

Regarding its contribution to society, Gas Natural Unión FENOSA sees the well-being and development of communities as a basic pillar in Corporate Responsibility practices. In this sense, the company has developed mechanisms to identify the principal social demands and seeks to respond to them with initiatives and alliances with strategic institutions in each country.

Gas Natural Unión FENOSA is recognized as a wealth generator in the countries where it develops its corporate activity. Its contributions to wealth generation are linked to salary payment, tax payment, investments and value creation. It also contributes in the community development where it operates with projects aligned with its own business. Particularly, regarding Latin America, it has developed initiatives to facilitate the access to energy, residual transformation, supply-chain development and the reduction of environmental contamination in some sectors.

Gas Natural Unión FENOSA's social actions are focused to contribute towards development through social investment, education and environmental preservation. One of the most important social responsibility strategies focuses on providing, in an efficient, sustainable and safe manner, the energy that a community, where it operates, needs; as well as its innovation capacity, together with its presence in new businesses, which benefits the group and society.

Gas Natural Unión FENOSA also promotes the Millennium Development Objectives; Gas Natural Unión FENOSA is part of an inter-sector alliance of multinational companies that promote support and fulfillment of these objectives. With this in mind, Gas Natural developed actions that are oriented to the Millennium Development Goals among the different interest groups in the company.

8. Gas Natural Mexico

Both Gas Natural (in 2002) and Gas Natural Mexico (in 2005) have joined the United Nations Global Compact (2009), where they have committed to adopt the 10 universal principles; these cover issues of human rights, work, environment, and the fight against corruption. The GRI-G3 guide is the reference in which Gas Natural Mexico (2009) presents its progress toward the fulfillment of the 10 principles declared in the Global Compact.

On a national level, Gas Natural Mexico has received a Socially Responsible Company distinction (ESR). According to its CSR reports, Gas Natural assigns approximately 2.5 million Mexican pesos to social actions investments. Its activities are focused on social, energy, cultural and environmental investment. Gas Natural's cooperation with other institutions is oriented towards sustainable development, human rights' protection and environmental conservation.

For Gas Natural Mexico, affiliated with Gas Natural Unión FENOSA, both sustainable development as corporate responsibility are key factors in a business. One of the principal challenges that it assumes is to contribute in improving the quality of life in communities where the company is located and directs to these through the modern, safe, and environmentally friendly distribution of this type of energy.

As part of its internal social responsibility, Gas Natural Mexico received a recognition of the Editorial group Expansion, as well as a "Super Company 2007" recognition, given by the business' Top Companies. This recognition was offered thanks to the good work environment kept by the company.

Through its CSR programs, Gas Natural Mexico, seeks to contribute to society by means of resources, technology and time, in order to create opportunities for educational, cultural, social, energy and environmental development.

The Mexican Philanthropy Center (2009) has granted Gas Natural México a recognition for best social responsibility practices in the category of value chain, for handling a win-win scheme between the company and society. The Gas Natural Foundation, in collaboration with the Mario Molina Center for Strategic Studies of Environment and Energy, has initiated a study to compare and evaluate the characteristics, environmental, public health and energy advantages and disadvantages of the different transport technology.

Likewise, it has the intention of offering recommendations to the Official Mexican Norms and the programs to promote alternate combustible materials to optimize its efficiency. Gas Natural Mexico declares that it has been capable of integrating its CSR efforts in a coordinated manner with Gas Natural Unión FENOSA (Spain), as well as having contributed to Mexico's economic growth for its impact on the gross domestic product.

9. Telefónica

Among its Performance Principles, Telefónica (2009) declared to be committed to sustainable development, environmental protection and the reduction of any negative impact that its operation could generate. To guarantee the development of a homogenous environmental process and policy, Telefónica created the Environmental Corporate Direction, and it developed a functional organizational model, with environmental committees made up of multidisciplinary groups in the different countries, in which it operates. Telefónica is looking for equilibrium between its own activities and sustainability, so that each of its services contributes to greater sustainable development. All of these have been captured in different international agreements signed in the past several years. For example, in the year 2002, Telefónica endorsed the UN's Global Pact (United Nations Global Compact, 2009). Since then, Telefónica has committed to work focusing on contamination prevention, encourage environmental responsibility, and favor the development of technologies that respect the environment. Although there is a scarce environmental impact generated by the telecommunications sector, in comparison to other sectors, responsible behavior with the environment and society demands that Telefónica be committed to reduce and control any impact generated by its activity. In this way, Telefónica's most significant environmental aspects, due to its social relevance, are related to: energy consumption, electric and electronic equipment residues, dangerous residues (batteries), electromagnetic emissions and visual impact. In response to this impact, Telefónica performs an operational control that seeks to minimize the environmental impact in a corrective and preventive manner.

Regarding the adequate disposal of residues, Telefónica categorizes them according to their level of danger and the alternatives available in the country. To fulfill this objective, Telefónica demands that its offices and points of sale follow environmental practices.

Additionally, Telefónica offers a mobile phone pick up and recycle service. A mobile phone may be recycled almost completely; leaving it in inappropriate places may produce environmental damage. With this objective, Telefónica has installed in its stores and offices containers to pick up recycled mobile phones and batteries.

In order to make a greater environmental commitment, Telefónica organizes specialized environmental education for its employees and campaigns focused on the importance of recycling practices and the use of resources. It also systemically adds environmental clauses in contracts with its providers, who must implement environmental practices.

Regarding the crisis, Telefónica notes that it has oriented its CSR objectives towards TIC (technology information and communication), especially through tele-presence, which reduces transportation and CO2 emissions. Its CSR orientation towards sustainability and credibility through report publications has merited the recognition of best practices given by the Dow Jones index.

10. Sol Melia

Sol Melia (2009) declares to consider, as part of its corporate identity, the inclusion of social, cultural and environmental criteria. It relies on a Sustainability Global Policy, a document that collects the criteria of this norm and that are conducted throughout the organization. Derived from this policy, a revision of the Sustainability Department manuals is included and social and environmental indicators in the organization are incorporated. Hotels with environmental norms and hallmarks are certified. Sol Melia collaborates with working groups to deal with climate change issues and its relation to energy, such as World Travel & Tourism Council. It is also part of Grupo de Empresa y Discapacidad y Empresa y Voluntariado (a group for organizations and disabilities rights and a group for organizations and volunteerism) Sol Melia has participated in diverse projects in Mexico to promote PYMES (small and medium companies) in marginalized areas; it is also part of the Strategic Committee of the International Organization against Sexual Exploitation. Sol Melia tries to guarantee that the most important parts of its social and environmental commitment could be assumed by the work-force through an educational strategy on the issue.

11. CSR of Spanish Companies in Mexico in the EUMFTA framework

Although there is no doubt of the importance of the efforts made by European companies in Mexico as part of their CSR agenda, it is necessary to question: Why are these projects chosen and not others? Was it the private interest what defined the issues of their CSR projects? Or were the CSR projects demanded by the society?

It may be assumed that any effort made by a company is good per se, whether it is oriented towards society or the environment or meant to fulfill human rights. Nevertheless, according to the principle of benevolence, it is not only important to do right what is being done, but to do good with things done right. Doing the right thing is not an easy job. First, it is necessary to define what is important for society and the environment? To answer this, it is not enough for the company to define CSR strategies by itself; its proposals must be dialogued with the government, academics, civil society and institutions.

The participation from these stakeholders to discuss and identify what projects should be carried out by the company does not only make CSR projects more effective, also establishes the company as part of the society. Companies that consider CSR investments as a tax-deductible expense should consider the stakeholders proposals. The reason is that the government receives fewer income taxes because of companies' tax deductions, which reduces the resources required for doing the public good. In this sense, civil society, government and academics have the right to participate in the definition of CSR projects.

Furthermore, the CSR projects that some companies undertake are strongly questioned, since some of them, instead of being CSR practices, are only a business strategy, a way to build entry barriers toward competitors, or a way to achieve market growth focusing on a specific niche. Only a few of them are oriented toward social well-being or environmental improvement.

Social responsibility should not be exclusively associated with doing business right, but rather, that through the business the social well-being is accomplished. In this sense, it is expected for companies to declare as Social Responsibility not only what makes the company look better before society, but what fulfills the internal needs of the company and legitimizes the company as part of society, in response to the company's mission.

Diverse critics have emerged with respect to social responsibility in the economic arena. For example, Salazar and Husted (2008) support the need to have a legal framework to assure that CSR practices truly are directed to resolve social needs, since these may not match with the stockholders' ideas. Additionally, Hanlon (2008) questions if CSR is nothing morethan a commodity to achieve a competitive advantage, get social legitimacy and consolidate and open new markets. Kuhn and Deetz (2008) supported by the critical theory, argue that companies' sustainability initiatives do not arise from a serious commitment but from regulations, competitive advantages or from the need to consolidate their public image. In their contention, there is a reduced possibility that the environmental improvements be taken seriously, unless there is an ideological change.

Also, the value of the recognition given by the CSR achievements is questioned, since they may deviate the attention from those social changes that are truly necessary. When being recognized as a socially responsible company for its CSR levels, a company may be prevented from the possibility to identify its own ethical flaws, since certain ethical aspects, which are not so visible, may be hidden. The organisms that grant these distinctions are usually supported by the same companies being evaluated, so their neutrality may be questionable. Also, their ties with NGOs may make them appear as altruistic organizations and hide their own private objectives. Although CSR is part of their agenda, they do not achieve the profound changes that society requires.

In this regard, Aguirre and Pérez (2007) argue that the social responsibility of European Union companies in Mexico, through the EUMFTA, do not respond to the social demands of the country. Both authors state that in analyzing the bases that support the EUMFTA, which are respect for democratic principles and fundamental human rights, a different relationship is expected between Mexico and the European Union. This relationship must reflect not only economic but also social development in Mexico.

According to Aguirre and Pérez (2007), when no legal mechanisms, norms of cooperation and political dialogue are available, the commitment toward this EUMFTA declaration stays on a level of good intention. According to these authors' judgment, the European Union, in signing international free trade agreements, seeks to deregulate as much as possible the economies of developing countries and to facilitate the penetration of European capital. Taking deregulation advantages, the European Union redefines its commercial policy and ignores its social and democratic ideals, which are part of the EUMFTA ends.

On the other hand, according to the Mexican Secretaría de Economía (Ministry of Economy) (2009), the European Union is Mexico's second largest commercial partner and the second largest source of foreign direct investment (FDI). Because of the EUMFTA, commerce between the two parties has grown 40% annually. In the past few years, Spain has been Mexico's second largest commercial partner among the members of the European Union.In addition, Spain is the first source of foreign direct investment to Mexico among the member states. Thanks to the EUMFTA, Mexico's industrial products pay no taxes when arriving in Spain (the rate went from 5.7% to 0%), an advantage that has benefited the acceptance of diverse Mexican products in the EU market.

Particularly, the EUMFTA has favored Mexican exports, which flow with more dynamism through Spain. Moreover, since the EUMFTA's implementation, the agricultural sector has had minimum tax limits. There is a great window of opportunity for Mexican agricultural products that is yet to be utilized. Also, thanks to the EUMFTA, government groups were formed to support small and medium businesses interested in exporting, expanding markets or increasing exports. Nevertheless, the agricultural sector lacks the infrastructure that could allow the possibility of exporting to Europe.

With the EUMFTA and the entrance of new countries to the European Union, Mexico's FTA network grew to cover 43 countries, with more than one billion consumers. Due to the expansion of the EU and the EUMFTA, Mexican businessmen now enter new markets in more favorable conditions than those of their competitors. Mexican businessmen may have the commerce and investment opportunities that are demanded by these countries. To take advantage of this position in the EU, there has been intense EUMFTA promotion.

Aguirre and Pérez (2007) critics the EUMFTA effects. According to both authors, besides its economic and social impact in Mexico, the EUMFTA has reduced the Mexico's capacity to promote adequate economic policies to fulfill a more integrated regional development. Mexican authorities assumed that the promotion of the free trade agreement would cause economic growth and with that, social development. Nevertheless, this assumption has not become a reality.

In addition, the Mexican financial sector, where European banks have the most important market share, has not fulfilled its function of granting production credits, which would give incentives for regional development.

The EUMFTA, in essence, should be a free trade agreement that seeks mutual benefits. Nonetheless, since extreme inequalities exist among the participant countries, the benefits usually help large transnational companies with the capacity to compete in the international arena. Consequently, there is a diminished capacity for the State to integrate economic development oriented to improve citizens' human rights. Although there is a constant search to promote cooperation and political dialogue, in practice, trade conditions are not equal for both parties.

As a political plan to attract foreign investments, Mexican governments generate proposals with attractive fiscal incentives for European companies. This is done with the objective of attracting investments that generate jobs and wealth to a particular Mexican state. Nevertheless, these plans do not always generate positive consequences. In some cases, these commercial deals are limited to buy-sell transactions of already existing assets (Aguirre & Pérez, 2007). This may benefit foreign investments, but it does not have the same effect on less developed regions in Mexico.

On the other hand, according to the Mexican Business Council for Foreign Trade, Consejo Empresarial Mexicano de Comercio Exterior (COMCE, 2009), the EUMFTA impacts approximately 7,200 companies. They also affirm that foreign direct investment is increasing. Before the EUMFTA, annual investments used to be USD$2.7 thousand of mdd, and after the EUMFTA, they are now $USD4.8 thousand of mdd. Based on this evidence, it is possible to state that foreign investment flow has increased substantially because of the EUMFTA. Just as the Consejo Empresarial Mexicano de Comercio Exterior (2009) figures report, the main states that are receiving foreign direct investment are the ones with the highest development in Mexico--Mexico City, Nuevo León, and Estado de México. The countries where the investments mainly originate are Spain, Holland, United Kingdom and Germany. Foreign direct investment in these states has increased their economies, but other less developed regions have been negatively affected by these investments.

The main sectors in which foreign direct investment (FDI) is focused are: financial services (24%), commerce (6%), chemical industry (6%), electricity (5%), and automotive industry (5%). Having FDI focused on financial services has helped maintain and increase employment in this area. For example, BBVA Mexico (with Spanish investment) is the main Mexican employer in financial services. This might be very important for the Mexican economy, but there is also the possibility of focusing FDI toward areas of more technological development, and as a result, technical competences among the Mexican population might be favored.

On the other hand, Mexico's main imports from the EU are capital goods and intermediate goods that incorporate productive processes and strengthen exports. As a next step, it is necessary to offer potential exporting companies infrastructure and services, which allow them to have strategic support, so they may take advantage of the European market, as part of the free trade agreement.

Although the EU has become the second source of productive capital in Mexico, with regard to respecting labor and environmental laws, European companies responsibilities are not always equal with those in the European countries. In some cases, European companies are limited to what is established by the Mexican labor and environmental law. Nevertheless, various Spanish companies in Mexico seek to follow the environmental policies dictated by their foreign parent company. The majority of foreign parent companies are affiliated to international pacts (the Global Compact, for instance), which are closely linked with human rights and the environmental issues.

Mexican financial services with European investment are services that have not had a direct impact on the base of the pyramid; there is not enough of a stimulus for economic growth in this sector. In keeping with the free trade agreement objectives, it would be expected that financial services from Mexican banks with European investment also be concerned with favoring the micro-enterprises offering micro-credits and with improving self-employment.

Certainly these types of banks offer efficient services focused on small and medium enterprises, but they could also offer credit programs with more accessible rates. This would allow micro-enterprises to invest in new export processes, new technologies, as well as to finance commercial strategies, among other activities. This type of support would result in a strategic and important social responsibility practice for the economic development of Mexico.

As it can be inferred, the lack of economic development at the base of the pyramid is not a particular problem that emerged from the EUMFTA, but it is expected that the free trade agreement between the two parties will reduce asymmetries. This is an important justification for why it is necessary for the government, civil society, and academics to assume their social responsibility, in order to study the evolution of CSR programs developed by European companies in Mexico.

Even though there are important advantages offered to Mexican companies as a result of the EUMFTA, there are significant impediments as well. According to Alcalá (2009), there are eight important causes that require tending to, in order to have a more effective free trade agreement with Europe.

First cause: Mexico lacks experience in the development of design processes. Mexico is characterized as being a manufacturer in many industries, for instance, the automotive and electronic industry. This has ensured that a good utility margin be given to countries that do have design calling. This design has a special impact on two aspects: 1) the development of new products, which could compete in the international market, capturing new market locations; and 1) in the development of better processes, which would allow for the products to be of better quality or to improve the product's price in the market. It is therefore important for Mexico to generate mechanisms so that manufacturing industries also have design processes and improvement of products. In order to do so, it is important to invest in areas, such as research and product development.

Second cause: There is a lack of promotion in the development of productive national chains. This lack of promotion is related to two aspects – the design and the bond created through the programs. 1) Design processes do not only apply to companies but also to government programs on the different levels. They should be designed to propel the country's productive sector, adjusting to the short, medium and long run, according to each specific scenario and any new implications, and in some occasions could not work well 2) A bond is required to achieved the government programs and some situations is not possible to access the promotional programs. It is important to generate teamwork in specialized areas of different sectors, such as commercial, technical and administrative, considering the possible relationship that would surge among divisions, such as public, private and research, for the negotiations of the processes. In several cases, the success of the industry depends on these relationships, more than on free trade agreements.

Third cause: Cultural differences in negotiations between Mexico and the European Union. The language employed by Mexican and European businessmen is generally different, not only the language itself (with the exception of Spain), but also certain cultural aspects and their context differ. Trying to find information on internet sites becomes difficult when it is written in the language of the State and no Spanish or English translation is offered. This creates the necessity of translators and other people related to the cultural aspects of these countries, in order to expand commercial connections. Language barriers generate distrust among Mexican businessmen in the promotion of strong, long-term relationships.

Forth cause: Scarce business financing. The current international situation makes financing a business difficult. This generates fewer investments in new export processes, since they imply additional costs. These costs are related to personnel, technological changes, specialized consultancy, sample shipping, client financing, product certifications and commercial activities, among others.

Fifth cause: Lack and inefficiency of infrastructure for the development of logistic activities in Mexico. The majority of Mexico's roads are asphalt and not concrete. The asphalt easily wears out, especially with heavy weight. Likewise, there are unpredictable costs in Mexico's ports, which depend on the functions of logistic and associated costs. Moreover, a recurrent subject is the insecurity of the roads, which generates excessive costs with respect to merchandise insurance.

Sixth cause: Lack of human and technological infrastructure to validate certifications. In Mexico, there are not enough technical specialists dedicated to the development of technical norms--neither technicians that participate in technical international committees for the development of international standards or those dedicated to evaluate the fulfillment of the norms. As a result, the physical infrastructure is to evaluate the compliance with normative aspects.

Seventh cause: Differences among the Mexican and European normative structures. The European Union has gradually changed its normative structure to the "New Focus" model. This model is orientated to separate the actors who participate in norm elaboration from those dedicated to norm verification. The model leaves the European Commission to regulate aspects regarding security, environmental care and quality. This is done through committees, which specify each aspect that should be taken care of but not the way in which it should be carried out. The technical organisms are then responsible for the development of optional directives that companies may use to abide by the established directives and to demonstrate their compliance with them. There are also the so-called "notified organisms." which act as fulfillment inspectors of the commission's established guidelines. In Mexico, these types of activities tend to be centralized in the Federal government through the different Secretaries. They generate obligatory norms, which specify aspects of security, environment, and quality; how they should be fulfilled; and the mechanism to demonstrate the fulfillment. The Secretaries have the task of verifying the fulfillment of norms as well. This situation increases the operation's complexity, which causes gaps in the norm actualization and in the mechanisms to evaluate norm compliance.

Eighth cause: Lack of market studies on products that have a chance to enter the European Union. It is common that Mexican businessmen interested in exporting goods to Europe encounter the following situation: they request information to know which country could provide the best market for their product, yet all they receive is the answer: "which country are you interested in exporting to?" This answer, of course, puzzles them even more. Mexican businessmen may be enthusiastic about exporting and may even have the resources to do so, but they also need solid information allows them to learn of the best markets for their product to be exported. This information depends on variables based on the product itself, the opportunities established through Mexican commercial, free trade agreements, and the advantages of the specific foreign market. There are cases where businessmen commercialize different products that represent a greater degree of complexity.

According to Alcalá's (2009) contention, these eight causes are the main explanations for why the EUMFTA's advantages have utilized by Mexican businessmen. Through this analysis, the lack of support for Mexican companies who try to export to the European Union is evident. In addition to the reduction of asymmetries between the European and the Mexican contexts, it seems that the main problem is not only related to how European companies took advantage of the EUMFTA, as Aguirre and Perez (2007) argue, but rather, the lack of infrastructure for technological development, cultural barriers, financial services, logistics, and marketing services, among others. This infrastructural support is very important for Mexican companies that intend to export to Europe.

12. Conclusion

Considering the economical, social and environmental issues that are part of the commercial relations promoted by the EUMFTA, the MDG objectives, and the lack of infrastructure for Mexican companies that want to take advantages of the EUMFTA, a constructive dialogue and transparent framework is required. Through social dialogue, the economic, political, academic and social sectors may discuss the EUMFTA's orientation toward the enhancement of economic, social and environmental development in a sustainable manner for Mexico. The market forces cannot be allowed to act in a free, unguided way; rather, as free trade agreements are established, the respect and promotion of human rights must be favored. It is intended that Mexico, through a participative dialogue with its stakeholders, assume a more autonomous position, in order to decide rationally what is best for the integral development of the country. Even if attracting large amounts of capital is important for Mexican economic wealth, it is expected that social development also be considered; CSR plays an important role in this issue. Regarding the environment, although foreign investment from European companies is necessary to exploit natural resources, this should not compromise the environment or impede Mexican society from accessing these resources. It is mandatory that in the search for private goods, public good be preserved. This can only be accomplished through an active and participative civil society that defends and guarantees its public goods. Finally, civil society, in conjunction with the government, academic and economic sectors, must ensure that in the search for private goods, public goods be balanced.

References

Aguirre & Perez. (2007). Siete años del Tratado Unión Europea-México (TLCUEM): Una alerta para el sur global. Red Mexicana de Acción frente al Libre Comercio. Retrieved from www.rmalc.org.mx/documentos/eumexicofta-s.pdf

Alcalá, X. (2009). "Algunas causas del desaprovechamiento del TLCUEM por parte de empresarios mexicanos". Multidisciplina. Retrieved from http://www.acatlan.unam.mx/multidisciplina.

ALIARSE. (2009). Responsabilidad social. Retrieved from http://www.aliarse.org.

BBVA Bancomer. (2009). Informe Anual de Responsabilidad Social Corporativa. Retrieved from www.bancomer.com.mx/

Brito, S. (2005). "La responsabilidad social empresarial navega en la oscuridad". Expansión. México: Grupo Editorial Expansión. September 28, 2005.

Cajiga, J. (2009). El concepto de responsabilidad social empresarial, CEMEFI. Retrieved from http://www.cemefi.org.

Centro Mexicano para la Filantropía. (2009). Información de RSE. Retrieved from www.cemefi.org

Comisión de las comunidades europeas. (2001). Libro Verde. Fomentar un marco europeo para la responsabilidad social de las empresas, Unión Europea: Bruselas. Retrieved from http://eur-lex.europa.eu.

Consejo Empresarial Mexicano de Comercio Exterior. (2009). Tratados Comerciales con la Unión Europea. Retrieved from www.comce.org.mx/

Corral, A. et al. (2006). Contribución de las empresas al Desarrollo en Latinoamérica. Capítulo 1. Los ODM en América Latina: Estado de la Cuestión. Estados Unidos: Banco Interamericano de Desarrollo. pp. 25-52.

Crawford, J.A. (2007). New Transparency Mechanism for Regional Trade Agreements, A. *SYBIL, 11*, 133.

ECLAC. (2005). Comisión Económica para América Latina y el Caribe. Retrieved from http://www.eclac.org.

Fundación Carolina. (2009). III Conferencia España-Iberoamérica de RSE. Retrieved from www.fundacioncarolina.es.

Gas Natural México. (2009). Responsabilidad Corporativa. Retrieved from http://Portal.gasnatural.com.

Gas Natural Unión FENOSA. (2009). Responsabilidad Corporativa. Retrieved from http://Portal.gasnatural.com.

Global Reporting Initiative. (2004). Communicating Business Contributions to the Millennium Development Goals. Retrieved from www.globalreporting.org.

Hanlon G. 2008. Chapter 7. Rethinking corporate social responsibility and the role of the firm-On the denial of politics. En A. Crane, A. McWilliams, D. Matten, J. Moon & D. S. Siegel (Ed.), The Oxford Handbook of Corporate Social Responsibility, pp. 156-172. New York: Oxford University Press.

Kliksberg, B. (2004). Más ética más desarrollo. Buenos Aires, Argentina: Editorial Temas.

Kuhn T. & Deetz, S. 2008. Chapter 8. Critical Theory and Corporate Social Responsibility Can/Should we get beyond cynical reasoning. En A. Crane, A. McWilliams, D. Matten, J. Moon & D. S. Siegel (Ed.), The Oxford Handbook of Corporate Social Responsibility, pp. 174-196. New York: Oxford University Press.

Lozano, J., Albareda, L., Arenas, D. (2007). Tras la CSR, La responsabilidad social de la empresa en España vista por sus actores. Barcelona, España: ESADE Instituto de innovación social Editorial Granica.

Mitchell, R. K., Agle, B. R., and Wood, D. J. (1997). Toward a theory of stakeholder identification and salience: Defining the principle of who and what really counts. Academy of Management Review, 22, 853-886.

Quiroga, R. (2007). "Garantizar la sostenibilidad del medio ambiente". Propuesta regional de indicadores complementarios al objetivo de desarrollo del Milenio 7. Santiago de Chile, Chile.

Ruíz, G. (2004). "Cuando ser bueno es negocio". Expansión. México: Grupo Editorial Expansión. September 15, 2004.

Ruíz, G. (2005). "Filantropía no es hacer cheques, Manuel Arango y su filosofía de negocios sanos en ambientes sanos". Expansión. México: Grupo Editorial Expansión. February 16, 2005.

Salazar, J. & Husted, B. (2008). Chapter 6. Principals and agents, further thoughts on the Friedmanite Critique of Corporate Social Responsibility. En A. Crane, A. McWilliams, D. Matten, J. Moon & D. S. Siegel (Ed.), The Oxford Handbook of Corporate Social Responsibility, pp. 138-155. New York: Oxford University Press.Sol Melía (2009). Plan Director. www.solmelia.com.

Santander. (2009). Grupo Santander lanza importante Plan de Apoyo a la Educación en México. Retrived from http://www.universia.com.ar.

Secretaria de Economía. (2009). Comportamiento de la Inversión Extranjera Directa en México. Retrieved from http://www.economia.gob.mx.

Telefónica. (2009). Informe Responsabilidad Corporativa. Retrieved from www.telefonica.com.mx.

Tevini, Anna G. (2011). Article XXIV. In Rüdiger Wolfrum, Peter-Tobias Stoll & Holger P. Hestermeyer (Eds.), *WTO – Trade in Goods* (pp. 616-661). Leiden et al: Martinus Nijhoff.

UNDP. (2008). United Nations Development Program. Retrieved from http://www.undp.org.

United Nations Global Compact. (2009). What is the global compact?. Retrieved from www.unglobalcompact.org.

World Economic Forum. (2009). Information about our Annual Meeting in Davos and regional activities. Retrieved from www.weform.org.

WTO. (7.2.1996). *Organization, Comittee on Regional Trade Agreements, Decision of 6 February 1996*. WT/L/127.